The Essence of
Business Ethics

...E OF MANAGEMENT SERIES

PUBLISHED TITLES

The Essence of Business Ethics

PETER PRATLEY

Hanzehogeschool, Hogeschool van Groningen

Prentice Hall

London   New York   Toronto   Sydney   Tokyo   Singapore
Madrid   Mexico City   Munich

First published 1995 by
Prentice Hall International (UK) Limited
Campus 400, Maylands Avenue
Hemel Hempstead
Hertfordshire, HP2 7EZ
A division of
Simon & Schuster International Group

Typeset in 10/12pt Palatino
by Keyset Composition, Colchester, Essex

Printed and bound in Great Britain by
Hartnolls Limited, Bodmin, Cornwall

Library of Congress Cataloging-in-Publication Data

Pratley, Peter
  The essence of business ethics / by Peter Pratley.
    p. cm. — (Essence of management series)
  Includes bibliographical references and index.
  ISBN 0-13-356544-0 (pbk)
  1. Business ethics. 2. Social responsibility of business.
I. Title. II. Series.
HF5387.P735 1995
174'.4—dc20   95-6669
                                                        CIP

British Library Cataloguing in Publication Data

A catalogue record for this book is available from
the British Library

ISBN 0-13-356544-0 (pbk)

---

1 2 3 4 5   99 98 97 96 95

To Christine

Ce n'est pas l'estomac qui réclame la soupe bien chaude, c'est le coeur.

René Char (1962), *La Parole en Archipel*

Contents

Preface

The rise of business organizations and global commerce has reshaped the world and has made traditional society obsolete. Until only a few hundred years ago the bulk of mankind lived in autarky; people earned their daily food themselves by hunting, fishing, agriculture or animal husbandry. Commerce and exchange of goods were mainly limited to local markets and were of minor importance. Producing goods in factories powered by combustion engines was still an unknown phenomenon.

Nowadays, a basic activity of modern mankind is the production and exchange of goods and services in order to earn money, money that allows us to purchase other goods and services. Our consumer needs have exploded and now cover a huge range of wants. Thanks to modern economy and technology, almost half of mankind nowadays lives in an epoch of unprecedented material prosperity: famine, war and epidemic disease seem banished from their lives. The new economic activities of private companies were fostered by government policies and could develop into the chief source of wealth.

A host of inventions, improved business organizations and worldwide commerce not only changed the way we earn our living, they also radically changed our whole way of life and even modified our ways of thinking, especially by the expansion of our perceived needs. These profound changes in our way of life also gave rise to a whole range of practical theories concerning the inner functioning and organization of business activities. One of these disciplines is business ethics.

In this book I postulate that business ethics provides a basic outlook to the training of a business manager. It is not just a new approach alongside the other tried methods; rather it has a general scope and purpose that cuts across several disciplines such as strategic marketing, organizational theory, and finance. Business ethics studies the moral quality of organizational policies. The main objective of this book is therefore to introduce general concepts and standards for moral behaviour in business; that is, to outline the basics of this discipline.

From the start it is important to caution against one particular erroneous expectation: people with immoral habits will not change by reading a book on ethics. Behaving with a sense of moral responsibility requires practice, it is a reflective activity. Ethics can only guide our reflection on such matters, but cannot actually reorient and shape the qualities of our character, commitment and mind. This is a matter of education, giving the right example, and learning to practise moral behaviour in honest dialogue.

This book covers the more fundamental issues of business ethics – especially the definition of ethics, the concepts of free choice, and personal and company responsibility – and provides an introduction to the relevant value systems. How these issues apply to specific cases is briefly exemplified in most chapters. Nevertheless the book does not examine in detail any one particular field of business ethics, but adheres to the general concepts. The cases illustrate these ideas, but also remind us of the importance of precise and accurate judgements that take into account the concrete facts and issues. Ethics contributes by highlighting basic principles in a systematic manner.

Reflective ethical insight is a very important and underestimated prerequisite for concrete moral action. It is only one element, for the moral quality of business actions also depends on vision, circumspection, experience and sensibility. Yet here progress can be made. Too little is known in business about adequate moral theories, and thus for reflective managers the great potential of these theories is not fully realized. The scope of this book, then, is to present useful ethical theories to business practitioners, and to improve the skills of reflective managers both in analyzing concrete moral issues and in deliberating and deciding upon stratagems for solving moral dilemmas.

1

The nature and purpose of ethical reflection

1.1 Introduction

This chapter starts with an example of a moral issue in a business environment, and then tries to answer the following questions:

- ☐ What is ethics?
- ☐ How does ethics study moral behaviours?
- ☐ What are the two practical purposes of ethics?
- ☐ Are culturally transmitted values relative?
- ☐ What is the moral syllogism?
- ☐ What distinguishes moral standards from other norms?

1.2 Autumn 1990: immoral supplies to Iraq?

1.2.1 Optical instruments for Saddam

During Christmas 1990 Iraqi troops from occupied Kuwait territory attacked the Saudi Arabian town of Khafdji. It took several days of heavy fighting for American troops from the UN force to end this attack. The American intelligence services soon announced that they were surprised to find night vision equipment on the side of their Iraqi enemies. These Western optical instruments allowed their Iraqi enemy to target well by night. The supplier of this equipment was soon found: it was the Dutch Delft Instruments NV.

1

In the 1980s Delft Instruments NV had found ways to ship their technology towards Iraq, relying on tacit or overt permissions by Dutch and Belgian authorities. Until summer 1990 such export methods were quite common practice. Even weapon sales to Iraq were permitted in silence by a number of Western countries until the Iraqi invasion of Kuwait in August 1990. Since the early 1980s Delft had shipped thousands of first-generation TP1MS image intensifiers, which was a legal export. In April 1990 they shipped two prototypes of sophisticated thermal-imaging technology to Iraq, and in December 1990 another model went for demonstration purposes to Jordan. These three high-tech products were equipped with infrared detectors from Hughes Aircraft Company and scanners made by Litton Systems. Here Delft Instruments made a mistake – they did not ask for the required re-export licence.

US intelligence must have known for a longer period that the TP1MS night-vision goggles were adapted to the tank periscopes on T-55 Iraqi tanks. But they had only recently learned about the illegal export of two thermal-imaging models, which was the first part of a $35 million contract with Iraq. Delft Instruments cancelled this contract the same day that Iraq invaded Kuwait, which was days before the UN debated imposing sanctions on Iraq. However, the true elements in the declarations after the Khafdji incident are made up from a cocktail of three isolated facts: first, American troops had found night-vision systems made by OIP Instrubel, a Belgian subsidiary of Delft Instruments; secondly, Delft Instruments had illegally supplied sophisticated equipment, as the two prototypes needed re-export licences.

Finally, in one other case it appears that Delft's Belgian subsidiary crossed the borderline of tacitly accepted but formally illegal exports. In December 1990, several months after the Iraqi invasion of Kuwait, the company exported the third model of this thermal-imaging apparatus to Jordan for demonstration purposes. This shipment was ordered by Jordanian authorities. Delft Instruments claims that the US authorities found no evidence that this demonstration model ended up in Iraq. It should be noticed, however, that high military authorities from Iraq assisted the demonstration in Jordan.

1.2.2 The US trade embargo

The detection of optical instruments in the possession of Iraqi troops triggered a very severe reaction by US authorities. The Office of Defense Trade Control withdrew at least two permits for licensing optical inventions owned by the American Hughes Corporation. A more costly sanction was the February 1991 trade embargo on all supplies made by American-based firms to this private Dutch company. This trade ban included every possible item, including the salary strips that used to come from a European IBM unit. Delft had to find other suppliers for thousands of items. These sanctions were also a setback for Delft Instruments' other core activities, the production of medical instruments, and industrial and scientific equipment.

1.2.3 Details on the export of optical instruments

In their newsletter of 21 February 1991 Delft Instruments contested the idea that they evaded export embargoes. At that time they were as yet unaware of the specifications of the captured optical instruments and suggested that these belonged to a completely legal supply to the Iraqi army in the mid-1980s. (This was not contested later, however, in the US court, although at that particular moment sources kept talking about illegal supplies.) The following week Delft Instruments learned that the captured equipment was the first-generation goggles, but they also found out that four managers in Belgium had committed several unauthorized actions. Especially, they had shipped two prototypes of thermal-imaging equipment to Iraq without applying for the US re-export licences, and this they acknowledged in their newsletter of 1 March 1991. Under the export licence of the Belgian authorities, OIP Instrubel did indeed export two thermal-imaging prototypes to Iraq, one in December 1989 and one in April 1990. They also recognized that they shipped one other model on 7 December 1990 for demonstration purposes, with alleged final use in Jordan, accompanied by the required Belgian export licences. However, the export to third countries required an American re-export licence. The newsletter then states: 'Contrary to the explicit company guidelines such a licence has not been demanded [by their subsidiary, OIP Instrubel].'

A more elaborate explanation of this unfortunate export event may be inferred from Dutch newspaper articles. For the time being, however, the status of these conclusions is not final, as authoritative reports are non-existent. The embargo affair was initially settled by a confidential agreement between Delft Instruments and the US government in July 1992, which coincided with the dropping of all legal prosecutions in the Netherlands. In fact, the Dutch authorities possessed a large file of original documents that they had seized in spring 1991 at Delft Instruments' main office. These files were handed over to the American authorities in order to help the US attorney Jay B. Stephens in the preparation of further American indictments.

1.2.4 Tentative conclusions concerning the export of optical instruments to Iraq

The following conclusions may be drawn regarding the export of optical instruments to Iraq.

(1) In 1983 Delft Instruments was prohibited by the Dutch Ministry of Economic Affairs from exporting to Iraq: its permission to export to 'sensitive destinations' was withdrawn.

(2) By a letter dated 3 September 1984 Dutch government officials permitted Delft Instruments to demonstrate SAMTOR at the Baghdad International Trade Fair 1984, adding: 'this is no guarantee that in the future we will give permissions for supplying the SAMTOR-system to Iraq'.

(3) Iraq placed an order for a few dozen SAMTOR systems in 1984. Note that the war between Iraq and Iran had started at that stage, and Iraq was then considered to be the ally of the West in the fight against fundamentalist Iran.

(4) The company exported several prototypes to Iraq in the period 1984–88. In practice this means that from 1984 onwards, Dutch authorities tacitly gave a new export permission.

(5) Since 1988, Delft Instruments used the Belgian OIP Instrubel product facilities in order to supply Iraq with legally exported TP1MRS night-vision goggles. Delft Instruments had bought OIP Instrubel in 1988.

(6) The Belgian authorities did not consider the supplies to be 'weapons or ammunition', but rather a non-strategic supply of optical equipment. Also, as Iraq did not fall under the embargo for strategic products imposed against pro-Communist countries, it was anyhow a fact that exporting optical instruments from Belgium to Iraq did not need any special permits. Export from Belgium was therefore completely legal.

(7) Although the export of SAMTOR technology was officially only permitted to Nato countries, Delft Instruments paid royalties to Hughes for their shipments to Iraq. Some sources allege that this was based on a covert industry-to-industry agreement between the companies about which the US administration had not been informed.

(8) Besides the SAMTOR technology, OIP Instrubel also shipped TP1MS night-vision goggles that could be adapted to the periscopes in Russian

T-55 tanks. US sources estimate that up to 5,000 pairs of night-vision glasses were exported by Delft Instruments to Iraq. This supply of first-generation goggles lasted until 1990.

(9) After the armistice between Iran and Iraq, Western governments became more hostile towards Saddam Hussein. The export of military equipment to Iraq, already forbidden by international law, now became less and less acceptable to Western governments.

(10) Even after the Kuwait invasion by Iraq and in possible violation of the UN embargo on all exports to Iraq, the Belgian company OIP Instrubel exported a model of thermal-imaging equipment to Jordan. This shipment was sent as late as December 1990 with Jordan as 'final destination'. It should be noted that in this period it was common practice for many firms secretly exporting to Iraq, even American, to list Jordan as the final destination.

(11) TP1MRS night-vision equipment was discovered by the US Army during the Khafdji incident (Christmas 1990) and the battle for Qaruh island (end of January 1991).

Despite all this, Delft Instruments claims that even the export of the prototype of new technology in December 1990 was not the result of intentional profit-seeking by the top management, but rather an unfortunate company mistake due to internal misunderstanding and a lack of control at top level. They fired the four middle-managers responsible for this action, who were also later prosecuted by the American Justice Department. Investigation amongst corporate middle-management circles reveals a final point that seems very feasible.

(12) The severe embargo imposed by the US authorities came at a time when US intelligence was probably aware that others, even some American firms, had violated the sanctions. The Delft Instruments affair served to dampen public interest in research on other violations. Newspaper coverage overkill on this isolated issue served as a lightning conductor. Also, by hanging a European sinner, they could stop other violators.

1.2.5 How Delft Instruments coped with the US trade embargo

From February 1991 onwards Delft Instruments had to deal with a new situation. At the end of February 1991 the American authorities had placed an embargo on all Delft Instruments imports into the United States and prohibited delivery of parts from US-based companies to Delft Instruments. These restraints stopped Delft Instruments from trading with the US market, and limited the number of their suppliers, especially in the medical branch.

The speedy decision by the US administration was made in a period of active warfare with Iraq, and served to set a salutary example if we consider the type of information held by US sources on Delft Instruments NV. At the moment of the embargo, US decision-makers were not aware that only three of the company's ten business units supplied the military market, and that most of the units produced medical, industrial and scientific equipment. As far as they were concerned, they were dealing with a Dutch firm that produced military optics. Thus the embargo on the seven other business units was an unintentional side-effect.

In 1991 Delft Instruments had an historical loss of DFl 34 million on a turnover of DFl 400 million. Their medical supplies business suffered especially from the sanctions as many American parts used in the medical equipment were considerably cheaper than those from alternative suppliers in Europe or Japan, and this cost Delft a lot of money.

In the beginning the communications between Delft Instruments NV and the American authorities were non-existent. The first bans ordered by the US Departments of Trade and of Foreign Affairs were followed two months later by sanctions from the Pentagon. The chairman of the Delft Instruments board, Mr R. V. Kingma, first became aware of these sanctions ten days later by reading an article in the *New York Times*. Until that moment in May 1991, Delft Instruments followed the advice of Dutch solicitors and kept a low profile. In our opinion this advice caused lasting damage, for the company replied only briefly and reluctantly to initial newspaper coverage and questions, which fuelled suspicion.

Mr Kingma then decided upon a different and more active approach. Following a phone call and a recommendation by the former Dutch attaché in Washington he decided to hire help in the United States. Two different bureaus of legal consultants were called in to carry out active lobbying and to implement a corporate code of ethics.

Five lawyers from Akin, Grump, Strauss & Hauer in Washington, DC covered the negotiations with the three US departments involved in the matter. Another bureau, Mudge & Rose, screened the Delft Instruments organization. They recommended the application of American norms for corporate controls and decision-making procedures concerning strategic equipment. Delft Instruments implemented these new norms, establishing a strict division between the units with military and non-military product lines. Also, they tightened controls. This whole operation was monitored by a third bureau from Washington, IPAC, which specialized in obtaining government contracts for private companies.

In November 1991 the ban on medical exports was lifted by the US authorities. Then in July 1992 the company paid a $3.3 million fine to the US administration, after pleading guilty in the federal court in Washington to the charge of illegally re-exporting the three thermal-imaging models.

By 1992 Delft Instruments had clearly set apart its defence industry units, and for all equipment of strategic value they had adopted a strict *strategic product control* programme. This convinced the US authorities that the holding company had implemented satisfactory controls and procedures which could prevent further incidents. From then on, most bans were lifted, except for another three-year embargo on the export of American supplies to the defence branch of Delft Instruments. The legal bureaus had done their job, and in the summer of 1994 Ronald Carlberg of IPAC finally persuaded the US authorities to lift the remaining bans, one year earlier than scheduled previously.

1.2.6 Preliminaries of ethical enquiry

This case illustrates several features of research in business ethics.

(1) Business ethics studies existing corporate policies that have an impact on human and environmental wellbeing. These actual policies and behaviours constitute business morality, which is expressed as a given set of convictions and activities, both inside and outside a corporation, on business issues.

(2) Business ethics is a comprehensive study of corporate policies and not the study of an isolated topic (e.g. one illegal export). Also, business activities have to be seen in a context of external and internal forces. For example, returning to our earlier study, as an isolated incident the delivery of thermal-imaging equipment to Iraq in 1990 appears to be an instance of improper corporate activity. Nevertheless, in order to see this incident in the right proportions one has to make a broader study of both the overt and tacit policies of government authorities. In our case, the extent of illegal transactions with the oil-exporting nation of Iraq in the 1980s has only now become evident. One quote from the Dutch *NRC Handelsblad* newspaper of 25 July 1994 may indicate the possible extent of secret bargains with Iraq:

> Over a period of twenty years Saudi Arabia has secretly tried to procure itself nuclear bombs. As a part of these efforts it has paid 5 billion dollars to Iraq. In exchange Baghdad had to share its nuclear technology with the Saudis. Even when the Iraqi president Saddam Hussein prepared his invasion of Kuwait, Saudi Arabia continued to pay him.

This information was published by *The Sunday Times* yesterday. It was based on the declarations of a Saudi diplomat and nuclear scientist, Mohammed al-Khilewi. Last June Mr al-Khilewi has applied for political asylum in the United States, bringing with him 14,000 documents that are said to substantiate the truth of his allegations.

(3) What seems to be totally scandalous behaviour at first sight, may later become just one minor excess amongst a multitude of many careless, unjustified, and even criminal deals. Looking again at our example, here the business environment was filled with a tradition of covert military exports to Iraq by many Western corporations, and encouraged by the Western governments until the beginning of 1990. In the late 1980s military exports to Iraq, especially by American, Chilean, German, French, Italian and British firms included cluster bombs, ammunition, Scud-missile electronics, equipment for nuclear (bomb) technology, chemical factories, and synthetic ingredients for poisoned gas. Some may remember the export by British corporations of huge tubes for the barrel of the Iraqi super cannon, though in this case every company involved will plead innocence, claiming that they understood these unorthodox tubes were meant for the Portuguese market. Until 1990 some of these strategic exports, such as shipping of Chilean cluster bombs to 'Jordan', were even encouraged by the US Bush Administration. It was only after the Kuwait invasion of August 1990 that the Iraqi regime was seen as the enemy and trade with Iraq was prohibited.

(4) A careful and broader study is necessary in order to set things in proper proportion. A more balanced understanding of the factual context is a basic requirement of any ethical evaluation. Business ethics often also requires an understanding of the political context. Thus we know now that the US embargo against Delft Instruments was meant to set an example. Yet, as Alan Friedman (1993) writes in his book *Spider's Web*, military exports to Iraq by US firms continued even after the occupation of Kuwait. Between the Kuwait invasion of 2 August 1990 and 4 October 1990 the Bush administration gave 14 permissions for weapon exports by American companies to Jordan. US Intelligence most probably knew that these goods would in fact transit to Iraq.

1.3 A definition of ethics

Ethics is a branch of philosophy. Its object is the study of both moral and immoral behaviour in order to make well-founded judgements and to arrive at adequate recommendations.

In this book 'ethics' refers to moral philosophy or normative ethics.

Ethics is not identical with its subject matter, that is, moral expectations and conventional judgements of moral behaviour. Ethics is a normative enquiry, not a purely descriptive science. Normative ethics does not make neutral inventories of given moral practices, but organizes the issue in a framework of explicit evaluations. If the activities of Delft Instruments were reported as mere facts without making any normative comment, it would be just a tedious list relating isolated behaviours and quoting various contradicting sources. Such a long-winded exposition is not yet a case study in business ethics. Descriptions provide material for a well-based ethical judgement, but are not its core activity.

1.3.1 A twofold objective

Ethics has a twofold objective: it evaluates human practices by calling upon moral standards; also it may give prescriptive advice on how to act morally in a specific kind of situation.

The first aim implies analysis and evaluation. It leads to an ethical diagnosis of passed actions and events. The analysis consists of clarifying standards and lines of argument. Already here ethics can be useful, as one is often unaware about most moral values and habits of thought. The basic assumptions behind our moral actions and judgements are mainly taken for granted. Normative ethics analyzes our judgements and makes our moral assumptions explicit, but it may also criticize them.

This first purpose does not limit itself to neutral description. It seeks to understand the real issues that are at stake in order to make adequate evaluations. The underlying moral issues may then often be represented as a dilemma. Such moral choices often confront us with painful choices, presenting options that each has positive and negative features. Moreover these features are not easily evaluated, because people have different objectives. These different goals may lead to different moral standards.

In front of such true dilemmas reflective practitioners have to make a stand. One has to choose a line of conduct in order to serve vital objectives. In this sense normative ethics is evaluative. The recommended guidelines may lead to a critical evaluation of actual or historical choices.

Normative ethics sets itself a second and more curative purpose. Ethics develops rational methods for answering the present and future issues. In order to achieve this second objective one has to be well informed. Balanced judgements are based on the careful assessment of relevant information; also one has to be quite specific when deciding upon appropriate normative standards. If both these conditions are met, ethical thought may lead to valid prescriptions.

So, the second objective is to provide therapeutic advice. It suggests solutions and policies when facing the present dilemmas and future dangers, based on well-informed opinions. This especially requires a broad-minded identification of relevant stakeholders and a clear under-standing of the vital issues at stake.

1.4 The subject-matter of ethics – moral behaviour

We distinguish the study or *discipline* (ethical reflection) from its *object* or field of study (conventional moral judgements and actual moral be-haviour). This distinction shows that ethics has its own approach towards morality, it is not swallowed up by its subject-matter. In any debate on practical moral issues it is possible to point towards certain ethical standards that should be considered, or to warn against the certain dangers of a too partial attitude. In this way ethical thought can actually make its proper contribution.

In practice, the distinction between ethical reflection and conventional moral behaviour is blurred, as the best examples of applied ethical thought are found amongst practitioners. In particular, those who live in situations where different cultural conventions make conflicting claims, develop ethical reflection. If we are immersed in one moral code we often take its moral standards for granted. The repeated experience of painful clashes between different codes may oblige us to look beyond conventions. People confronted with this experience show a great ability for moral philosophy, transcending the limits of the moral code they were brought up in. Thus ethical thought about the foundations of given moral codes is not the prerogative of some library philosopher, for its crucial problems are often posed by intelligent practitioners facing conflicting codes of behaviour.

Due to their social position, especially good examples of ethical dilemmas are formulated by emigrants like expatriate writers, businessmen and diplomats. Persons in these positions often develop personal ideas on how to cope with conflicting codes of behaviour.

Nevertheless, knowledge of reflections developed by schools of moral philosophy provides a useful supplement, for it offers a general guide on how to question, organize and reformulate the practitioners' insights and dilemmas. Some philosophical reflections from past and present on the issue of ethical relativism may illustrate this.

1.5 One major ethical issue – relativism

1.5.1 Herodotus on cultural diversity

A story related in the two-thousand-year-old text of Herodotus (1972), *The Histories*, confronts us with the ideas of cultural and ethical relativism.

Everyone without exception believes his own native customs, and the religion he was brought up in, to be the best; and this being so, it is unlikely that anyone but a madman would mock at such things. There is abundant evidence that this is the universal feeling about the ancient customs of one's country.

One might recall, in particular, an anecdote of Darius. When he was king of Persia, he summoned the Greeks who happened to be present at his court, and asked what they would take to eat the dead bodies of their fathers. They replied that they would not do it for any money in the world. Later, in the presence of the Greeks, and through an interpreter, so they could understand what was said, he asked some Indians, of the tribe called Callatiae, who do in fact eat their parents' dead bodies, what they would take to burn them. They uttered a cry of horror and forbade him to mention such a dreadful thing. One can see by this what custom can do, and Pindar, in my opinion, was right when he called it 'king of all'. (pp. 219–20)

This anecdote leads to the conclusion that habit makes the man. Starting from the assumption that our ideas about right and wrong depend upon the moral code we are raised in, Herodotus shows what happens to people when they are confronted with a totally different custom. In this case it seems impossible to overcome the differences between opposing cultures, and we are tempted to conclude that there are no transcultural values. One is lured towards ethical relativism: moral behaviour must only be judged according to its proper cultural standards.

Yet this is a much too hasty conclusion. A more critical analysis starts by portraying the true problem, which is based upon two facts. First, the rites of incineration and of body-eating are conflicting rules of behaviour that exclude one another. Secondly, both parties show great respect towards their own traditions and the holy rituals they use to honour their dead fathers. Due to this second fact we can maintain that the first fact does not force us to become relativists, because both moral codes share the same fundamental commitment: they both hold their parents' death rituals to be sacred.

1.5.2 Applying the distinction between norms and values

To elucidate further, we will apply a distinction Dutch sociologists make between concrete *norms* and basic *values*. Both concepts have to do with our *expectations* about behaviour (opinions), which is not the same thing as the actual behaviour. Norms can be defined as specific expectations about concrete behaviour, also serving as a criterion for judging the quality of human behaviour. In this case the norms are completely different: the Greeks practise incineration as a funeral ritual, while the Callatiae appear to have a sacred ritual of eating their dead parents' bodies.

Values are more general expectations and representations about human behaviour, which may be either conscious or so deeply embedded that they are not formulated verbally. As such, values can be defined as abstract, collective representations of what people believe to be just, good and worthwhile to pursue. The basic values of a society constitute the core of its culture. In the case of the Greeks and the Callatiae, neither party wants to bargain about their concrete norms: this more general attitude is a value they share. They both show a deep and sacred belief in the rituals they use for helping their fathers pass from the world of the living to the world of the dead. In short, they share a value of unconditional respect concerning death rituals.

1.5.3 The cornerstone of culture: transmitted survival methods

This interpretation of value as something more general and more fundamental than norms points in the direction of what the sociologist and consultant Fons Trompenaars (1993) calls the 'core of culture'; in particular, our basic values refer to our assumptions about existence. Each traditional civilization can be seen as a specific way of dealing with the challenges in our natural and social environment. Culture is, then, a socially transmitted method for satisfying vital objectives. The same conception of culture can be found in the introduction of this book. Core values of existing cultures relate to the traditional methods people found to survive. It would be wrong to describe this as reductionist thinking, since the urge for group survival is connected with deeply engraved rules and taboos. To quote Fons Trompenaars (1993):

> The problems of daily life are solved in such obvious ways that the solutions disappear from our consciousness. . . . From this fundamental relationship with the (natural) environment man, and after man the community, takes the core meaning of life. This deepest meaning has escaped from conscious questioning and has become self-evident, because it is the result of routine responses to the environment. In this sense culture is anything but nature. (p. 24)

1.5.4 A position in the relativism debate

We accept as given fact that cultural norms and values vary a great deal. This is a fact of life. Yet, from the point of view of normative ethics it would be very dangerous to endorse ethical relativism, which claims that all normative rules can only be judged according to their own criteria. A significant consequence would be that one has to accept all kinds of local habits that inflict severe injuries and death: examples are the widow burning (suttee) in India, slavery, political terrorism or the customs of tyrannical warlords. On the other hand, we are aware that it is dangerous to simply apply our concrete norms to other cultures, which would amount to blinkered ethnocentrism, a belief that one's own local customs provide a universal standard. At the level of descriptive understanding of other cultures, anthropological relativism is valid when it claims that one should first thoroughly understand customs as they are perceived and practised by the local people before making any judgements about the ethical quality of the various local practices.

Our position tries to respect both sides of the debate by drawing on the difference between concrete norms and more general values. Some of these values we hold to be true. For example, we firmly adhere to the basic values of human decency, which may best be understood in the general objective of protecting relevant stakeholders against serious injuries. These stakeholders are other people or, according to some, even animals or environmental qualities. This is a normative point of view. In order to make appropriate judgements about the ethical qualities of concrete practices, one has to study carefully whether, in each specific case, the practised norms live up to these more general standards. Being humane is an attainable ideal; it contains transcultural aspects although it has to be realized in specific circumstances.

1.6 The difference in methods with moral theology

Moral debate in Europe is no longer the privilege of theology. Although we do not want to exclude moral theology from moral debate, it is important to stress some big differences between ethics and theology. Normative ethics is part of philosophy. Many moral philosophies hold that we can formulate moral standards on the sole basis of reason: that natural reason and mutual agreement are the only foundations needed to elaborate moral guidelines.

Contrary to this, moral theology ultimately refers to revelation and religious tradition, formulated by a venerated spiritual guide or prophet and laid down in a sacred text.

This does not imply that in practice both approaches lead to contrary findings. A brief discussion of one vital principle may illustrate this. The normative principle of reciprocity – the 'golden rule' of treating others as you would like them to treat you – is present in many religions and is also accepted as a line of reasoning by most ethicists. It is part of human heritage.

The expression of this rule – that is, treating other people as you would like to be treated – is not only found in many sacred texts, but also exists in precepts based on natural reason.

The specific feature of moral philosophy is that it can expand on this idea in a very systematic way. For instance, this principle of reciprocity is just one part of a more general principle found in the teachings of Immanuel Kant, specifically in his *Foundations of the Metaphysics of Morals*. His expression has become famous in ethics as the unconditional or absolute norm, the *categorical imperative*. The first formula runs as follows:

> Act only according to this moral guideline, if at the same time you would want it to become a general rule. (1965/1785, my translation)

Normative reciprocity is only part of this imperative of generalizability. For Kant ethical rationality goes beyond the altruism expressed by religious precepts. Ethical behaviour according to Kantians consists of applying only those moral guidelines that stand the test of the categorical imperative. The motivation of a moral guideline in this rational tradition has to pass one test: Can this guideline be generalized in comparable situations?

Kant pretends to define one single general principle. He accepts that it still needs a lot of fine-tuning in order to determine whether situations are comparable, but the thrust of his approach is universalistic. Testing concrete rules and policies by applying the litmus test of his ultimate guideline is the one and only moral check needed, according to Kant. His categorical imperative can be applied to the whole range of moral guidelines. He shows how his test not only applies to mutual obligations (reciprocity), but also to the duties we owe towards ourselves (making the best out of ourselves) and the non-reciprocal guidelines for benevolent support and charity.

Although the Kantian approach is just one of many in normative ethics, it is exemplary in many respects. Moreover it has been very influential, having been invoked by others who have propounded doctrines on universal human rights.

1.7 Moral judgements are normative judgements

The next two sections deal with the analysis of the formal aspects of argumentations used in moral judgements. First, we explain the idea that *ethics only studies one type of normative judgements, the moral judgements.* Secondly, we turn to the specifics of moral standards, namely that *moral judgements result from the evaluation of facts by means of a moral standard,* and that *these standards most often remain implicit and are commonly taken for granted by moral agents.*

1.7.1 Descriptive statements and normative judgements

Moral judgements never simply describe: they also judge and prescribe. They refer not only to facts, but also call upon norms and standards in order to make recommendations about how or how not to behave. Just like other judgements that apply a standard, moral judgements are *normative*.

A *descriptive statement* describes a state of affairs; it claims only to formulate factual information. Descriptive statements do not call upon norms or values; they do not comment, but simply state how things are. Examples of such factual descriptions are sentences like 'DAF small trucks division went bankrupt in 1992' and 'Clinton became President of the USA in 2001'. Obviously, the second example contains false information: it is an incorrect description since Clinton was first elected President in 1992. The descriptive statement 'Clinton became President of the USA in 2001' may be disproved by two methods: either one checks whether the statement corresponds to facts or one tests the consistency of this statement with taken-for-granted descriptive statements. Therefore a fundamental characteristic of descriptive statements is that their truthfulness can be verified.

A *normative* (or *prescriptive*) *statement* contains a judgement. It expresses an opinion or attitude about some topic. It makes an evaluative assessment about a subject. It may express a command, an expectation, a request, an encouragement, a prohibition, a warning, or another opinion. A normative sentence will never just relate a state of affairs, it always colours reality by adding some judgements about its correctness or desirability.

Normative statements apply normative expectations or standards. This element will be italicized in the following examples. 'That was a *mean* thing to do'; 'The directress of this nursing home for the elderly claims she is *not responsible* for the food poisoning'; 'The presence of salmonella germs in the shrimps was due to *lack of hygiene and severe negligence* by the kitchen staff, the cook in charge *ought to be sued for manslaughter*'.

It is important at this point to avoid a basic misconception: normative is *not* identical to subjective or arbitrary. Comparable to descriptions, which can be true or false, one can say of normative judgements that they are valid or unfounded. But although individuals make normative judgements, these individuals may express standards and do refer to facts. Normative standards can be shared, communicated and discussed publicly. In general, the fact that individuals make these judgements does not necessarily make them arbitrary. The following example may illustrate this. 'The directress of the nursing home is responsible for the hygiene in their kitchen; in this case a lack of supervision gave rise to the cook's abusive behaviour' is a normative statement containing moral standards. The facts can be verified and the standards may be tested for their validity.

In this example, the validity of the judgement could be checked by answering questions such as:

- ☐ On what basis can we hold the top management of this nursing home accountable for staff failures, and to what extent?
- ☐ Could the actual abuses have been prevented by better quality controls and staff training, and by improving other procedures?
- ☐ Or was the food poisoning basically a matter of a one-off act of negligence on the side of the cook, beyond all management control?

In this way the study of the relevant facts and standards goes way beyond arbitrary thinking and impulsive decisions.

In moral debates people refer to moral standards that can be elucidated and tested. The relevant facts and standards can be identified and we may then find differences that go far beyond private arbitrary opinions and whims. Of course many standards and norms concerning moral questions may vary. But it would be a mistake to believe moral debate impossible because 'everybody has the right to think what he or she likes'. Expression of thought is fine, but rational debate and control of impulsive behaviour by use of argument and analysis should remain possible. For instance, some overtolerant ideas like 'in your sexual behaviour you may do as you fancy' may contain dangerous ideas concerning others. It is not being arbitrary to warn adherents about these views, especially those who practise them without seeing the damage they are doing. Likewise, promoting opposing values that foster individual growth together with care and concern in human relationships, is not of arbitrary importance. It is the backbone of civilized society.

1.7.2 Legal normative judgements and moral normative judgements

Moral judgements are only one of a whole range of normative judgements. Every human activity with well-defined rules has its norms. For instance, normative judgements can be made during a sports game (e.g. 'That ball was in, I tell you!'). Here we will only discuss details of legal and moral normative judgements.

Legal normative judgements apply accepted legal norms to a specific situation. For example, 'Menacing a citizen from another country like Rushdie with death is contrary to accepted rules of international law.'

Moral normative judgements, on the other hand, apply moral standards accepted by a community, group or individual. These standards may refer to various topics and their use may depend on many circumstances.

Examples of moral judgements are: 'Boeing was responsible for the plane crash in Amsterdam', 'Publicity for alcoholic drinks should be forbidden in all European countries', 'The fees charged by the public notaries in the Netherlands until July 1994 for deeds of sale were disproportionate; for those who believe in fair pay for a real effort this was legalized robbery'.

Of the whole range of normative judgements, the legal judgements are those most related to morality. In fact there is quite an overlap. An example that is both a moral and a legal judgement is: 'This toy helicopter should not have pointed wings'.

There are also differences. First, we often see legislation lagging behind, while moral opinions or judgements take the lead: for example, 'The manufacturers should have stopped producing CFCs right after the first alarming evidence about the hole in the ozone layer became public'. Secondly, law regulates areas of human behaviour that have no direct concern with morality. An example of a morally indifferent rule is: 'In Great Britain traffic drives on the left-hand side'; another example is the European Community legislation standardizing the outside measurements of tomato crates.

The example of the tomato crates can also serve to explain why these apparently value-neutral regulations may indirectly concern basic human interests. The Italians used to get more EC subventions than the Greeks for their tomatoes, as these subventions were paid per crate and the Italian crates used to be smaller than the Greek ones. So, again we return to an issue where ideas of justice are at stake. The motive for the legal standardization of crate size was a moral one, allowing the Greek peasants to claim equal pay with the Italians for the same quantities of tomatoes.

This overlap and these differences may be explained by a simple definition of law: *law codifies rules for human behaviour*. This codification is made in a society by an authoritative institution that has the acknowledged right to legislate. Law stipulates all kinds of rules and guidelines for behaviour. Some of these rules cover moral issues, but others regulate issues of no direct moral concern. As laws have to be laid down by authoritative bodies, it becomes clear why legislation so often lags behind. Certainly future generations may suffer because of negligent behaviour in the case of banning CFC production, but if we examine the history of CFC production we must conclude that a more timely legal prohibition was almost impossible. Only in 1987 were the estimates for ozone reduction conclusively verified, and at that stage there was no existing international legal network capable of enforcing a prohibition on CFC production. Moral pressure by environmentalists was effective initially in arousing public interest in the matter, but it was only later, when national politicians acted and leading manufacturers were forced to adopt a phase-out policy towards CFC production, that a worldwide ban became possible. Here a moral awakening took and kept the lead; legal bans have only followed at a later stage.

Personal morality does not rely only on inner conviction: networks in civilized society have an important role to play in socializing people. During our moral education people experience coercion and habit training. Doing what one ought to do on the basis of personal conviction is only the desirable outcome, the goal of moral education. This is an ideal which requires personal experience and wisdom and should not be taken for granted. In summary, we believe morality needs compliance based on mutual care and agreement and on reciprocal controls. But these controls should not have to be voted in and enforced by public authorities. Indeed, it is preferable when the public laws are compatible with the beliefs to which the civil society is wholeheartedly committed.

1.7.3 Legal, strategic and moral norms in international export business

Within one nation the distinctions made above between pre-existing moral requirements (moral standards) and their codification by law (legal norms) do hold. However, in modern society there are increasing international exchanges in which dominant powers try to impose their rules. After the Second World War one of the overriding issues that caused conflict between the United States and minor European nations was the implementation of American export codes concerning the export of strategic goods to Communist countries.

In his thesis, Roodbeen (1992) records the implementation of multilateral export controls aimed against the Communist block. After the Second World War, the Dutch government was very reluctant at first to follow sanctions inspired by the United States. Roodbeen explains that the Dutch authorities had other priorities, and in particular they wanted to rebuild their economy. There were differing opinions about what the United States defined as 'strategic exports': for example, Dutch authorities encouraged a shipbuilder to export a whaling factory ship to the Soviet Union in 1954, while the United States indicated that this export could endanger Dutch–American relationships. This friction of policies caused problems for local corporations, and in the 1950s, as a result of their strategic exports to Communist countries, several Dutch companies appeared in American exclusion lists.

Contrary to the hesitation on the part of the Dutch national authorities, one Dutch firm scrupulously applied the 'US 1A List for strategic deliveries' from 1948 onwards: Philips Eindhoven. As a result of their wartime activities with Nazi Germany and trade with Eastern Europe up till 1948, Philips figured on the American 'List of denial of access to classified army, navy and air force contracts'. The company wanted to regain and maintain access to the important American market. Yet it was only after two years of repeated mediation by Dutch authorities that the Americans declared Philips to be safe. Until 1950 they stayed on the exclusion list despite their overtly good conduct. Over the years Philips has understood the danger of having a bad image in the eyes of the federal American administration, because of the sheer weight of the US market and their coherent trade policy. By experience Philips was already aware of the risks of an American trade boycott. Mainly driven by strategic corporate interests they now have a long tradition of maintaining their reputation for reliable and safe partnership with American corporations. This tradition prevents risks and keeps them away from the financial losses and damaged reputation that, for example, Delft Instruments NV incurred in 1991 as a result of the US export boycott.

So the motives for Philips' 'good behaviour' appear to be mainly strategic. This leads us, however, to a core question of moral enquiry: What are the specific characteristics of moral behaviour? Before answering this, we will first explain the distinction between moral judgement and the underlying criterion, the moral standard.

1.7.4 The moral syllogism: facts, standards and judgements

In general, all normative judgements refer to standards. Now, ethics studies moral behaviour and moral judgements. Thus in order to formulate a productive approach to ethics, we have to discard the idea that moral judgement is something completely individual or arbitrary. Just as for the other normative judgements, we have to distinguish facts, standards and judgements. This approach offers considerable opportunities for a further study of normative decision-making.

In order to draw conclusions on moral issues, we apply a (hidden) moral standard for evaluating relevant facts. This standard can be expressed as a *moral norm* or a more vague and general *moral value*. Often the underlying motives, interests or objectives are taken for granted. Turning these unarticulated attitudes into explicit standards may often even transform their very substance.

As already mentioned, moral judgements are not true in the sense that we speak about the truth of factual descriptions. Still, we can reach an understanding about the validity of a normative claim as soon as we open our minds to shared standards. Mutually subscribing to the same rules is possible first by proper education and later by reasonable understanding of the principles governing respect for others.

Table 1.1   Three moral syllogisms based on one single fact

Factual statement	Moral standard	Moral judgement
This mushroom is poisonous	I want to stay in good health	I do not eat this mushroom
This mushroom is poisonous	I want to attempt suicide	I do eat this mushroom
This mushroom is poisonous	I want to punish my ex-wife	I put this mushroom in her soup

Humans can test moral judgements by communicating about the truth of facts and the validity of applied standards. This can be explained by reference to the *moral syllogism. Facts* have to be evaluated by *moral standards* in order to arrive at a *normative moral judgement*. These standards express the norms and values that back up our judgements. Such standards contain the affirmation of positive interests or preferences; they also give the reason for a negative attitude by explaining motives for rejecting a specific practice.

The example in Table 1.1 shows that if one applies different standards to the same facts, opposite guidelines for action might follow. Conversely, the presence of an edible mushroom (other factual evidence) might incite the health-loving person to adopt another conclusion: 'I will eat this mushroom'. Different facts judged according to the same standard may lead to contrary moral normative conclusions.

The bottom right-hand statement in Table 1.1 contains a rather shocking and immoral judgement. In a more neutral sense ethicists call this a 'moral normative conclusion' – because it affirms a course of action – or a normative attitude. Moreover the syllogism, 'This mushroom is quite edible, I want to stay in good health and I have an appetite, so *I choose to eat it*', does not shock anybody. It does not pose a moral problem – in ordinary language, it is a non-moral statement.

Here our next question comes in: What characteristics are typical for moral standards and moral judgements? In other words, what are the common characteristics of moral consent or indignation?

1.8 Characteristics of moral standards

First, it is important to stress that in a very practical sense *moral standards contain a normative appeal*. Moral standards set claims on human behaviour, they express a criterion for what *ought* to be done. Even if moral rules are violated, those that adhere to these rules continue to maintain them. Thus the fact that rape happens does not invalidate the moral interdiction of sexual violation. Likewise, the fact that other export firms broke the UN embargo is not a valid excuse for Delft Instruments NV's exports in 1990. In general, moral standards to which people feel deeply committed are strengthened by the fight against those who violate rules.

Besides this characteristic of deeper moral standards, namely, that *their normative validity remains in spite of, or is even strengthened by, violations,* Velasquez (1992) identifies five other standards. Especially concerning the first, third and fifth characteristic we will make additional comments and change their very meaning.

(1) *In general, all moral standards deal with matters (that are thought to be) of serious consequence for human wellbeing. They also deal with the wellbeing of animals, and the respect we owe to our natural environment.* There are many rules about how to prevent serious injuries and how to share benefits. Thus all rules of criminal law refer to moral norms and are codified in legal documents. These moral norms express our condemnation of murder, rape, stealing, child abuse, slavery, slander, and fraud. Such moral norms specify values concerning which injuries should be prevented and how individual benefits ought or ought not to be obtained. Yet these benefits and injuries do not only concern *human* wellbeing. Our moral norms also cover serious injuries and benefits towards other living beings and even nature. 'You should not treat bulls that way' is a moral conclusion if it is made by someone protesting against bullfights or by somebody criticizing bio-industrial breeding. This first characteristic also explains one basic reason for the indistinct borders of moral issues. Because of different ideas about the quality of individual life and social duties, because of the differences in opinion about animal wellbeing and environmental duties, it is possible that one group may call a matter a moral issue, while in another culture some people might feel that the benefits and injuries at stake in that matter are not part of a moral debate.

(2) *Moral standards cannot simply be established or changed by the decisions of particular authoritative bodies.* This aspect opposes moral rules to legal guidelines, and has already been discussed separately (see section 1.7.2).

(3) *All moral standards are supposed to override self-interest.* This statement is too general. It is relevant for blatant egoism, which is indeed immoral, but does not hold for other-including self-interest and enlightened egoism (see Chapter 5). Nonetheless, this statement does explain a crucial distinction between strategic norms and moral standards: strategic norms do refer to private interests. Thus most readers would question the morality of the motives behind Philips' tradition of following US regulations (see section

1.6.3) as they are mainly motivated by corporate interests. In fact, this third characteristic will be amended in Chapter 2 in order to meet the specific task business ethics has to face: mediating between moral demands and strategic interests.

(4) *All moral standards are based on impartial considerations.* The idea of equal treatment for comparable cases is fundamental to moral reasoning. It refers to the concept of impartial justice. Most civilized people do in fact formulate impartial norms and values based on the basic conviction that all members of the human species have equal rights. The universal declaration of human rights expresses that conviction, as does the rule of law in most constitutional states.

(5) *All moral standards are associated with special emotions and a special vocabulary.* However, special emotions and vocabulary do not guarantee that we make the right judgements. When people act contrary to a moral standard, strong emotions of dissent arise in others. Normal persons with an internalized set of norms and beliefs are quite liable to react this way. This characteristic remains valid if we stay within one accepted moral code. However, it is dangerous simply to apply our own moral norms when we judge the behaviour of people with a different conventional moral code. If we do so, we practise *ethnocentrism* or *moral absolutism*: that is, we take our own moral code to be the only *valid* code. Moral absolutism will prevent us from opening any *ethical* dimension in our moral convictions; we will not really try to understand 'strange' behaviour, since we refuse to analyze the norms behind that behaviour and do not want to check on deeper values. People in uncertain situations that rely on an aggressive kind of ethnocentric moral code are quite capable of inflicting murder, torture and genocide on those they consider to be 'not one of them'. In this way, strong moral feelings may be completely misguided and even unethical. Nevertheless, even though the emotion does not always indicate whether the moral issue is estimated correctly, this fifth characteristic has a certain value: under normal circumstances it helps to detect topics of public interest in conventional morality.

1.9 Synopsis

1. Ethics only studies one type of normative judgement: the moral judgements entailed in everyday moral practice.

2. Moral judgements result from the evaluation of facts by means of a moral standard. These standards most often remain implicit and are commonly taken for granted by moral agents.

3. Moral standards are distinct from other normative expectations, although overlap exists. From a practical point of view it is important to appreciate that deeply felt moral expectations may even be reinforced by a feeling of revolt after a serious violation. More generally, moral standards:
   (a) deal with matters of serious consequence for human, animal and environmental wellbeing;
   (b) are not established by the mere decision of a legal authority;
   (c) override egocentric interests without consideration for others;
   (d) express some impartial ideal of equity and justice; and
   (e) may involve feelings of particular emotion and thoughts of revolt and anger.

4. Descriptive ethics simply describes moral behaviour and judgements.

5. Normative ethics formulates philosophically coherent theories with a prescriptive thrust. A normative ethical theory is not merely descriptive as it judges existing practices on the basis of explicit moral standards indicating what ought to be done in that situation.

6. Normative ethics is a branch of philosophy studying moral judgements. It aims at evaluating past moral behaviour by applying clearly defined moral standards, and it seeks to formulate advice for new situations. By elaborating explicit moral standards that can be applied to concrete moral issues, ethics may provide frameworks for a thorough understanding of these moral issues. Thus, normative ethics is a philosophical reflection on conventional morality.

7. Our general idea of normative ethics maintains that in fact concrete guidelines vary to a great extent, and moral norms differ. However, certain general values do 'exist'. Civilized human beings, including many business people, adhere to basic values of human decency and respect. These basic values can best be formulated in a negative way: do not murder, torture, rape or exploit.

8. Ethical or normative relativism is rejected, as it claims that moral behaviour and moral norms should only be judged according to the particular standards of one's own culture. Contrary to this we maintain that certain transcultural values should prevail. These values belong to the backbone of humanity.

9. Anthropological or descriptive relativism is quite acceptable and belongs to a basic skill in human communication. It stipulates that in order to acquire a valid perception of our interlocutor, we need to be well acquainted with his or her cultural norms, values and customs. Consequently, foreign habits should not be judged by simply applying our own norms.

10. The practical use of normative ethics lies in the careful study of specific cases often exploring dilemmas between conflicting values. Ethical analysis and judgement is possible by developing well-informed ideas on how to mediate between the various values and strategic concerns when facing moral dilemmas.

1.10 References

Friedman, A. (1993) *Spider's Web*, New York: Bantam Books.

Herodotus (1972) *The Histories*, transl. Aubrey de Sélincourt, revised by A. R. Burn, Harmondsworth: Penguin Classics.

Kant, I. (1965/1785) *Grundlegung zur Metaphysik der Sitten*, K. Vorländer (ed.), Hamburg: F. Meiner Verlag.

Roodbeen, H. (1992) *Trading the jewel of great value: the participation of The Netherlands, Belgium, Switzerland and Austria in the Western strategic embargo*. Unpublished thesis, University of Leiden, ISBN 90-9004642-9.

Trompenaars, F. (1993) *Riding the Waves of Culture*, London: Nicholas Brealey Publishing Ltd.

Velasquez, M. (1992) *Business Ethics, Concepts and Cases*, Englewood Cliffs: Prentice Hall.

2

Business ethics: mediating between moral demands and interest

2.1 Business ethics is normative

Business ethics adapts the methods and purpose of normative ethics to the specific requirements of moral issues in business. It studies the specific moral demands that apply to this particular sphere of modern civilization. Here, business ethics studies both profit and non-profit corporations.

Although business ethics has to base its conclusions on careful studies of factual norms and values, the core activity of business ethics is not descriptive. What pertained for ethics in general is also relevant here: business ethics is equally normative. Existing practices are judged on the basis of knowledge of what ought to be done in a given situation. Business ethics has both the diagnostic and therapeutic aims of general normative ethics. It evaluates moral behaviour in business environments by applying clearly defined moral standards, and it elaborates specific moral guidelines suitable for actual business issues.

One specific feature is vital to business ethics. Business ethics has to account for strategic concerns. More than in many other branches of moral philosophy we face the task of developing well-informed ideas on how to mediate between moral demands and strategic concerns. In the business sphere, ethical reflection has to allow for the interest at stake, in order to avoid being so high-principled that one disregards all consequences for the corporation's future.

A principal reason for including strategic concerns in business ethics is explained in the following section, which also shows how this can be done without sacrificing justified moral demands to inflated economic concerns.

25

2.2 The relative autonomy of business morality

2.2.1 The position of business in modern society

Business ethics evaluates and prescribes moral standards that match a specific sphere in modern society: the business environment. Business is now a prominent part of modern society, with its own rules and a relatively independent status. The very basis of business ethics refers to an idea of how business fits into modern society as a whole: a social philosophy of business. We now will outline three different social philosophies of business, and show that two of them lead to untenable concepts of corporate responsibility.

First, we indicate the 'unitarian' danger of regarding business as a diffuse or non-distinct part of society. This view leads to a false idea of accountability holding that public claims apply to business in an indiscriminate way. Secondly, we expose the opposite view which separates business completely from any ordinary moral concern. This separatist view leads to the equally false consequence that business is never directly accountable, i.e. the only business of business would then be to do business within the boundaries set by the non-moral rules of law and market.

Chapter 4 will elaborate our idea that business has at least a number of well-defined public responsibilities. Here, we lay the foundations for that theory by means of a more adequate social philosophy of business: the integration view, which holds business to be a relative independent part of modernity. This view allows for moral claims on business behaviour, as long as one gives credit to the particular position of business organizations. We claim that private enterprise is a relative independent sphere in modernity, but at the same time we regard corporations as involved in the broader sphere of moral society by means of three integrating social mechanisms: market constraints, national legislation, and personal responses to the appeal for socially responsible behaviour.

Most of this section refers directly to a paper by Ronald Jeurissen (1995). The novelty of his paper lies in its clear definition of the relationship between private business and public morality. Jeurissen outlines a *social philosophy of business*, explaining why business ethics is not the simple application of general codes of ethics to business. He does so after showing that business morality belongs to a relatively autonomous sphere of modern society, the market system. By a social philosophy of business Jeurissen means a philosophical reflection on the actual role and functioning of business in our society. In order to explain this role and function he expands on Max Weber's definition of modernity.

Modernity stands for a process of differentiation in society resulting in several relatively autonomous spheres, each with its own logic, procedures and rules. Primary examples of such social spheres are:

☐ Our private lives in the sphere of family and friendship.
☐ Our economic life in the sphere of the market.
☐ A political life in the sphere of the state.

Modern society is a fragmented society, which has lost its sense of unity. It is based on the growing of functional distinctions between various social spheres: a new phenomenon in human history. This phenomenon is in contrast to pre-modern society which more closely resembles an undifferentiated whole. In European history, there is the example of the Middle Ages where close ties existed between church and kingdoms, art and religion, family and economic autarky. Whereas the non-modern man of the Middle Ages did not yet make a clear distinction between earning one's living and family life, or between art and religion, modern man does. The differentiation in distinct social spheres is the first characteristic we need to recognize in order to obtain a better understanding of the role and function of business in modern society.

The second and related characteristic is the fundamental dichotomy between two large, distinct realms in modern civilization. One part of our life happens in a cultural and social sphere called lifeworld ('*Lebenswelt*' according to Weber). This is the overall sphere of cultural tradition with its basic outlooks and values forming the common cultural world people live in. It provides people with strong bonds of solidarity. Its basic values are warmth, recognition and support. Jeurissen refers to this *Lebenswelt* by the expression *moral community*. The norms of each moral community originate from pre-modern local traditions; they date back to the period when most societies survived by means of almost autarkic economies.

The other realm of modern social experience consists of a number of highly specialized functional spheres, each performing one task within society. The main examples are technological research, medical science and care, the economic market system and the organization or bureaucratic sphere. They all seek to perform their specific task by applying strictly formal procedures and rules, and expressing target-oriented values such as efficiency, procedural rationality, emotional neutrality and task differentiation. As far as these separate functional spheres do their specific jobs well, they operate 'rationally'.

It is vital to understand that this rationality belongs to what Charles Taylor (1991) calls instrumental reason: 'the kind of rationality we draw on when we calculate the most economical application of means to a given end. Maximum efficiency, the best cost-output ratio, is its measure for success' (p. 5).

Two functional spheres play a dominant role in modern society:

☐ The market system aiming at the rational production and allocation of products and services.
☐ The bureaucratic sphere which aims at the rational organization of institutions and services.

The core maxim of organizations working within the market system is to reduce costs in order to maximize profits. Here, we also propose a core principle for the means and objectives of the bureaucratic sphere: standardize procedures and impose a system of controls which is instrumental for the institutional goals.

Business corporations fall within the large zone of overlap between the functional spheres of the market system and bureaucracy. However, it should be noticed that our use of the word 'bureaucracy' does not have the negative connotation that may be found in expressions like 'In the 1980s IBM and General Motors had become bureaucratic elephants, unable to anticipate market shifts'. We follow the more neutral and sociological meaning of *bureaucracy* which originates from Max Weber, and that we describe as *conducting an organization in a manner that is characterized by formal guidelines, instrumental expertise, a hierarchy of tasks and responsibilities and, finally, recruitment and promotion on basis of acquired skills and accomplishments.* In this sense, bureaucracies are rational organizations dominated by instrumental reason. They apply the values of procedural rationality, emotional neutrality and task differentiation. Following this meaning of bureaucracy, one may rightfully say that the bulk of private business organizations are both market-oriented institutions and bureaucratic organizations. The present growth of these functional spheres has led to feelings of alienation: modern organizations operating within functional spheres have broken away from the safe routines of the *Lebenswelt*.

Now one of the major problems of business ethics has to do with the existence of relatively autonomous spheres of instrumental rationality. The rationality of the systems of market and bureaucracy is quite different from the solidarity and moral warmth of the moral community. It seems as if the functional spheres of modern society 'colonize' and dehumanize the moral community. Following this line of reasoning, both Aldous Huxley and George Orwell gave their powerful satires of a dehumanized society monopolized by instrumental reason in *Brave New World* and *1984*.

Jeurissen (1995) formulates the issue of modern society in a more reflective way: 'How can a society that is based on two radically different principles still remain in one piece? How can modern society be protected from disintegration?' Replies to these questions can be organized under three headings, according to their different perception of modern society: the *unitarian view*, the *separatist view*, and the *integration view*.

Moreover, each of these views entails a different outlook on the relationship between business and public, which leads to three contrasting answers to a vital question in business ethics, 'May we simply apply public morality to judge business activities?' Unitarians agree to do so, separatists are strongly opposed, while integratists adopt an intermediate position. For separatists and integratists a second question then follows: 'If you may not simply apply morality to modern business, by what means is it possible to contribute to human wellbeing in the economic sphere?'

The unitarian and separatist view are presented as one-sided, because they are based on erroneous views of modern society, although both contain useful elements. But Jeurissen's central thesis is positive. The chief aspects of modern society are more coherently formulated by the integration model. It presents an adequate description of modern society.

2.2.2 *The unitarian view*

This view ignores the idea that modernity is a basic feature of present society, but still regards society to be based on one unifying social–cultural principle. This is a pre-modern view. It does not recognize the distinct character of functional spheres in modern society, and resolutely applies the general values and standards of the overall culture to evaluate activities in newly developed areas of technology, economy and public administration.

The social philosophies of Marxism and Catholicism are good examples of this view. Marxism projects solidarity values in the Communist utopia of a classless society, without recognizing that large segments of modern society have become disconnected from the moral community. Thus Marxism is not able to cope well with the difference in principles between moral community and the functional spheres. When Marxist morals and political values are applied in practice, the end result is the perversion of both realms.

The Catholic church projects its idea of the church as a 'familia dei' – the family of all God's children in emphatic solidarity – to the whole society. It looks upon society as an organic whole, a familylike moral community based on feelings of solidarity and love between its members. This perception of society as only a moral community creates blind spots for those concerned. Consequently, the Catholic clergy tends to underestimate the differentiated character of modern society. Rome prefers to see new commodities and services as threats to the moral community and the outcome of their unitarian outlook is found, for example, in encyclical letters on contraceptives, on bio-technology, and even on the basic principle of modern finance, that is, charging interest when borrowing money (see Figure 2.1).

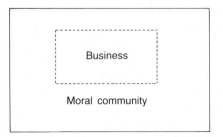

Figure 2.1 The unitarian view: Moral claims apply directly to business.

According to Jeurissen (1995), the unitarian or pre-modern view of society is quite influential in business ethics:

> The influence can be seen most clearly with those business ethicists who conceive of business ethics as applied ethics. There are moral principles that have universal validity, such as the principles of rights and justice. The task of business ethics is simply to apply these principles to business. (p. 4)

He agrees that business cannot escape from public debate on moral issues, but he criticizes the underlying assumption of identity between the morality of the lifeworld and the morality of the business sphere. The business system does not operate in an unbroken unity with the moral community. This unitarian view is unable to provide guidelines for corporate governance:

> Moral principles alone, for example, cannot tell business how much it should invest in environmental protection, what it should do for the unemployed and what kinds of anti-competitive practices are morally permissible. To get answers to these questions, moral principles must be confronted with the internal logic of the economy, but this the unitarian approach fails to do. (Ibid., p. 4)

2.2.3 The separation view

Classical economists like Adam Smith were prominent in the development of this view. It contradicts the idea of an undifferentiated unity, and represents the functional spheres in modern society as radically independent and disconnected islands. And it was already Adam Smith that introduced the invisible hand argument in order to explain how the open market system may lead to socially beneficial communication between the egoistic private pursuits. For classical economists, this is the non-moral means that explains how business companies pursuing their own isolated interests may contribute to human welfare.

The separation view looks upon business as being part of the *completely autonomous* market system. It exists totally separated from the cultural–ethical sphere of the lifeworld. Separatists dismiss the application of moral appeals to business. For them, business has a normative principle of its own: 'maximize private profits, reduce costs'. It is alleged to be an amoral principle falling beyond direct moral claims.

Critics of business ethics often follow the separation view of modernization. Here Jeurissen (1995) sketches the view of Milton Friedman on business responsibility:

Managers should single-mindedly pursue only one goal: the maximalization of profit for the benefit of their shareholders. The invisible hand of the market then guarantees that their actions contribute to social welfare in the best possible way. According to Friedman, the idea that you cannot beat the market is also true in a moral sense. (p. 5)

The separation view of business does not exclude all controls by society, but the controls should not be based on direct moral appeals. In order to ensure that business activities do not become utterly harmful and disruptive, the larger community still has two non-moral means of influencing business: law and the market. For example, a separatist comment on the Delft Instruments exports would not contain any moral condemnation, but would highlight the illegal aspects and the financial consequences of the US embargo. In the separation view those that simply apply the underlying moral concepts to the specific business environment actually muddle quite distinct categories: legal guidelines and market rules are quite different from moral claims.

Jeurissen introduces a metaphor to explain how the separation view looks upon the function of law and the market. They serve as *transformers* between the moral community and the business system. In our case this means that the UN sanctions of August 1990 as well as the US embargo against Delft Instruments from February 1991 are perceived as legal devices with a commercial impact. So these market-regulating laws transform moral claims to match the business context. In this case the embargoes transformed the moral support for the Gulf War into legal sanctions against private corporations supplying a wartime enemy.

In the separation view, therefore, *law and the market* transform:

'moral inputs from the lifeworld into outputs that the non-moral system of business can understand and deal with. If the public is clever enough to translate its moral demands into the language of law and market, it will obtain a response from business to conform with its moral demand. The response from business is not in itself a moral response.' (Jeurissen, 1995, p. 6)

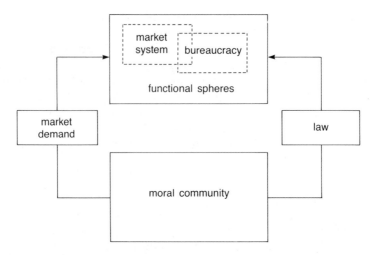

Figure 2.2   The separatist view: Moral claims can only apply indirectly to business, by means of transformers.

These two transformers *modify values* which originated from the moral community into non-moral normative guidelines that fit well into the language of business: *the language of strategic orientation towards self-interest*. The first transformer, law, refers to this language, but also has its proper merits. Law is mainly the instrument of public administrations. As we have seen in the Delft Instruments case, such administrations may impose embargoes in order to *compel* a business corporation to respect their law. Due to this feature of compliance even corporations and individuals that do not feel committed to the idea behind the law have strong strategic motivations for respecting it (see Figure 2.2).

According to the separatist one has to modify moral demands into legal rules. Most separatists agree to enforce law on business, especially when individual human rights and national security are at stake.

The second transformer is the market demand, which belongs to the proper sphere of business, the market system:

Sellers and buyers strategically adapt themselves to each other's behaviour, in determining the prices and quantities of supply and demand. This adaptive mechanism makes market demand a second instrument for the public to communicate moral messages to business in a strategic language. Consumers can translate their moral demands and appeals to business in the strategic language that business understands, by demanding products in accordance with their moral preferences. (Jeurissen, 1995, p. 7)

The example Jeurissen gives here seems less adequate. The activities of anti-apartheid activists who attempted to mobilize the public for a boycott against Royal Dutch Shell, did not only use the transformer of the market demand. Certain activists were so convinced about their own cause that they cut off refuelling hoses at Shell filling stations. This technique was similar to the successful fire-raising by anti-apartheid activists of RaRa in the 1980s. RaRa activists burned several huge Macro stores in the Netherlands owned by the SHV wholesale firm, demanding the withdrawal of SHV investments from South Africa. Although suspects were known, legal proof of their involvement was not available. After a few more big fires the insurances backed out. Facing the risk of further fires and without any fire insurance, SHV decided to withdraw all their activities from South Africa. They felt that they had been blackmailed and terrorized by fanatics, people who do not adhere to the separatist view. The RaRa activists may be seen as a violent group of unitarians.

Jeurissen then explains that the separatist view gives an inadequate idea of modern society, because not all moral anxieties in society are included under either market demands influencing corporate strategies or legal rules enforced by public authorities. Morality cannot be simply reduced to strategy:

> What about firms that develop and implement moral codes, that organize ethical training programmes, that set up an ethics board, that make charitable donations, that adopt a highly sensitive stakeholder policy? . . . A sceptic might view many of these appearingly moral actions as strategy in disguise, or as based on self-interest on the long run. . . . But if you want to reduce it all to strategy, the concept of strategic action will be stretched so far, that it will become meaningless. (Jeurissen, 1995, pp. 7–8)

2.2.4 The integration view

This view is neither overoptimistic nor oversceptical. It knows that one cannot directly apply demands from the moral community to the functional spheres of modern society, but it does not exaggerate the distinctness of the functional spheres, thus avoiding scepticism: instrumental reason is not all there is.

In common debate people often remain committed to fruitless opposition between these inadequate views. Simplifying moralists fight against cynical moneymakers. In business ethical debates during the 1970s and early 1980s, a similar opposition was dominant: either you were in favour of unitarian ethics or you declined to apply moral considerations to business and reverted instead to separatist cynicism.

The point made by the integration view is that economic activities not only have an inner logic based on profit maximalization, but are also part of society and are controlled by moral claims. Jeurissen portrays the economic sphere as a relatively autonomous part of modernity, but still a part that to a certain extent has to reply to moral demands. He follows the classical theory of modernity as expressed by Max Weber and Talcott Parsons in order to formulate his integration view on business.

Max Weber first expressed the idea that modern Western capitalism is fundamentally different from non-Western and pre-modern forms of capitalism because of its elaboration of a characteristic economic order. His famous study Protestant Ethics and the Spirit of Capitalism was first published in 1904.

> Modern capitalism is founded, according to Weber, on a methodological –rational way of life; an ethos that values hard work, postponed consumption and the use of accumulated capital for productive invest-ments. It also involves moral norms such as honesty and fair dealing. (Jeurissen, 1995, p. 8)

Weber stressed that modern capitalism has an ethical foundation; its goals referred to Christian Protestant culture. Calvinists developed utility maximalization in business that was inspired and motivated by religious creeds.

> Weber's theory of the cultural roots of modern capitalism makes a strong point against the separation-view of modernity. It is not the separation of the economy from the ethical lifeworld that has created modern capitalism. On the contrary, modern capitalism is the result of a close connection between the economy and a cultural-ethical tradition. (Ibid., pp. 8–9)

We have to make a comment here. In recent times another great cultural tradition has performed a similar job in the Far East under authoritarian rule, developing a new type of capitalism. In particular, President Lee Kuan Yew in Singapore and General Chiang Kai-shek in Taiwan estab-lished a fruitful link between Confucian traditions and modern free market capitalism. By imposing authoritarian political regimes aimed at public welfare they established maximum economic liberties for certain economic entrepreneurs. Weber had thought that such a phenomenon would be impossible in Chinese cultures, as he maintained that Mandarin Con-fucianism and free enterprise were mutually exclusive. Now, however, developments in the Far East show evidence of successful combinations between Confucianism and state leadership, while a non-Confucian country like the Philippines lags behind.

In the 1950s Talcott Parsons added a new dimension to Weber's theory of modernity. Parsons is the founder of the integration view of society, which gives a more adequate idea of the unity-in-difference between the moral community and the evolving functional spheres. He saw the functional spheres as subsystems with a relatively independent internal logic of their own. Each subsystem had developed its own rules and conventions, prescribing how people have to conform with the internal demands of the sphere.

> Each sphere is characterized by a specific social role. Parsons distinguished between three main spheres of society: a socio-cultural sphere, an economic and a political (bureaucratic) sphere. People can move from one sphere to the other, by changing social roles. (Jeurissen, 1995, p. 8)

The crux of the integration view of society runs as follows:

> If social action can be described in terms of social roles that people take within different social spheres, then it is possible to study social action as a system of social roles. Society can be seen as an overall system, that consists of a number of subsystems which are each characterized by a specific social role. (Ibid., p. 9)

Parsons looks upon the interconnections between the subsystems as *internal connections*, the *'zones of interpenetration'*. The concept of *interpenetration* is based on overlap between the various social subsystems: the subsystems communicate through these overlapping zones where they are interconnected.

> In these overlapping zones, exchanges take place, through which the subsystems communicate through each other, and maintain their mutual relations. Through these interpenetrations and exchanges, the integrity of the universe of subsystems – society itself – is maintained. (Ibid., p. 9)

In his Sankt Gallen lecture, Jeurissen proposed to use the term *'integration'* instead of interpenetration. This new term insists on the *internal* type of relation between the different subsystems. Economy and public administration do not interpenetrate externally like plug and socket, but may fuse and mix. In this book, we will use the expression 'integration view'.

Our example on Delft Instruments in section 1.1 can illustrate this *integration* of subsystems. The possible reasons for the US embargo show internal connections between economic interests and national policies. Some important possible topics for further enquiry are:

☐ The US administration seems to have preferred to strike a blow at some foreign firm competing with their national industries.

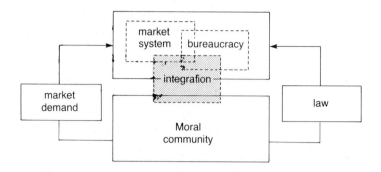

Figure 2.3 The integration view: Moral claims may often be applied directly to business, provided that they are mediated with strategic interests.

□ The same administration was very lenient towards their own illegal exporters.

□ Why did the Bush administration not punish the department members that had allowed the export of military goods made in the United States to Jordan after the UN embargo against Iraq in August 1990?

2.2.5 How moral demands generate in the business sphere

The internal link between business and society, between profit maximalization and moral demands, is exposed by Jeurissen in his theory of *justice requirements*.

To start with, he explains why economic rationality cannot provide moral criteria for economic activities. The expression of instrumental reason in the open market sphere is 'maximize utility, reduce costs'. Here, 'utility' is a vague term with no precise meaning. It can refer to a variety of goals ranging from private consumption to altruistic charity, and it also allows for very different means: 'The objectives of rational economic actors can be achieved through gifts, mutually beneficial exchanges, unilaterally beneficial exchanges, or through manipulation of demand, fraud, bribery, theft or coercion. . . . As utility maximizers and cost reducers, economic actors are completely unreliable, both in terms of the goals and the means of their actions' (Jeurissen, 1995, p. 10).

The vagueness of the term 'utility', combined with our impression that economic actors most often seek private advantages, is the reason why we introduce here our proper expression for the principle of economic efficiency: *maximize corporate profitability, reduce costs*. 'Corporate profitability' is more precise, but still does not provide us with a clue on how to behave morally. It is a non-moral principle, without any clear criterion referring to social integration. The reader should note that the term 'utility' has a vaguer meaning than the ethical concept of utility in Chapter 5.

The demands aiming at social integration stem from within the very functional spheres – they arise from within the order of the market and of public administration.

At this very point we start to draw conclusions leading in other directions than those exposed by Jeurissen. Certainly, we do not want to limit this book to the specific overall direction in which he points, for we would then confine our investigation within the scope of Chapter 6, that is: 'Is this policy honest, right and just?' Rather, we will also examine other important approaches to moral standards for business in Chapters 5 and 7. Nonetheless, we have to concede that the next conclusion in Jeurissen's paper is indeed vital, as it shows that moral demands exist already within the functional spheres:

> It is crucial to see that both the market- and the hierarchy-type of economic order are based on a moral principle of justice. Neither the market nor the hierarchical order are conceivable without this principle. Market exchange systems and hierarchical decision procedures must be considered as just or 'fair' by the participants in order to be stable and sustainable. (Ibid., p. 10)

Also, we subscribe to the further arguments he uses to expose the validity of the integration view of society for finding basic moral standards for business activities:

1. In business, actors that systematically pursue profits in ways that harm exchange partners will see the willingness of others disappear. A good example in the early 1990s is the collapse of the market order in Nigeria due to repeated thefts, intimidations, bribes and murder of foreign businessmen.

2. In general, the contrary is equally true: 'Whatever the precise formulation of economic justice requirements may be, it is evident that the compliance with these principles is a necessary condition of the stability of the economic order' (Ibid., p. 11). A moral basis of trust is necessary for business.

Yet we do disagree with his formulations concerning the basic principles of justice concerning public bureaucracies. We maintain that distributing 'burdens and benefits unequally over organization members' is not the root cause for feelings of moral revolt. Injustice is not a matter of unequal distribution, but results from the feeling and the experience of being systematically and repeatedly ignored. People may accept playing a minor role in society, but they do want to have the right to participate and to make meaningful contributions to society.

Finally, let us return to the main thesis of Jeurissen. His idea of the internal link between modern society and economic activities leads to several very fruitful insights into how public morality is already immanent within business:

> The interpenetration [:integration] view of modernity can explain actions and attitudes of business that cannot be reduced to strategic legalism and market conformity. Take the simple example of legal rule following. If all economic actors would react purely strategically to legal regulations, the legal machinery would soon be exhausted by calculated lawbreaking and by a constant stream of fraus leges issues. (Jeurissen, 1995, p. 11)

> From the perspective of an interpenetration [:integration] view of modernity, the advice to the morally concerned public is this: 'Be neither naive nor pessimistic about the moral response of business. Word your moral demands in terms of the fundamental justice principles that govern the exchange relations and hierarchical relationships on which the institution of business is built. Combine this moral approach to business with the strategic instruments of law and consumer demand.' (Ibid., p. 12)

2.3 The limited scope of normative business ethics in this text

2.3.1 The general goals of this text

Ethical study starts by elaborating moral standards that are relevant for concrete business issues, which implies careful and attentive case study. This is the true test of the theory, as concrete moral judgements and choices have to be justified by formulating the appropriate mix of moral standards.

This text on business ethics will scarcely go into such detail, although one attempt was made in section 1.1, and others will follow. The main objective of this text, however, is to provide the basis of a conceptual framework. In this sense, our scope here is threefold:

1. To define the nature and purpose of business ethics.
2. To outline basic concepts (e.g. free choice, responsibility).
3. To sketch three key outlooks on moral behaviour in business.

2.3.2 Promoting a pluralistic use of ethical outlooks

Modern philosophers often favour *pluralism* in ethics. Pluralism implies tolerance towards present codes and practices. Quite different local cultures may practise codes and conventions that are truly humane and moral.

Pluralism is also a reaction against dangerous oversimplified ideologies. Experience shows that the road to moral disasters is paved by blind adherence to so-called noble intentions. In an ideal world it may be that truth is a simple and noble intention, but in daily decision-making it is dangerous to apply one oversimplifying outlook. The policies of Stalin and Mao especially were applauded by many Western Marxists of the time as great leaps forward for humanity. These 'progressive' comments over-looked the genocide, a modern tragedy in which several tens of millions of human beings became both adherents and victims of these great and simple designs.

From such monomaniacal efforts we might learn a lesson. When assessing a policy, we should be wary of the immediate current effects on concrete human wellbeing, without being blind to possible future conse-quences.

In moral affairs pluralism of methods is essential. In defining moral options the use of three different outlooks, as detailed below in section 2.3.3, may avoid one-sided ideas and set things in a more balanced perspective. We will try to show later that a plurality in outlooks does not lead to confusion, as the different angles may complement one another. Adequate ethical evaluation and advice require that we look at the issue from several perspectives.

We believe that our multifaceted understanding of ethics in combination with an open eye for strategic concerns is well worthwhile. When applied by competent and sophisticated persons this approach should lead to mature, composed and beneficial corporate actions.

The three corresponding questions in section 2.3.4 may open minds to other ethical viewpoints. On top of the methodological concern, this is a perceptive advantage. By using different angles of approach we can balance the risk of a too partial consideration.

2.3.3 Three different normative approaches fit for the economic sphere

Chapters 5, 6 and 7 formulate a first step in answering a vital question: How can business ethics improve moral decision-making in corporations? They will formulate general criteria for moral decision-making, by pointing to three independent ethical outlooks. Each outlook has its proper merits and limits as an evaluative and prescriptive tool. The criteria we define are specific replies to the needs of business ethics, as exposed by the integration view.

This chapter tries to disqualify the unitarian view, which leads to an approach full of blunt and overmoralistic claims. We hold that one cannot indiscriminately apply ready-made moral standards to business corporations. We also refuted non-moral separatist views. The more adequate integration view has introduced what we call the *mediation requirement*. Business ethics should lead to moral standards based on a well-informed and sensible mediation between strategic corporate interests and moral concerns.

This implies that private interests do count in business ethics, provided corporations have a sophisticated idea of what looking after private interests implies. Thus, the main task of this book is to redefine moral outlooks in such a way that they can perform the mediation task. This may lead to sophisticated and morally responsible corporate strategies. Chapters 5, 6 and 7 each discuss a specific outlook and will try to define corresponding standards. By studying these three different perspectives reflective managers can acquire a pluralistic idea of how to overcome the pitfalls of narrow-minded instrumental rationality. It may help them to define what morally responsible behaviour might mean in their specific business situation.

Each of these chapters has a quite different focus. This can best be understood by looking at the main questions they seek to answer. These questions are also the title of each chapter. They are listed below in section 2.3.4.

Some of our discussions contain criticisms. For instance, in Chapter 5 we will show that utilitarianism is not relevant for moral decisions by private corporations. Also, we will point to the fact that many authors stress only one outlook: for example, duty-ethical writers seem already satisfied when they can point towards the underlying moral standards, without explaining how to balance the interests of the parties concerned and without giving much consideration to undesirable effects on personal habits, moral discipline and beneficial skills.

2.3.4 *The corresponding three questions*

In order to evaluate whether a certain option in business is morally good, one has to ask three different questions, which correspond to:

1. What is in it for all parties concerned? (Chapter 5)
2. Is this policy decent, right and just? (Chapter 6)
3. Does this policy foster desirable skills? (Chapter 7)

In each of the Chapters 5, 6 and 7 a detailed discussion will lead to the definition of ethical guidelines for business. Chapter 5 studies an outlook based on interests or stakes; Chapter 6 discusses criteria for formulating duties and obligations in a corporate environment; and Chapter 7 develops concepts referring to common public purposes based on intellectual and moral virtues. In each case we will try to formulate guidelines that should help to answer the relevant question. Knowledge of these different outlooks should help in the assessment of concrete options on the basis of a deeper ethical understanding of the underlying issues.

Our aim is to define valid business ethical outlooks that can check and balance each other. But that is only one element of morally sound business practices. Moral decision-making requires more.

2.3.5 Other factors in the moral decision-making process

Besides ethical value systems, many other factors play a role in the decision-making process. To illustrate this, we briefly refer to the 'model of ethical management behaviour' formulated by Stead, Worrell and Stead (1990) in which they list the following ethical philosophies: utilitarianism, rights, and justice. In addition, they mention various other factors that contribute to moral behaviour in business. These factors are organized under the following headings: individual factors of personality and socialization; ethical decision ideology; external forces; past reinforcement of ethical decisions; ethical decision history; and organizational factors.

It is crucial in a text on business ethics to apply adequate general ethical insights and criteria. Therefore, we would reiterate that the philosophical discussion and the definition of these criteria are our priorities here.

2.4 Special studies in business ethics

Many texts on business ethics expand on particular issues. According to this last approach, business ethics is mainly *special ethics*; it studies separate clusters of moral issues in business. This text will draw upon various special studies on moral issues in business, mainly to exemplify basic insights.

It should be noted, however, that even texts on special ethics can fall into the fallacy exposed by Ronald Jeurissen as the unitarian view. Some authors indeed make in-depth studies of particulars, but seem to forget that general moral claims cannot simply be imposed on business policies.

2.4.1 Business and its internal stakeholders

This problem area is dominated by employee issues like job discrimination, affirmative action, the use of genetic passports for personnel selection, moral issues in human resource management, and the use of personnel incentives (see Table 2.1). An internal stakeholder often neglected by business ethics is the investor, especially for the way they are treated in cases of company bankruptcy.

2.4.2 Business and the end users or consumers

This problem area covers core issues of marketing ethics, such as product responsibility, consumer safety, and advertising ethics (see Table 2.2). Some issues related to product responsibility are discussed in Chapter 4.

2.4.3 Business and its social environment

This problem area contains various social and political issues referring to general shifts in the global environment. These issues (see Table 2.3) may emerge through technology change, and cover subjects like privacy and the use of data banks by direct mailers, the use of genetic manipulation for food production, and so on.

Campaigns on many issues are launched by action groups, covering a variety of political and social issues such as export boycotts to Iraq, boycotts on investment in South Africa, and consumer boycotts directed against countries with a poor reputation for human rights. This field, and that

Table 2.1 Moral issues involving internal stakeholders

Example of moral issues	Direct stakeholders
Positive discrimination against women employees for top jobs.	Directors, male and female staff.
Discrimination against employing members of coloured minorities.	Directors, staff, public administration.
The rights of small shareholders after the DAF bankruptcy, compared to those of banks and debtors.	Trustees, directors, banks, debtors, shareholders.
Does the Health Horizon programme of Du Pont contain guarantees against abuse (i.e. will the health data of employees influence their future career)?	Du Pont, health service, personnel department, employees.
What is a fair salary?	Directors, employees, competitors.

Table 2.2 Moral issues in marketing ethics

Example of moral issue	Direct stakeholders
Do employment agencies have to comply with discriminatory employee profiles made by a company?	Employment agency, directors of company, candidates.
Was Boeing mainly responsible for the 1992 aeroplane crash at Amsterdam?	Boeing, El Al crew, Schiphol Air Control, inhabitants of the flats.
Should Ford have installed safety devices around the petrol tank of the Ford Pinto?	Ford, Pinto owners, victims of Pinto car burns.
Do we accept the way Benetton campaigns (picturing an agonizing AIDS patient, a kissing nun and priest, or a war victim, together with 'united colours of Benetton') blur the moral border between independent news and corporate publicity?	Luciano Benetton, Oliviero Toscani, billboard spectators, committees controlling ethical codes in the publicity branch.
Is the microwave oven manufacturer responsible for the bursting apart of a poodle, when the ignorant owner puts the poodle in there to dry?	Manufacturer, pet owner (acting as an unintentional pet tormentor), poodle.

Table 2.3 Moral issues and the social environment

Example of moral issue	Direct stakeholders
Do coffee roasters and distributors like Nestlé and Sara Lee have to do anything about the prices offered to the small coffee farmers for their products in the 1990s?	Nestlé, Sara Lee, other distributors, coffee farmers, intermediates.
Should Norwegian fishermen stop hunting about 300 minke whales a year in the North East Atlantic, given a total minke whale population of approximately 86,700?	Sea biologists, whalers, consumers of whale meat, Greenpeace.

covered in section 2.4.4, opens perspectives for 'ethical' marketeers like the Body Shop.

2.4.4 Business and the natural environment

This field covers environmental issues related to corporate production and trade. It involves topics on resource depletion, green marketing and pollution control. Its core issues relate to the responsibilities of private enterprise when faced by political goals such as sustainable growth. For example:

1. How to prevent national industries who comply with strict environmental regulations being squeezed out of the market by less scrupulous (foreign) competitors with low environmental priorities.

2. Why, how, and to what extent should a company respond to moral concern about environmental harm?

This field is of particular interest for the ethical reflection on modern business activities; it obliges us to innovate and to adapt received views. It was environmental issues that obliged private corporations to reconsider their separatist ideas about the relationship between business and physical environment, and separatist views have now lost their hold on environmental issues. Over the last thirty years there has occurred a fundamental change in our perception of the link between private corporations and social responsibility in this field. The ethical wave that hits business is mainly a green wave.

Instead of yet another table, let us briefly outline the antagonist view, a separatist philosophy that claims business is a separate sphere which should not be linked directly to its moral, social and natural environment. Understanding the significant features of this separatist view – a culturally transmitted myth of an isolated vocation for private enterprise – is very important.

Here we refer to Buchholz (1993), from which the following extended quotation illustrates the five main points of the separatist perspective leading to environmental mismanagement:

> In final analysis, the cause of our environmental problems is probably the culture we live in, a culture based on certain ethical perspectives with regard to economics and the environment and central values that guide decision making in both the public and the private sectors. Economic values are dominant in our culture and provide the basis for decisions about the uses and abuses of the environment. We do not have an ecological perspective that informs our decisions and guides our actions. Our approach to nature is dualistic, our vision of reality is fragmented, and we view resources and technology as infinite in some sense. According to Kenneth Watt, there are five basic beliefs at the heart of our culture that inform our thinking and practice. [These five ideas are thus outlined by Buchholz:]
>
> **1. The fixation on money**
> . . . The old-growth forests, for example, have no value in their natural state, and preservation of that particular ecosystem has no monetary or economic value. The only value these forests have is their lumber that can be used for construction. Money [present value in our economic sphere] determines whether these forests have any worth in our society.
>
> **2. The belief in omnipotent technology**
> . . . If we run up against limits, we look for a technological solution that

will extend those limits beyond the present. We do not have a plan for the future, as the future will take care of itself through more technological developments. . . . We believe that on the whole technology is good, and we exploit new technologies as quickly as possible before their environmental effects have been thoroughly researched.

3. The belief in management through fragmentation
The way to approach and manage reality is through fragmenting a large task into many small ones that can be controlled and managed. We do not want to worry about the whole, but concentrate on doing manageable tasks that do not require holistic thinking. We believe that the whole is nothing more than the sum of the parts. We do not think of communities and interdependencies, but are individualistic in our approach to reality and attach more value to private property than we do to public property. . . .

4. The belief in force
If something doesn't work, perhaps it is because we haven't tried hard enough or applied enough force to the situation. . . . We will to master nature rather than work in harmony with nature, and we are drawn in the direction of big [powerful] activity rather than the little activity. Our power-generating systems, for example, release massive amounts of energy at a point of source rather than lots of little systems producing energy where it is needed.

5. Growth is good
Economic growth is the bottom line of our society, as is the measure of all progress, both economic and social. Our measure of success as a society is gross national product (GNP), and we do not bother to factor out the environmental damage this growth may have caused or take account of the natural capital that was depleted to attain this growth. We do not particularly care about maintaining a diversity in nature that would lead to a more stable world, but promote uniformity with our emphasis on economic growth and the promotion of an economic lifestyle that is based on the accumulation of more and more material goods and services. (pp. 69–70)

The protest is clear, but the positive alternative is not. What we do know is that environmental pressures force us to reshape our values. Also, the moral community has already defined the general aim: sustainable growth. However, what this means for the reshaping of business operations remains to be seen.

The relationship between product liability and natural environment will be discussed in Chapter 4, and in Chapter 7 sustainable growth will be a prominent theme.

2.5 Evidence from surveys on the role of ethics in business

2.5.1 A survey by Ulrich and Thielemann

The study by Ulrich and Thielemann (1993) is a good example of a recent survey on how business managers conceive the role of morality in business. It confirms findings from other surveys from the 1960s onwards showing that managers generally subscribe to the statement that 'Sound ethics is good business in the long run'. Only a minority (10 to 15 per cent in the various surveys) affirms the statement that 'Whatever is good business is good ethics'. This latter view may be seen as the practical expression of the separatist view.

Other notable findings from this survey are:

1. Most managers subscribe to the idea of the moral or social responsibility of business, parallel to, and sometimes in conflict with, its market orientation.
2. Purely strategic legalism is not a dominant attitude amongst managers.

This survey by Ulrich and Thielemann amongst European managers seems to offer an interesting empirical argument in favour of Jeurissen's integration view of business.

2.5.2 Bird and Waters identify the absence of moral talk

Contrary to these findings, Bird and Waters (1989) insist on 'the moral muteness of managers'. They start by pointing to one dominant fact in business culture: while individual managers are often aware of moral issues, they prefer not to word them as moral issues.

The phenomenon of using non-moral strategic or legal talk when coping with moral issues often goes together with quite moral practices. The combination of moral practice and absence of moral talk is called 'moral muteness'. In studying this aspect, they explain why business does not cultivate ethical debate and indicate what business may gain from using moral talk in corporate communications.

Through interviews Bird and Waters identified three main reasons for avoiding moral talk, besides the more general (separatist) view that moral talk was dysfunctional in business environments.

1. Threat to harmony
Moral talk is said to be intrusive and confrontational and to invite cycles of mutual recrimination.

Business people seek to avoid the interpersonal confrontation that goes with moral talk. The Holland Casino example (see section 2.7.1) may illustrate this issue. The unorthodox activities of croupier Van Duren raised questions about effects of the casino's policies for preventing gambling addiction. The casino did not want to discuss their actual policies, but sacked Van Duren for organizational and business-oriented arguments. Bird and Waters concluded that 'Managers typically avoid any such confrontation, experiencing it as difficult and costly – as witnessed, for example, by the frequent avoidance of candid performance appraisals' (Bird and Waters, 1989). They also underpin their final statement on this first reason:

Many managers conclude that it is disruptive to bring up moral issues at work because their organizations do not want public discussion of such issues. We interviewed or examined the interviews of sixty managers who in turn talked about nearly 300 cases in which they had faced moral issues in their work. In only 12 per cent of these cases had public discussion of moral issues taken place and more than half of these special cases were cited by a single executive. Give-and-take discussions of moral issues typically take place in private conversations or not at all. (Bird and Waters, 1989,[1] p. 77)

2. Threat to efficiency
Moral talk is said to assume distracting moralistic forms (praising, blaming, ideologic profiling) and is held to be simplistic, inflexible, soft and inexact.

'Moral talk is associated with several kinds of exchanges that obstruct or distract from responsible problem-solving.' This sentence is illustrated by the words of Harlingen hospital director de Rouw, defining the issue of the second case, in section 2.7.2, as the clash between moral talk and strategic concern:

Morally the only right thing to do would be to end our relationship with the neurologist, but will people still be grateful about this if ethical behaviour means that an entire hospital department has to be closed? (*Leeuwarder Courant*, 1994)

Bird and Waters continued:

While moral talk may be legitimately used to praise and blame people for their conduct, praising and blaming do not facilitate the identification, analysis and resolution of difficult moral conundrums. . . . Blaming, praising and ideological posturing do not help to clarify issues. Moreover, such moral talk frequently seems to be narrowly self-serving.

[1]Copyright © 1989 by the Regents of the University of California. Reprinted from the *California Management Review*, Vol. 32, No. 1. By permission of the Regents.

Those who praise, blame or express ideological convictions usually do so in order to protest and advance their own interests. (Bird and Waters, 1989)

They also explain the vital role of strategic interests in what we call ethical decision-making. Notice that managers with separatist ideas will say that heeding strategic concerns is merely good business beyond moral talk: 'In addition, managers shun moral talk because such talk often seems to result in burdening business decisions with considerations that are not only extraneous, but at times antagonistic to responsible management.'

3. Threat to image of power and effectiveness

Moral talk is said to be too esoteric and idealistic; morally mute managers think that moral talk lacks rigour and force.

Most virile managers are afraid to lose their image of potency, power and effectiveness as decisive leaders, whenever they open the door to moral deliberation.

Many managers experience futility after they attempt unsuccessfully to change corporate politics which they feel are morally questionable. They privately voice their objections but feel neither able to mount organized protests within their organization nor willing to quit in public outcry. *De facto* they express a loyalty they do not wholeheartedly feel. (Bird and Waters, 1989, p. 70)

Bird and Waters go on explaining the common failure of managers to apply ethical considerations in their everyday business practice, by pointing to the poor skills of managers in this field. They do not suggest at all that the mainly duty-based and unitarian outlook of several ethics workshops in the 1980s has anything to do with this inadequacy. Their explanation starts by pointing to the actual predominance of non-moral normative expectations.

Moral expressions recede and are replaced by discussions of organizational politics, technical qualifications, competitive advantages as well as costs and benefits measured solely in economic terms. In the midst of these kinds of practical considerations, moral terms are abandoned because they seem to lack robustness. They suggest ideals and special pleadings without too much organizational weight. (Ibid.)

Furthermore, 'At best they [the managers] received instruction in juvenile versions of ethics as children and young adults in schools and religious associations. They have little or no experience using ethical concepts to analyze issues.' Most managers 'do not know how to use ethical terms and theories with intellectual rigour and sophistication to identify and resolve moral issues.'

2.6 A theory on voluntary mediation: participatory ethics

Henk van Luijk (1994) makes a plea for *participatory ethics*. This ethical outlook expands on the voluntary participation of business in a shared interest, the co-operation of parties to produce a public good. van Luijk characterizes such common goods by three features:

> first, the good can only be realized through the participation of all parties; second, participation cannot be enforced – there is no explicit moral obligation to take part in the project; and third, although participation may be profitable for participating parties as well as for the community at large, none of the participants has to participate in order to survive, every possible participant can abstain without risking a lasting damage for him/herself.

This sounds like charity duties, the promotion of public goods beyond the call of legal duties. Participatory ethics expresses a perspective on how moral agents interact with great potential for the business environment. It indicates a positive role for business in developing moral communities by performing beyond strict self-interest and corporate duty.

All in all, van Luijk distinguishes three general ethical outlooks, each with a different view of the way moral demands are expressed. Besides participatory ethics, van Luijk identifies *transaction ethics* and *recognition ethics*. Both express the moral commitments existing inside the business environment, based on deals between egocentric interests or on the recognition of existing duties. We will review these two briefly, in order to gain a better understanding of participatory ethics.

2.6.1 Transaction ethics

Transaction ethics regards moral interaction as a defence of private interests and bargaining whenever there is a conflict of interest. It does not accept that we recognize others' interests in an altruistic way, and does not allow for feelings of solidarity and loyalty. Sacrificing individual interests goes much too far according to this outlook, as the moral agents are seen as egocentric rational individuals seeking to optimize their private profits. This approach may have positive results in win-win situations, where arrangement can benefit participants. To us this ethical attitude is a typical expression of instrumental business rationality, starting from the idea that economic agents are independent egotists, without roots and loyalties towards their moral community.

2.6.2 Recognition ethics

Recognition ethics regards moral interaction as a matter of protecting individual liberties and guaranteeing public welfare. Here, two dominant issues are at stake for individuals. Each person is regarded as a member of society with, on one side, rights and positive claims to a fair share of the common wealth, but on the other side, each member owes certain duties to society and its other members. According to this view the rights of individuals and our duties to them override personal egocentric interests. Moral agents are bound to the whole of society by a tacit social contract. Moral issues are explained as asymmetrical relationships with, on the one hand, agents with moral claims or rights and, on the other, agents with moral obligation or duty. This view presents a fair idea of what it means to be a member of a moral community, in which the rights and duties of members supersede egocentric calculations. Van Luijk applies this view to the business environment. A recognition approach to moral issues looks upon private corporations as moral communities where loyalty and solidarity values should dominate. For instance, a labour union activist may expect support from his employer when he is prosecuted by justice, even if the imputed activities of that employee did undermine the strategic interests of the company. Recognition ethics holds that duty overrides private interest.

2.6.3 Participatory ethics

In business environments van Luijk sees great potential for his third view: participatory ethics. Here moral agents start voluntary co-operations on the basis of mutually agreed targets. This implies that moral agents choose to involve themselves in freely endorsed moral obligations. Participation ethics distinguishes a specific type of social duty, appealing to personal commitment and involvement to common causes. Such a voluntary and benevolent participation goes beyond both private interest and the call of duty.

Participatory ethics is present in business policies that show proactive and legally unenforceable involvement in various issues. Some may belong to the direct competence of the private company, having immediate effects on the corporation's competitive opportunities. This kind of issue may vary from voluntary waste reduction and limitation of resource input as a part of total quality management, to benevolent policies for employees' health care or a positive discrimination policy. Other participatory activities by business companies may go beyond the sphere of direct concerns, that is, the company involves itself in public charity. Two examples of participatory involvement are job programmes for retraining long-term unemployed and the covenant on Heineken beer crates in Chapter 4.

Thus participatory ethics gives a fine idea of how moral demands and strategic interest can mix on a basis of partnership assent, and without legal sanctions. It creates opportunities for proactive projects that serve the public good in an innovative way, and expresses a dimension of moral commitment where moral activities are agreed upon for the sake of our moral community: in other words, they foster the construction and further development of feelings of solidarity and loyalty. In participatory ethics one contributes to public purposes by free assent.

2.7 Two examples illustrating the predominant role of interests

It is a major task for business ethics to find ways of mediating between moral demands and strategic corporate interests. The following two case studies illustrate the dominant role of these strategic interests whenever moral issues are at stake in the business environment. Our narratives will first describe the *direct circumstances*, and secondly, the *moral issues*, that is, the *larger setting*. We will then delineate *appropriate moral standards*, and finally conclude with a *critical evaluation* of the adopted policy. This sequence serves our specific objective of studying the relations between moral values and strategic interests.

2.7.1 Croupier Van Duren versus the Holland Casinos Foundation

Direct circumstances and moral issues
Mr Van Duren has been a croupier at Holland Casino Valkenburg for 15 years. From 1985 onwards he approached addicted gamblers on his own accord. These activities went beyond the Casino regulations. His motive was compassion with clients who were ruining their lives through their addiction. At the playing-tables he overtly voiced his concern to addicted gambers when they started to lose heavily. Such a direct approach in the early stage of addiction *was not done*, according to the Casino rules. Another activity of Van Duren which flouted the regulations was paying home visits to addicts to discuss their problem.

On the basis of their code of conduct adopted in 1990, Holland Casinos started a lawsuit against Van Duren at the Roermond cantonal court, seeking his complete dismissal. One reason given for dismissal was that

Van Duren's actions had isolated him, and he no longer functioned as part of the team. Also, Van Duren had violated the company's rule against personal relationships with casino guests. Finally, they claimed that Van Duren would not accept orders from his superiors, he refused to stop his warning remarks to the guests, and also he continued to visit addicts at their homes. The court decided to allow this dismissal in March 1994.

The issue here is a particular kind of employee insubordination motivated by noble intentions. The concrete dilemma concerns whether it is morally acceptable that a croupier working for Holland Casinos should be sacked because of his altruistic care for gambling addicts, and because he uses unorthodox methods in this process that go against corporate regulations.

The larger setting
Holland Casinos is a non-profit-making foundation, with eleven establishments all over the country. They have the legal monopoly on casino games in The Netherlands; the total amount of their profits goes to the Dutch government. The mission statement of Holland Casinos is the canalizing of the gambling drive in a socially acceptable way and the public control on gambling. They are part of the two-track policy against gambling abuse. The first track is the suppression of illegal casinos, and the second is the creation of legal alternatives that meet strict conditions. Holland Casinos promotes gambling as a respectable leisure activity, and has always been concerned about gambling addiction since it started in 1976.

Mr Van Duren was trained as a croupier by Holland Casino Valkenburg, an establishment in the south of The Netherlands. He had a well-paid job. About 1985 he became an active member of a Christian church, and his concern about the problems resulting from gambling addiction forced him to take action.

The problems of gambling addicts should not be minimized, for gambling can disrupt their lives completely. In the final stage of gambling addiction the addict is completely obsessed by the accumulated debts and problems and finally realizes the futility of hoping for the lucky strike. In this phase four options remain: seek professional help; run away; plead guilty and accept the sanctions (for instance, a jail sentence for thefts); or commit suicide.

Holland Casinos is not the chief cause of gambling addiction. It only allows in adults over 18 years old; it does not lend money to visitors; and it does not hand out free playing-chips to encourage gambling. The bulk of gambling addicts (88 per cent) stem from other environments. An important source of juvenile crimes is due to the gambling habits of minors operating slot machines. These machines are legally installed in many Dutch bars. Holland Casinos is the only non-profit-making foundation with an explicit mission concerning gambling addicts. Their objective is to canalize the drive for gambling and to create an environment where the harmful aspects of gambling habits are reduced to an acceptable minimum. One may, however, claim that they too create gambling wants. They organize several events to promote their hazard games as a morally acceptable leisure activity in a sophisticated decor. These activities have considerably changed the general public's attitude towards gambling, and for many it has now become an acceptable new excitement. The average expenses per visitor – about 150 Dutch guilders – may illustrate this.

Several Holland Casinos' regulations are important on the issue of addiction prevention. For example, in the work contract it is stipulated that employees should not establish personal relationships with guests, primarily in order to prevent any conspiracies between a croupier and a guest.

In 1990 Holland Casinos formulated an *explicit* policy for dealing with gambling addiction – although they had applied most of the following regulations since 1976. This policy has passive and active aspects. Through the active aspect they oblige all employees to take courses on how to detect gambling addiction. On top of that, game supervisors like croupiers have to follow additional training courses. This active policy also indicates who may address guests about their addiction, and confines this role to specially trained former police officers with experience in dealing peacefully with distressed persons.

Identified cases of addiction have to be reported to a member of the Casino contact group. Every six weeks the contact group runs through the reported cases and decides whether to take action or not on each individual case. Only in cases of great urgency is direct action allowed without previous reference of the case to the contact group meeting.

The passive policy consists of informing the public by leaflets about the possibilities for finding help and support. The leaflet called 'The Risks of the Game' has a cover that is almost identical to their most popular leaflet, 'The Rules of the Game'. At the end of the risks leaflet is a coupon that the addict can sign with a request for entrance reduction or refusal. Experience shows that these written constraints will only be applied when the guest starts to realize the irresponsibility of his or her prolonged addictive behaviour.

Holland Casinos can impose entrance bans against addicted gamblers after having consulted that person. This more compassionate and friendly attitude differs quite a bit from another entrance barrier put up by Holland Casinos. The Casino doormen can refuse admission to inebriated persons. So, when they ban gambling addicts from their premises they take much more time and allow the guest to have a say. Holland Casinos explains the difference by pointing to the difficulty of identifying gambling addiction. Whereas drunken people can be detected by their breath, gambling addiction is a less detectable habit. All employees have been trained by a Dutch addiction clinic to recognize the possible signs, like a sudden change in gambling behaviour or a much greater frequency of casino visits.

Appropriate moral standards and interest
For Van Duren:

1. Employees with unselfish intentions may go beyond corporate regulations, especially when giving altruistic support to addicted guests.
2. Charitable duties towards these guests override employers' requests for compliance with existent regulations. This is my duty as a Christian, according to the Sermon on the Mount.
3. The croupier's job is well paid and Van Duren does not want to leave of his own volition, since he then also loses his right to additional unemployment allowances.
4. Van Duren thinks: 'maybe I will get sacked if I disobey, but by behaving this way I blow the whistle. The Casino will have to reconsider its policies towards gambling addicts, and my present behaviour might oblige them to practise due care.'

For Holland Casino Valkenburg and the holding, Holland Casinos:

5. Employees should stick to the rules stipulated in job contracts and in the code of conduct towards gambling addicts.
6. Repeated refusal to comply with these guidelines is already a sufficient reason for dismissal.
7. In front of gambling addicts we wish to appear as, say, a friendly fire brigade; the problem must first become a nasty fire before we act and we prefer to act after an agreement with the guest.
8. Gambling addiction is more respectable than alcohol abuse; gambling addicts have to be tolerated initially, but drunken guests should not be admitted to the casino.

The declarations by Van Duren did insist on standards 1 and 2, whereas Holland Casino stressed the importance of standard 5.

A critical evaluation of all these standards will have to state priorities. We have to put one of the following two objectives first:

1. The maintenance of corporate discipline and team spirit.
2. The unorthodox care for gambling addicts as practised by Van Duren, which expresses a noble concern for human wellbeing.

Critical evaluation

According to one's priority in this specific case the evaluation will differ. When the job contract and its obligations is placed first, the insubordination and the lack of team spirit shown by Van Duren will lead to acceptance of the claim made by Holland Casinos. The judge's verdict will be held to be correct. However, when one emphasizes the ethical value of the croupier's intentions and maintains that this case of independent behaviour is morally acceptable for various reasons, then an opposite conclusion might be drawn.

Reconsidering the mediation requirement

Van Duren's actions were guided by altruistic intentions, which is considered to be a highly respectable moral demand in the Christian moral tradition. Thus the adherent to the unitarist view will see Van Duren as a lonely just man, operating in a corrupt environment. Both a separatist and an integrationist would look at his behaviour with less compassion and wonder for instance what Van Duren might have done to change the inner rules of the corporation in a more co-operative way.

The mediation requirement is expressed by the integration view. In this case it will probably lead to some critical comments about the actual regulations of Holland Casinos. At first sight, these regulations seem rather reactive and not very efficient. Their policy in the earliest stage of drug addiction is rather *laissez-faire*. However, this criticism of the Casino policy does not mean endorsing the methods used by Van Duren in his care for the addicted guests' wellbeing. Recent scientific reports indicate that the method of approach adopted by Holland Casinos is rather effective. Conversely, visitors who were criticized at the playing-table by Van Duren expressed their resentment and complained. These visitors felt publicly dishonoured, and were less disposed to cope with their addiction problem. So, probably the Van Duren method at these tables was counterproductive.

2.7.2 The petty theft of patient donations in Harlingen

Direct circumstances and moral issues

In spring 1994 the director of Oranjeoord Hospital in Harlingen, a small public health institution in the north of The Netherlands, learned that some member of their personnel must be stealing patient donations from the personnel pool. It was a petty theft, as the stolen amounts were probably a few tens of guilders each week. Still, the director took this affair very seriously, because the money from this pool was destined for Christmas parcels for their nursing personnel. Stealing from this pool was felt to be very disloyal towards colleagues. After consulting local police authorities, the board secretly installed a video camera. Beforehand the director decided that whoever the culprit might be the only sanction could be dismissal. At the end of June the truth came out. The video tape had registered the actions of the only neurologist at the hospital, tiptoeing towards the donation box and removing the paper money with his pincer.

The hospital board was at first flabbergasted and then quite furious when they found out that their respected specialist had committed this petty crime. But soon they realized that they now faced a big dilemma, with a strategic dimension. Dismissing this man would quite probably have serious consequences for the immediate future of the hospital. They are negotiating a merger with a far bigger partner, Medical Centrum Leeuwarden (MCL), in which Leeuwarden had already proved that they have some hidden agenda. Most probably MCL would use the firing of the neurologist as an argument for closing down the Harlingen neurology clinic. Consequently, at least twenty persons would lose their jobs without any prospects of future employment, and patients would be obliged to go to the Leeuwarden hospital twenty-five kilometres away.

Their actual dilemma combined moral demands and strategic concerns. It can be expressed in various ways:

☐ Should we be ethical in the eyes of the public and sack our neurologist, while accepting the probability of the closing down of the neurology department?

☐ Should we submerge our original intention in the best interests of our hospital and retain the man because of the worth of his contribution to the hospital?

☐ How can we explain to our personnel that we now want to keep the man? Surely they will expect justice to be done, and insist that rules should apply equally to everybody?

☐ How can we communicate this news to the outside world? How should we present this whole thing to the newspapers? How should we reply to the charge that we practise discriminatory justice?

The larger setting

Harlingen Hospital is a small town hospital engaged in a fight for survival. The Ministry of Public Health wants to concentrate special clinics in main hospitals, removing entire services from the small ones. In Harlingen, the whole staff supports the board's defensive fight. All members of this hospital community want to keep the existing clinics where they are now.

The neurologist was a well-known person in this town, with an excellent professional record, although as a private individual people find him rather arrogant and awkward. In press releases the board directors remained very discreet about his motives, and they asked him to behave equally discreetly on this issue. On his side, the neurologist asked that the director should not announce the sanctions the board was imposing on him.

The hospital board also refused to comment on the man's motives, but they did explain why they did not dismiss him. This decision was first communicated to their personnel in group sessions of 20 to 25 persons, during which it was stated that sanctions had been imposed. The reaction of the personnel went through the same three stages that the board had experienced initially. First, astonishment, then anger or even outrage, and finally strategic and moral reasoning. Several months later only some of his peers, the medical specialists, still harbour hard feelings against him.

The reasons for not sacking the neurologist were frankly expressed in terms of strategic concerns involving severe moral consequences. They would probably lose their neurology department, which would cause job losses for at least 20 members of the nursing staff. But also the director expressed his concern about the merger negotiation, and the fact that the fewer services they could offer, the weaker would be their bargaining position.

The board took time to discuss and present their decision, before bringing the whole thing to public attention. They explained that confidence had been damaged, and that they recognized the risks they were taking by keeping this man in place, but insisted on the predominance of the organization's vital interest. The director, Mr Albert de Rouw, declared that almost everybody present backed the board decision and thought it to be the wisest, although it seemed contrary to principles of justice. Only four days after these corporate briefing sessions, the first journalist phoned Mr de Rouw with some probing questions about a rumour. The journalist agreed to keep it silent, but had the right to publish his scoop as soon as another journalist should contact Mr de Rouw. This happend a day later, and the next morning the story was published in local and national newspapers.

Appropriate moral standards

For the hospital board:

1. (*Beforehand*) Stealing from the personnel pool is wrong; it should be punished by dismissing the culprit.
2. (*After seeing the video tape*) We cannot find another neurologist, and that will mean the closing of the neurology department. Because of these considerations we must apply a second standard: namely, that

applying the same justice to all is not as important as looking after the future of the hospital and the survival of our public services.

3. From a unitarian point of view dismissing the neurologist would have been morally the only acceptable thing to do.

For the personnel council:

4. From the point of view of retributive justice, punishment should be imposed without regarding the culprit's position.
5. The consequences for our organization overrule the need for doing justice.
6. As a professional he has a good reputation.

For the culpable neurologist:

7. Being caught is a very painful experience; I understand other people's feeling of indignation.
8. I prefer to stay and weather the community feelings for private reasons, and because I feel strong enough to work this out with my colleagues under the conditions set by the board of directors.

For the main hospital:

9. We should have been informed about this incident by our future merger partner, as we might have provided practical assistance.
10. It is ridiculous to keep somebody who undermines public confidence in the entire medical profession, just because of the consequences for the other 20 members of the Harlingen neurology department.
11. Justice should be the same for all: a member of the hospital nursing staff that is caught thieving would be sacked, so why make an exception here?

Crucial choices by the hospital management
The board of directors decided not to apply equal justice, and to give priority to the short-term strategic interests of their hospital. They did this by means of open but firm corporate communications, first, with the personnel directly involved inside, and later, when they had gained inside support, with the press, although they did not seek publicity.

Three months later
In October 1994 the hospital directors still felt that this choice had been the best in the given circumstances. The decision was well accepted by

the nursing staff; only some of the medical specialists and the big merger partner were dissatisfied. The event had also been the talk of the town, people felt it to be discriminatory justice. Most probably the decision would have been better understood if the hospital board had made the sanctions public. From his point of view, firing the neurologist would have made it practically impossible for him to work again as a neurologist. The man is therefore thankful for the board's clemency, but seems to have underestimated the strong pressure he still has to weather each day. Harlingen Hospital functions also as a moral community.

2.7.3 Concluding comments

Both cases referred to employee dismissal. In both situations it seems as if mainly strategic concerns took priority over purely duty-based moral demands. The consequences of this apparent dominance of strategic corporate interests had quite opposite effects.

In the case of Van Duren his good intentions were not sufficient reason for the cantonal court to refuse his dismissal. A man of relatively high moral standing was dismissed because he used unorthodox methods, refused to comply to his superiors' requests, and did not function as part of the Casino team.

In the neurologist's case, the petty theft itself is of a very poor moral standing. Yet he was not dismissed, as his removal would have caused even more serious trouble for the organization. This indicates that in this case community survival standards took priority over equal justice standards. We maintain that both standards are moral standards, and that a reflective business ethicist can quite well defend the actual decision. In fact, the hospital board actually explained to us that in their opinion one serious consideration was paramount. They chose to maintain the neurologist because they had serious indications that their bigger merger partner would otherwise use his dismissal as an excuse for closing down their neurology clinic, which would make some 20 members of the nursing staff jobless. This consideration is not only a strategic concern: it also refers to the moral principles of being a good employer.

Our final conclusion
Especially in the Holland Casinos' case the integration view may help us to understand how moral demands related to corporate discipline and corporate identity can override the more easily expressed moral demands (i.e. to help your fellow human being). We even may accept that most probably the now existing procedures for dealing with gambling addicts are more effective than the head-on confrontation provoked by croupier Van Duren's remarks at the playing-table. Yet an issue remains which

should serve as a reference value: corporate strategic concerns should not corrupt the pursuit of moral purposes in the corporate mission. More specifically, one of the utimate criteria for evaluating the actions of this casino staff is the quality, efficiency and impact of one's efforts for preventing and solving the harm done by gambling addiction.

On the other hand, opting for strategic interests in the Harlingen Hospital case clearly entailed pursuing morally beneficial consequences. Expressing them as corporate goods is considered here to be, in fact, moral talk.

2.8 Synopsis

1. Business ethics adopts the methods and purpose of normative ethics to the specific requirements of a particular kind of moral judgement, i.e. judgements that are concerned with business policies, business norms and values. It evaluates and prescribes moral standards that fit to a specific sphere in modern society – business.

2. Business is a relatively autonomous part of modern society, having its proper inner logic, a principle we formulate as 'maximize corporate profits, reduce corporate costs'. Business ethics has to deal with a situation in which the inner logic of business rationality creates tensions and may injure the moral community. Business ethics elaborates valid moral demands concerning business by basing its function on a valid theory of the relationship between business and society. Private enterprise is integrated into the sphere of moral society by market constraints, national legislation, and by the personal commitment of managers to a sense of moral and social responsibility.

3. A primary task of business ethics concentrates on finding ways for reconciling strategic corporate interests with moral demands. Strategic interests are not completely separated from moral feelings, but carry within them morally beneficial consequences that have to be assessed carefully.

4. In business one often prefers the 'strategic' option over purely value-based stands. One reason for choosing a strategic option is proper to the logic of this subsystem, i.e. the profitability or continuation of a business unit. However, a 'strategic' course can also be quite acceptable from a moral point of view, whenever this option contains a strong moral appeal based on arguments referring to beneficial consequences. Examples of such arguments are the prevention of severe harm and injury for a constituency or the inspiring example it may create.

2.9 References

Bird, F. and Waters, J. A. (1989) 'The moral muteness of managers', *California Management Review*, **32**(1).

Buchholz, R. A. (1993) *Principles of Environmental Management: The greening of business*, Englewood Cliffs: Prentice Hall.

Jeurissen, R. (1995) 'Business in response to the morally concerned public', in H. van Luijk and P. Ulrich, *Facing Public Interest: Ethical challenge on business policy and corporate communications*, Dordrecht: Kluwer Academic Publishers. Reprinted by permission of Kluwer Academic Publishers.

Leeuwarder Courant (1994) 'Stelende specialist nachtmerrie voor Oranjeoord (Stealing specialist a nightmare for Oranjeoord)', 20 July.

Stead, W., Worrell, D. L. and Stead J. G. (1990) 'An integrative model for understanding and managing ethical behaviour in business organizations', *Journal of Business Ethics*, Dordrecht: Kluwer Academic Publishers, **9**, 233–42.

Taylor, C. (1991) *The Ethics of Authenticity*, Cambridge, Mass.: Harvard University Press.

Ulrich, P. and Thielemann, U. (1993) 'How do managers think about market economy and morality? Empirical enquiries into business-ethical thinking patterns', *Journal of Business Ethics*, **12**, 879–98.

van Luijk, H. (1994) 'Business ethics: the field and its importance', in B. Harvey (ed.), *Business Ethics: A European approach*, Hemel Hempstead: Prentice Hall.

3

Moral responsibility in general

3.1 Introduction

The notions of free choice and responsibility are the cornerstones of moral reflection. This chapter gives definitions of these concepts.

The chapter starts by taking one step backwards, and considers what makes humans really human. Modern science shows how close our common natural abilities are to those of certain primates, and the minor physiological differences are not sufficient to explain the presence of humans capable of creating complicated cultural patterns. Our natural abilities are clearly not able to explain the unprecedented affluence in modern society. The existence of modern man and the way our life changes has to be explained by calling upon other causes, namely, our participation in civil practices and human culture. The core of human abilities may seem natural, but by training the human animal in a cultural setting new and unprecedented abilities can be shaped.

3.2 The idea of man behind free and conscious behaviour

3.2.1 From free choice back to our idea of man

Any claim to responsibility relies on the conviction that people are capable of acting willingly. People have to answer for *their* actions as we hold them to behave as conscious living beings.

Before discussing the notion of free choice, we will first take one more step backward and study what allows man to act knowingly and willingly.

3.2.2 Closing in on human nature by comparing humane and bestial abilities

A general scan of what really makes the difference between humans and other animals may help to understand what abilities really make the difference. The argument will start by establishing a common ground: the skills and abilities we share with other intelligent living beings.

One of the core functions that distinguishes human individuals from dead objects and merely sentient animals, is our capacity to choose consciously. People pursue goals in life and they can formulate them more or less consciously. Being conscious also means awareness of the present conditions. In order to obtain results, people have to make an assessment of their present situation and of the potentials in their environment.

Acting with premeditation and knowledge of circumstances is not a characteristic we associate with robots, plants, or with the lower animals like fish, insects or reptiles. These beings do not aim at achieving objectives by the use of rational and conscious procedures.

Conscious behaviour seems more probable when we study the higher species, especially mammals like dogs, pigs, dolphins or great apes. For instance, domesticated dogs can be trained to act as guide dogs. One may say that these dogs are capable of making judgements in complex non-natural situations, enlarging the scope of action for their master. Yet one may effectively doubt whether dogs act with conscious premeditation. It is more plausible to maintain that an effective guide dog simply is trained to respond (with pleasure) to the needs his master expresses. Modern scientists and ethicists do not study dogs in order to find characteristics of personal or near-human behaviour.

Traditionally, philosophers held that human beings were the sole animals capable of speech and language. They claimed that language with an inner structure and with artificial symbolic meaning can only be found amongst humans. Apes were supposed to utter yells and cries associating emotions with meaning, but only man was held capable of articulating propositions. So, an ape was thought totally incapable of formulating, say, 'Mistress, give me a piece of banana'. But these ideas have been questioned quite recently.

Until the 1970s, certain fundamental insights about human nature still stood firm and even now remain uncontested. Thus it is a given fact that humans do share a very important part of their nature with other living beings. If properly raised, humans are able to function in small groups, share values and even reshape norms whenever the environment confronts us with new challenges. All these are common characteristics that we share with certain other animals, but there remains something unique. Until recently, two specific capacities have been regarded as unique to human behaviour and have served to make us understand how human beings act with a conscious will:

1. Humans speak complex symbolic languages. Language provides a much more sophisticated means of representing, expressing and exchanging ideas.

2. Humans participate in organizations structured according to self-made rules. These rules are the object of public attention and debate whenever they are violated, inadequate, obsolete or too vague to meet current demands. Organizations may then adopt new rules and new systems for control and enforcement.

The first characteristic especially is now being contested. Recent research has revealed the capacity of certain mammals to use symbolic speech in propositional language. Already in the 1970s' studies it was shown that chimpanzees like Washoe are capable of making sentences by using deaf sign language, and the more recent example of Kanzi has shown evidence of even more astonishing language abilities.

3.2.3 Our nearest kin: the great primates

In the early 1990s we become even more aware that the human species has mute nephews. Kanzi, a member of the smaller chimpanzee species, the dwarf chimpanzee or Bonobo from Zaire, is indeed capable of symbolic speech. In the Georgia State University Primate Research Center he learned to combine icons on a computer into complex new expressions and he can understand the corresponding English expressions.

Researchers have therefore become more aware of what primates can do and have started to look at them afresh and with greater respect and consideration. Researchers even become opposed to the artificial and un-apelike behaviour we impose on them as pets or as research objects.

A remarkable story that may help humans to understand how near the great apes are to humans stems from Bernard Rollin, philosopher and biologist of Colorado University. It describes a significant event during a small group seminar where animal researchers discussed the management of stress for persons working with laboratory animals.

The most extraordinary story was told by the chief technician at a major government research facility. Apparently, he had been closely involved in raising a baby chimpanzee who was to be used for research. Eventually, the animal was moved to a different laboratory, to be used for invasive studies. Having developed a rapport with the chimpanzee, the technician deliberately avoided following the animal's fate. One day, he was in a different portion of the institution, walking down a corridor with another technician, when the other technician called his attention to a cage, where a chimpanzee appeared to be gesticulating to them. He approached the cage, read the card affixed to it, and realised that this was the animal he had raised. It had just been used for a terminally invasive experiment. As he stood there, the animal reached through the cage, met his eyes, grasped his hands tightly, and holding on to him, died. As extraordinary as the story was, the reaction of these laboratory animal people was equally surprising, for every single member of the seminar was crying. (Rollin, 1993, p. 213)

The feelings of grief and sorrow felt by this audience remind me of a reaction of Mr Emile Looman, president of the largest Dutch company for television studio broadcasting facilities, NOB. He was relating a previous experience as a business consultant operating in eastern Groningen where industry was closing down and people were laid off without any real future prospects. Following my question about how he thought the members of a certain factory felt when they heard they would lose their job, he did not say much, but he was very close to tears. Both chimps and humans inspire sympathy, and both merit respect as persons, not simply as objects for experiments or as mute victims of a cost reduction.

It is on the basis of this and related evidence regarding our similarities with great apes, especially chimpanzees and gorillas, that Peter Singer enunciates his moral rights for great apes, which I propose to apply also to human beings:

☐ The Right to Life.
☐ The Protection of individual liberty.
☐ The Prohibition of Torture (which includes certain scientific experiments).

3.2.4 On the uniqueness of humans

For the purpose of our subject, it is important to understand how little our natural abilities are specifically human. Apparently, what distinguishes man is less a matter of nature, and more a matter of nurture and of education within a human culture. Chimpanzees like Kanzi are not yet capable of understanding sentences like 'You have won the first prize: tickets for two people to travel for 14 days to Japan', and people wonder whether they might be trained to do so. And even if some scientist succeeds in achieving this result, I doubt whether the experiment is ethically proper: such advanced chimps have difficulty in socializing with their fellow chimps; they remain unhappy loners. To summarize, one has to doubt whether even bright animals like chimps will and should be capable one day of civilized activities requiring the tremendous amount of skills and concepts an average sane 12-year-old child can handle when it has completed primary education.

The second philosophical idea about the specific nature of our human condition is the capacity to reshape and reorganize relationships and environment on the basis of common plans and verbal agreements. This second characteristic remains more or less unchallenged. Man is still held to be the only 'political animal', a being that lives within organizations with *self-imposed* rules and norms. Animals are capable of learning and changing by imitation, but they are not able to ponder about what one should do *in public debate*. Nor has research revealed evidence of human legal practices amongst animals like public trials or life-long imprisonment.

Human beings share many capacities and needs with other living creatures. Their specific abilities, however, lie in the field of articulated speech, the use of symbols, the capacity to represent meanings in complex and changing languages, and the ability to interact with others, to discuss, debate and decide, and to act accordingly.

Though in principle the difference between humans and mammals like chimpanzees is less than we once thought, human education is capable of developing skills and mental abilities we do not meet amongst other animals in a natural environment. As the result of his life in a cultural environment man is able to develop and shape his unique abilities. The reader should be aware that 'unique' is used in a morally neutral sense. Humans can be educated to perform willingly and knowingly various kinds of behaviour, ranging from music and dance to torture and genocide.

Contrary to our emphasis on the cultural factor alone, it could be said that studies reveal whole lists of natural innate capacities that are unique to humans. This list contains characteristics like the ability to walk upright, the opposition between thumb and the other fingers of the hand, the sexual availability of female humans, or the fact that we have little fur. Still, there is a big difference between the naked apes of a hundred thousand years ago, which already had the same innate capacities, and modern man. It is not a difference in natural abilities, but rather a matter of trained and culturally transmitted norms and skills, which in turn cause the variations and diversity between humans. At the same time it is important to understand how much, in terms of affections, values, physiology and sensory abilities, we share with our primitive ancestors.

Civilized humans have both natural and cultural capacities in common. Speech, ways of organizing, and custom may vary, but they all refer to certain cultural abilities and mental skills. This statement is based on the concept of *disposition*. A cultural ability or disposition may result in a well-functioning capacity to perform specific tasks. It is not completely innate. Education, reinforcement, and shaping, all play a role during the process of learning to perform well. By use of the concept of cultivated disposition we arrive at some general ideas on human morality. These ideas will result in the general idea of civilized beings. At a descriptive level this idea of culturally shaped humans does *not* imply the presence of specific transcultural moral norms.

3.3 Towards a balanced concept of freedom

One of the human core abilities underlying our civilized activities is the capacity for making choices autonomously: that is, free choice or freedom. Our definition of free choice claims to express a general truth about the human ability to make choices whatever the cultural setting. Its philosophical simplicity reveals the conditions for a normative idea about people: fully grown and reasonable persons are able to make free choices.

Moral behaviour presupposes that people have a choice to make. The most fundamental idea in the debate on responsibility and accountability is free choice. Thus, our philosophical question here is: What ideas of free choice are a necessary part of any moral claim on individual and company responsibility?

A sane person integrates education and life experiences. Humans naturally believe that their specific civilized life is not completely determined by outside factors. They see their own activities as at least partly dependent on personal initiative. Especially people from Western civilizations believe that most of their conscious actions result from a personal choice. Such human beings say: 'I choose to do X', 'I did Y'. This results in the feeling that healthy persons know and want what they do. We are beings capable of conscious behaviour. In particular, we feel our actions express personal choices.

3.3.1 The example of the Andes air crash

In 1972 an aeroplane with members and supporters of a Uruguayan rugby team crashed high in the Andes mountains of Chile. Some passengers survived, but soon found themselves in a situation without any food supplies. Their environment consisted of cold snow slopes with no natural food except the bodies of other passengers, their dead friends or relatives. They faced a terrible dilemma.

The crash survivors in the Andes mountains had a clear choice in these circumstances: either starve to death or eat their dead relatives and friends. Even though they chose the latter option, it is clear that they did it with remorse and a sentiment of utter revulsion. Westerners with a modern conscience, which emphasizes our natural goodness, may add that their actual line of conduct was forced upon them by overwhelming conditions. A more traditionally educated person would insist on a sense of assuming responsibility for one's own actions in tragic circumstances. The survivors had to face a choice between two dreadful propositions.

This example will serve to illustrate our concept of free choice. In this case the survivors consciously made their decision. Though the actual options were extraordinary, this example highlights the general principle that people have to choose, while circumstances restrict their options. This example also indicates the essential objective of moral human behaviour, and the essential reason why we have to make choices: survival, in a way which respects relevant others as much as possible.

3.3.2 Two basic constituents for free choice

A mature and balanced concept of free choice has to include two apparently contrary principles that are both part of human experience. The first principle stems from the idea that what we really choose to do is not merely determined by external pressures and conditioning, but that normal people *are* capable of making personal choices, of acting upon their proper decisions. Thus in all ordinary life situations with which people are confronted, they are capable of making autonomous choices.

The first constituent states that action results from a personal choice or deliberate will. Mentally healthy people are capable of saying 'I choose to do X'. So, man has the ability to choose for himself, an *ability* for free choice. Contrary to this, people acting in a fit of rage or individuals suffering from total mental deficiency are not held wholly responsible for what they do, because they lack moral consciousness and wit. Becoming a responsible adult person has certainly a lot to do with acquiring self-possession, which includes a whole range of trained skills. It may be seen as the ability to handle one's personal priorities: that is, 'I know where I want to go to now.'

The first constituent of free choice is an acquired sense of identification between who I am and the actions I take. Sane people are fully aware when they really choose to do something. People have a conscious will that enables them to say, 'I choose to do X here and now'.

The second principle within a philosophical concept of free choice relates to the fact that choices take place here and now. The options we have relate to the given circumstances and our present abilities and talents, either evident or latent.

Experience teaches us that clever choices do not simply depend on stating that 'I' want to achieve something. Clever action includes *a well-informed appreciation of the possibilities that are offered*. Understanding the potentials of a given situation and training yourself or your team to make the best out of it, is simply a crucial part of effective training. Action takes place *within a given situation*.

This second constituent stresses the importance of making a *well-informed* choice. The free choices of sophisticated humans are not blind and uninformed. Rather they are based upon a valid understanding of the possibilities present in the given circumstances.

3.3.3 A popular but inadequate definition of free will

'Free' enterprise and 'liberty' are commonly interpreted as referring to a very peculiar concept of free will that regards freedom as not being constrained by external factors. If this were so, then free choice would only depend upon what the decision-maker wishes. It can be found in common expressions like 'Feel free to do as you please'. If we interpret such an expression along the lines of this concept of freedom, we end up with 'You may try to do as you wish without any consideration for present abilities and limitations'.

Here, freedom is simply regarded as being free from any exterior authority or circumstance. Such a concept of freedom is entirely negative, as it only affirms one element of decision-making: that is, I can make choices on my own behalf. It expresses individual wants or wishes without recognizing any actual circumstances. This abstract concept of un-restrained liberty overlooks the given situation in which we have to operate. It disregards the conditions that we are confronted with whenever we aim at the fulfilment of our real choices.

Ideas of unconditional freedom soon lead into strange consequences and false dilemmas. People may then use expressions like, 'Shall I opt for a steady relationship or shall I choose my freedom'? Here 'my freedom' only implies that I am not yet bound to anything. Ultimately, such a concept of abstract freedom that refuses to come to grips with given realities may lead to the moral vacuum expressed in the famous quote of Janis Joplin: 'Freedom is just another word for nothing left to lose.'

The abstract idea of 'free from' reflects an attitude which overlooks the second constituent of our definition of free choice: that is, *choices are always made in the context of a given situation, including the present cultural environment with its variety of norms, values and practices*.

Many similar fallacies about liberty and free choice obstruct a clear understanding of the issue of public accountability. Five such cherished sophisms that are dominant in the hedonistic and wealthy part of our modern world are:

1. Free enterprise implies absence of moral obligations.
2. Liberty implies being totally free from social bonds.
3. Freedom implies not reckoning with any circumstance.
4. Free and conscious choice equals doing what we fancy or wish.
5. The only influence on our free conscious choice is our subjective feeling, our personal likings – in other words, our often egoistic and narcissistic whims.

3.3.4 A more balanced definition of free choice

We should now formulate our fundamental concept of free choice, which is essential for understanding responsible behaviour by both individuals and corporate officials.

The issue is that both constituents of free choice have to be respected when we claim responsibility for a conscious action. The first constituent requires that the action should result from a *personal choice* or will. In the following definition we use the expression 'autonomous choice'. Here autonomy does not imply that humans are independent from external circumstances or social norms, but rather it insists on the ability to determine as an innate capacity. Sane human beings can decide for themselves and stand by their choice. Whether somebody perceived that option first or absorbed it naturally from their environment is less important here. What matters is that people can choose for themselves, can make decisions.

The second constituent stresses the importance of making a *well-informed choice* based upon *an understanding of the possibilities present in the given circumstances*. The present possibilities and the limitations cover the physical and biological nature of our environment, our personal capacities and skills, and the skills and habits of people around us.

The word 'autonomous' literally means 'assuming one's proper rules and standards'. It means that, even if we feel the urge of our inner desires or the pressure of external events, in the end we consciously follow a line of conduct because we decide ourselves that it is the best course of action.

Freedom, therefore, is the ability to choose autonomously while considering the given circumstances with its opportunities and limitations. 'Circumstances' are both external and internal: they involve physical constraints, the direct social environment and personal skills.

The crash survivors in the Andes mountains faced a tragic dilemma: either starve or eat the dead bodies of their relatives and friends. Confronted with these two options, the majority of them positively did choose to follow the second line of conduct. They wanted to survive, and eating the corpses of their loved ones was the only way to achieve that end. According to the popular definition of free will, some may think that they had no choice. The line of conduct they adopted seems forced upon them by overwhelming conditions. Still, they did choose positively to follow one specific line of conduct, assuming responsibility for what they did under these conditions. The circumstances left them only two options to choose, and as the majority wanted to survive, they actually could only go in one direction. At a deeper level of reflection they made a vital assumption: *We wish to survive.*

Such a line of conduct can be reformulated in a practical syllogism:

1. *Intention*   We want to stay alive (and we want to show respect for our dead friends and relatives).
2. *Major premiss*   We need carbohydrates and proteins in order to meet this goal.
3. *Minor premiss*   In this case these corpses are the only sources of carbohydrates and animal proteins available in this neighbourhood.
4. *Practical inference*   We have to consume their dead flesh.

So, they did make a free and conscious choice, however hard it may have been to make it. In these dramatic circumstances eating the corpses of their beloved was the only means to achieve their goal.

3.3.5 *Application to choices in strategic management*

Our balanced definition of free choice may be applied to marketing strategies. In order to clarify this idea we will briefly refer to a very old philosophical tradition: a Stoic image on how to reconcile individual freedom with universal necessity.

The following image expresses how Stoics like Zeno, Chrysops and later Epictetes and Seneca saw the solution of the apparent paradox between individual freedom and the overwhelming global trends. I will use it to illustrate how proactive marketeers and strategic managers may understand their job. Strategic marketeers have to anticipate shifts of overwhelming importance and seek niche opportunities. They have to decide on the right marketing strategy, in face of uncertain and sometimes terminal trends, in order to reshape and implement the required corporate activities.

The Stoics' most drastic example of how individual choice can go together with the apprehension of global necessities runs as follows. A dog is solidly attached to a cart that rolls on forever in directions the dog cannot change. Now the dog (the individual person) may adopt two basic attitudes. First, it may try to do what it wants to do, but as the cart keeps rolling on, what actually happens is that the dog is dragged along in a sad and painful way. In this case the dog did not take advantage of any opportunities it was afforded as it totally failed to anticipate the turns made by the wheels of treacherous fortune (the cart). Secondly, the dog can accept the inexorable progress of the cart as a given, and simply walk alongside the cart. This causes the dog far less pain and sorrow, and it is able to use the span of the rope to run towards anything that might come within range, and smell or even eat whatever can be reached.

This image can serve to shed new light on the need to anticipate the shift in the external business environment. The proactive behaviour of the dog that anticipates the next movement of the cart in order to sniff, smell and eat what it can reach is comparable with the strategic insight that allows excellent companies to create opportunities for the future. Entrepreneurs anticipate global shifts in requirements: that is, the actions they take depend on their local efforts to sniff, smell and eat. The future is contingent: one is never completely sure about what lies ahead. Sometimes an apparently interesting opportunity will turn out to be a waste of time. Usually, however, perseverance, a clear mission, and anticipation of the slings and arrows of fortune are the best formula for creating good prospects.

3.4 Further remarks on the given circumstances: life areas

This section explains an approach applied in management consultancy which fits in with our concept of free choice. Here we only use it to highlight the second component of our definition of free choice: the given circumstances that we have to take into consideration.

3.4.1 A universal human intention

The Dutch philosopher and management consultant Annette Huiberts (1994) voices an elementary idea about our objectives in life: 'Every second in our life we strive towards optimal survival. But we do not achieve this objective only by caring about ourselves. We are also willing to improve human survival by improving the survival of others.'

So, responsible humans aim at human and environmental wellbeing. The next step is to identify the areas in which we have to operate in order to achieve this optimal wellbeing.

Before reviewing Huiberts' view of six life spheres, I should explain that her view has the best fit with the moral outlook described in Chapter 7: virtue ethics. Virtue theory regards virtue as leading to true happiness, a flourishing or optimal state of life. The separate virtues are not good in themselves, but only as far as they are constantly adjusted in order to reach the attainable optimum, which is the flourishing state called happiness, or more literally well spiritedness – eudaemonia. Expanding on this relationship falls beyond the scope of this text.

3.4.2 The surrounding circumstances: six spheres of life

Huiberts defines six spheres of life, represented as a hierarchy of concentric circles. The smallest circles are those most important directly to the individual; the larger the circles spread, the smaller is our capacity to influence either through injuring or through caring. Each circle requires individual input in order to realize our optimal survival. The circles are:

1. The individual person.
2. Their primary group of family (partner, children, parents): the small tribe.
3. The groups and organizations they participate in (tribes and coalitions).
4. Our common future as mankind.
5. Life on earth (the biosphere of plants, animals, humans).
6. The physical universe (sun heat, water, forces such as gravity).

Now every person has to play on each level simultaneously, and should realize that our moves have consequences for the survival and wellbeing of others in all these areas. Ultimately this also ensures the quality of our own wellbeing and survival.

Here we have a method which maps given circumstances in a relatively sophisticated way. This approach involves an idea of free choice that comes close to ours. On a voluntary basis each individual decides for him- or herself what it is best to do or leave undone while relating to these different areas of life.

3.5 A partial definition of individual responsibility

From the notion of free choice we now turn to concepts about individual responsibility. We will start with a simple idea, which has more truth in it than we commonly might believe. But first we have to define some terminology.

The *intention* is the will or the project someone has in mind, either conscious or subconscious. The *action* is the individual behaviour of a person. It may also consist of the absence of activity, *inaction*. The choice not to do anything in a certain situation is a way of responding. The *event* is the actual and overt chain of facts that happened in connection with the actions of all participating agents. The *injuries* are the harmful results that are somehow related or thought to be related with that event. Besides *injuries* results may also be positive; these are *benefits*.

Now, our first definition of *individual responsibility* runs as follows. *A person is only responsible for the things that he or she actually plans and does, not for what comes afterwards.* So, a person is only responsible for his or her intentions and what he or she does or does not do, but not for the related events and the subsequent harm and damage. What comes afterwards is never simply caused by one actor, but is regarded as the outcome of a complex interrelation between several agents, means and circumstances.

This definition has two positive features:

1. It boldly distinguishes the aspects of human behaviour that we as individuals may control fully from the other aspects that are not completely in our own hands.
2. It may help people to realize that harmful results are never caused only by the mistake of one individual. Harm and injury are produced in a complex setting where several conditions have to be met. This latter aspect may help people with strong feelings of guilt to arrive at a more equitable idea of what really is their own fault. Likewise, for people who are prone to blame others, this definition may help them to see the dangers of blaming one single agent for the harm inflicted.

3.6 A second and more complete definition of responsibility

The following definition is not completely new, although the formulation is: it contains basic ideas from classical Roman jurisprudence, as expressed in modern codes of criminal law.

A person is not only responsible for his or her plans and activities, to a certain extent he or she can also be held responsible for the subsequent events and resulting harm and damage, provided that two conditions are met:

1. *That the person acted willingly and knowingly, and in principle he or she was able to foresee this possible outcome (subjective criterion).*
2. *That any reasonable person with a comparable cultural background would be capable of forecasting that the intentions and the adopted course of action quite probably might result in certain damage or harm, considering all circumstances as far as they could be perceived (objective criterion).*

Here we concentrate on principles for moral responsibility in business. The next chapter will apply this second definition to a normative sketch of what entrepreneurial responsibility can mean.

3.7 Direct implications relevant to modern issues

Though the second definition states that to some extent agents may be held directly accountable for subsequent events, a second look at both definitions reveals some common characteristics. These features can best be expressed by reviewing some important consequences supported by at least one of the two definitions of individual responsibility.

3.7.1 Individuals remain responsible for their actions

Even if they are under pressure from their environment, each individual has to choose, since he or she is capable of acting knowingly and willingly. Many psychological and sociological theories point to the impact of socialization, external human pressure, and organizational reinforcement systems. Nevertheless normative ethics maintains that human individuals can make choices for themselves while evaluating situational pressures and factual conditions. Due to this normative appeal upon the individual's resources for autonomous situation assessment and decision-making, it remains valid to maintain the idea of individual responsibility.

3.7.2 In the final analysis, people always have a choice

Even if a bullying boss orders us to do something, we still have a choice. In the case of bullies the choice may be rather radical, but it exists even there: 'Either you do what I tell you or you quit this job.'

Only in the face of a fatal chain of events, where the mortal outcome seems inevitable, does the insistence on individual autonomy appear futile. *The Satanic Verses* by Salman Rushdie starts with such a fatal situation. Two of the main characters are falling towards earth immediately after the explosion of their aeroplane. As the plane was high in the air a mortal crash is inevitable. At this point the author portrays two contrary reactions towards fatality. One is already sulking and mourning about the prospect of his imminent death, the other sings and laughs because of the wonderful experience of flying through the air. This second person enjoys his present pleasure, the first only anticipates his future ordeal.

As some readers will feel indignant about this citation, one more additional remark. Salman Rushdie is a Muslim originating from Bombay. He did choose to write a novel containing some very nasty allegations about the Prophet's motives. A person following the most credulous and conventional interpretation amongst the 99 possible interpretations may feel very hurt, especially if he is unaware of the very early Islam tradition which included jokes and humour about religious zealots. So we respect the feelings of pain and injury caused to some Muslims. What is totally unacceptable, however, to most Western minds is the declared intention of fanatical Muslims to murder Rushdie. There has been no legal and fair trial condemning him on the basis of an equitable judgement of documents. There are also other reasons why Khomeini's fatwah should not be followed. Religious fanatics intent on terrorizing citizens from other countries should not be treated with great compassion and understanding.

3.7.3 Organizations should be clear about their basic values and norms

In order to control and develop their corporate philosophy they may use various means and skills. Not only sanctions and coercion, but also education, skills training and behaviour reinforcement are important.

Whenever individuals transgress beyond the vital interests in their community, the community can employ various sophisticated instruments. For example, some may try law enforcement, while others may seek motives, or try to develop reasonable debate and mutual respect for human rights.

Here again, the Islam fundamentalist example may illustrate this basic point of moral and political philosophy. The organization at stake here is the global community respecting all human beings. Either individuals accept the basic principles of the rule of law as they exist in civilized states, or they do not. In the latter case, modern societies should give themselves the means to confront transgressors with the undesirable consequences. Fundamentalism already obliges modern states to develop new jurisdiction and law enforcement in order to cope with religion-inspired violence and terrorism.

Another aspect would be ideologic combat. Expose fundamentalism as it really is – an unethical, paranoid and immoral abuse of a great religious tradition. Its credulous activism abuses religion for political purposes. In the final analysis it even refers to nineteenth-century Western ideas of injustice and resentment, as it presents itself as a poor people's revolt against the unjust exploitation by state authorities. The fundamentalists prefer to see their opponents as the servants of corruption emanating from the modern West.

A more theological criticism of the basic ideologic distortions perpetrated by Muslim fundamentalism may be an effective instrument for convincing Muslims who follow the basic rules of human decency to redefine their public attitudes. On a practical level, however, existing Muslim versions of entrepreneurial performance provide the hard proof that modern business can be reconciled with their religious values and commitments. An article by James J. Lynch (1991), 'The future shape of ethical banking', gives an essential insight into Islamic banking practices in accordance with the principles of the sharia.

3.7.4 Beware of stigmatization and idealizations

When we attribute responsibilities people often overstate the role of specific human agents. It makes life easier to think of morality as a combat between good and evil, in which some esoteric inside knowledge provides the means of salvation for the enlightened few, whereas the majority of modern society will have to rot in hell. The Persian prophet Mani formulated this extreme philosophy in the second century before Christ, creating a scene of cosmic struggle between the bad Satan dominating man on earth and the heavenly Kingdom of Light.

Christianity and many popular beliefs were influenced by this doctrine, which also fostered some paranoid habits of thought. In modern times the most influential example has been Communist Marxism, which converted Manichaean schemes into the historic and 'scientifically proven' struggle of the oppressed against the evil forces of capitalism. The institutions that backed this ideology have recently collapsed, but the habits of thought remain. Personal experience and talks with consultants dealing with Eastern European authorities indicate a dominant belief in evil conspiracies. Many attribute all kinds of intentions and purposes to projects that are mainly inspired by a vague combination of generosity and self-interest. In Russia people were exposed to more than 70 years of

Marxist propaganda, which attributed all kinds of evil human practices to a basically economic system called capitalism. Hitler killed at least 5 million Russians, so he was regarded as 'the valet of German capitalism'. Stalin, on the other hand, was seen as a good Communist, although his methods were not always adequate, and the 12 million or so victims of his regime were regarded merely as sacrifices to the progress of history.

3.7.5 Commit yourself to your limited but real responsibilities

The contribution business can make to the common wealth does not essentially consist of fraud, bribing, cartel deals and cronyism. Trust, work of high quality, regular tough competition and impartial procedures are more vital for national business economies. Corresponding differences in actual business ethics explain why the Nigerian economy is suffocating, while the Confucian nations in the Far East boom.

3.8 Synopsis

1. Humans have many abilities in common with the great primates. Decent human behaviour and sophisticated survival skills are not natural, they are formed in a process of iterative shaping by the interaction between the trainable individual and his or her cultural environment.

2. Sane persons have the ability to make autonomous choices while considering the given circumstances.

3. Sane persons are above all responsible for what they plan to do and for their actions, but they may also be held accountable for resulting injuries.

3.9 References

Huiberts, A. (1994) 'Afscheid penningmeester' (Farewell to our treasurer), *Dilemma*, Netwerk Bedrijfsethiek Nederland, **4**(1), 11.
Lynch, J. J. (1991) *Ethical Banking*, London: Macmillan Academic and Professional.
Rollin, B. (1993) 'The ascent of apes: broadening the moral community', in Cavallieri, P. and Singer, P. (eds), *The Great Ape Project: Equality beyond humanity*, London: Fourth Estate.

4

Moral responsibility in the business sphere

4.1 The gist: public accountability and entrepreneurial responsibility

The fundamental notions of free choice and responsibility were described in the preceding chapter. The inference for business ethics will now be drawn. Also, I will outline some psychological phenomena that obstruct a sound perception of entrepreneurial responsibility.

Our discussion on entrepreneurial responsibility in Inference 2 (see section 4.5 below) highlights the purpose of this book. It allows the application of the general ideas of free choice and responsibility to a rather evident and essential idea of entrepreneurial performance. We present a minimalist view of moral corporate responsibility, identifying moral demands as they are presently articulated in terms of quality requirements. Corporate quality programmes aim at fully satisfying agreed consumer requirements. Now, these agreed consumer requirements correspond to three moral commitments.

As the corporation engages in quality management, it accepts specific moral responsibilities. At a minimum level, the corporation commits itself to three such corporate responsibilities:

1. Consumer care, expressed by satisfying demands for ease of use and product safety.
2. Environmental care.
3. Care for minimum working conditions.

There is an important feature about moral commitment to risk prevention. It indicates the potential for a participatory ethical effort on the part of a business branch. By committing itself voluntarily to the reduction of personal and environmental damage, a branch of corporate activities can obtain a better bargaining position. For example, it may draw up covenants with public authorities, defining on a bias of partnership how to prevent vital environmental and health damages. This may lead to more effective policy-making, with considerable public benefits.

This chapter outlines arguments for concentrating efforts on those aspects of performance which companies can actually learn to handle and influence themselves. For example, prevention of accidents and public accountability do not call for cover-up strategies, but do point to the quality of the processes within the business. Here lies the main task for business ethics. Its function is not to deplore catastrophic results due to immoral or unconscious business activities nor to start witch-hunts against the evils of capitalism. Rather, business ethics can encourage entrepreneurs to define corporate commitments as responses to agreed moral demands. With such a mission it can guide and counsel practitioners.

Moral performance in business may be described in a negative way as the ability to limit risk of severe harm and damage, not only inside the company, but also amongst end users and other stakeholders. In order to inspire employees and outside stakeholders, though, it is better to formulate a more positive and appealing mission statement, while still referring to this 'negative' goal.

Our definition of three moral corporate responsibilities formulates a feasible and constructive programme for existing corporations. The moral minimum consists of business providing quality services and goods to the public, without endangering either basic public wellbeing or our common future. In our view, making money can be combined with responding to a limited number of highly moral demands.

4.2 Can a company be held responsible?

The main question in this debate is the 'moral agency issue': Does company responsibility belong to a separate moral agent which is distinct from the accumulated responsibilities of its individual members, or are corporate actions just accumulations of individual activities, no more?

4.2.1 The individualist reply

The last alternative concludes that only individuals bear responsibility, and that corporations can never be held responsible for what they do. Persons who adhere to this philosophy might even accept legal practices that charge corporations for damage provoked by their individual members, but will explain that such legal practices are based on a false assumption. According to the individualist philosophy, only human individuals can be moral agents; this is why corporations are not morally responsible for anything they do (Velasquez, 1983).

The individualist view considers all moral judgements about a company to be in fact shorthand expressions about individual members of that company. This reply takes an extreme position, although Velasquez is partly right in insisting on the responsibility of the individual. It is vital to understand this positive aspect: individual managers are also responsible, whenever they knowingly and willingly comply with harmful and immoral policies.

Nevertheless there is more. Corporations are durable organizations with core objectives and complicated sets of means, controls and procedures. W. Michael Hoffman (1986) charges the individualist view of leading to a mistaken extreme:

> To say that only human individuals are morally responsible is to fail to recognize that collective entities like corporations, armies, nations states, faculties and committees do bring things about in ways that are not just reducible or explainable by aggregates of individual actions. The whole of the collective entity is more than just the sum of its parts because the individuals who make up the collective (and whose actions are clearly necessary for the collective to act) are organized around cooperative purposes, goals, strategies, mission statements, policies, charters or whatever you call that which gives the collective its identity and spells out its function. People act on behalf of the collective purpose and according to its collective directives. (p. 233)

4.2.2 The collectivist reply

The other extreme position only looks at the collective features of corporations, insisting on the morality of corporate goals, strategies, procedures and controls. They refuse to see how the whole organization is supported by human beings, individuals capable of deciding for themselves whether and how they comply to the collective's requirements.

This reply has a positive aspect. It considers a corporation to be more than just the sum of its parts. Collective organizations have always existed because humans were willing and able to help achieve collective goals. But, the collectivist view is also one-sided and overstates the issue of distinct corporate responsibility.

> Attributing moral responsibility to collectives like corporations blocks us from going inside the corporations to get at praiseworthy or blamewor-

thy individuals who in the most fundamental sense intentionally cause the action to come about. If individuals within Ford knowingly and willingly produced an unsafe car, then they should not be allowed to escape legal or moral judgement by hiding behind a veil of corporate agency. Furthermore, to view the corporation as some sort of large-scale moral organism is not only anthropomorphism at its very worst, but also creates a situation where individual interest and autonomy can easily be submerged under what is perceived as corporate good. (Hoffman, 1986, p. 234)

4.3 Moral corporate excellence

4.3.1 The intermediate position of W. M. Hoffman

M. Hoffman not only indicates two ingredients of moral corporate excellence, he explains how they have to be mixed in right proportions in order to produce the desired corporate cultures. These two ingredients are moral corporate culture and the moral autonomy of the individual. In this way, Hoffman shows the moral dimension which remained dormant in the famous *In Search of Excellence* by Peters and Waterman.

Hoffman insists on the moral dimension of corporate excellence: 'The nature of the moral corporate culture is the key. It must be created in such a way that definite ethical goals, structures and strategies are clearly put forward to form a conceptual and operational framework for moral decision making.' Hoffman then explains how this key factor should be tuned towards well-tempered individual autonomy:

It must be made clear to all its individual members that it values and will not tolerate any deviation from the moral point of view. But at the same time, this moral culture, which gives meaning, identity and integrity to the whole corporate collective, must also value and encourage the moral autonomy of its individual members. (Hoffman, 1986, p. 241)

Earlier Hoffman referred to an example of corporate excellence by Peters and Waterman to illustrate the respect of moral autonomy expressed by some of the best companies in the United States.

For example, Hewlett-Packard, having one of the strongest cultures, referred to as 'the HP-way', is proud of its people-oriented philosophy.

The introduction to its revised corporate objective statement concludes: 'Hewlett-Packard [should not] have a tight, military-type organization but rather ... give people the freedom to work toward [overall objectives] in ways they determine best for their own areas of responsibility.' It seems, then, that one of the essential features of the cultures of the excellent corporations is the respect that is given and the space that is allowed for personal expression and initiative. Rather than the culture snuffing out the individual autonomy, the culture itself is actually built on and around such autonomy. (Ibid., p. 239)

Individuals remain responsible for what they do. Adherence to whatever organization does not reduce individual members to irresponsible cogs in a great machine. This ingredient should be allowed for in any truly moral corporate culture:

To deny such moral autonomy is to cut off the possibility of rationally developing and examining the ethical principles of the culture itself and to fail to respect the persons making up the culture itself – both being vocations of the moral point of view to which the moral culture is committed. (Ibid., p. 241)

When applied to the case in Chapter 2 ('Croupier Van Duren versus Holland Casinos') we may now understand better the failures on both sides. Van Duren felt sincere concern for gambling addicts, but with his colleagues he could not establish a moral dialogue based on respect and an effort for rational debate. The Casino directors formulated their policy code four years after Van Duren had started to act in his unorthodox fashion. Prior to the dismissal of this croupier the directors did not show much respect and sensibility for the moral concerns which Van Duren had highlighted, and applied for his dismissal on mainly professional grounds.

Holland Casinos has the mission to promote gambling as a socially responsible leisure activity. The Casino direction was very critical about the rather extreme attitudes of croupier Van Duren towards gambling addicts. Mr Van Erve, director of public relations at Holland Casinos' main office, expressed this in a discussion with me by using a parallel with selling alcohol in public houses: 'If you are a teetotaller you simply should not get involved in selling alcoholic drinks.' This expression overlooks the barman's code of honour, which also imposes constraints on the way you serve already drunk customers. In the case of Holland Casinos it seems as if the promotion of gambling as a socially acceptable leisure activity largely overruled corporate concern about addiction.

Such corporate policies are contrary to the moral standards expressed

by Hoffman. Corporate excellence includes respect for the moral autonomy
of the individual.

> Individuality is not being abolished through coercion but rather con-
> verted into an individual commitment freely to adopt the demands of
> the organizational imperative and to be willing to substitute organiza-
> tional values to personal values. . . . Having a strong corporate culture
> does not necessarily eliminate individual autonomy. (Ibid., p. 239)

4.3.2 A corporate excellence programme with a moral dimension

A major Dutch specialist on moral corporate excellence programmes is
Johan Wempe of the Erasmus University, Rotterdam. As a consultant of
Schiphol Airport NV he supervised the conception and implementation
of their programme. The Airport authority's requirement might have
seemed limited. They had problems with service personnel, resulting in
high costs for corporate car repairs, small thefts of corporate property and
other irregularities. At first sight, what they needed was simply a neat
strict code of conduct.

During the phases of problem definition and programme conception the
authority insisted on relating normative expectations and resulting moral
codes to the vital corporate objectives. Therefore, instead of defining a code
as a separate instrument functioning alongside other management tools
and controls, Schiphol Airport directors decided to adopt a more integrated
perspective.

Schiphol Airport already had a marketing policy and a mission
statement. Now they developed a moral excellence programme closely
allied to their main corporate objectives. Two chief components of their
mission statement are: (a) that Schiphol Airport becomes and stays one
of Western Europe's five main airports; and (b) that Schiphol Airport
should profile itself as the very best airport for service quality.

The feature of openness was identified as a crucial value. Consequently,
they introduced an elaborate training programme, facing their personnel
with relevant concrete issues in open debate. Senior manager commitment
to open debate went beyond their own staff: it also led to frank and
respectful relationships with several outsiders. Especially, they communicated directly with environmental activists fighting against the construction of a new runway – an atmosphere of respectful opposition prevailed,
in which the two sides stayed on speaking terms. Such programmes
insist on the *process* of getting corporate members committed to moral
guidelines.

4.4 Inference 1: attribution theory on managerial mistakes

4.4.1 Attribution of responsibilities is often biased by self-deception

Chapter 3 contains two definitions of individual responsibility. Both state that sane persons can be held responsible for what they plan or intend to do and for what they actually do or neglect. This implies accountability for damage done to others. In the following section, we study how managers explain failing business performances. Often they show self-deceiving optimism.

Starting a philosophic discussion on entrepreneurial performance with this inference has a definite purpose. It points to this psychological pitfall of optimism founded on self-deception. Our second definition of responsibility remains valid in principle, but in practice the attribution of responsibilities stands open to self-serving bias.

4.4.2 Failing entrepreneurs blame the circumstances, not themselves

Statistics and reports show that senior managers often refuse to accept the negative side of senior responsibilities. Entrepreneurial mistakes are commonly interpreted by senior managers as not their fault, and excuses are found by pointing to difficult circumstances.

A survey by Mathieu Weggeman and Ton Berendsen of Twijnstra Gnudde consultants reports on how entrepreneurs with recent bad results explained corporate failure. More than half the explanations blamed external circumstances. The main causes of failure cited by the managers were unfavourable market conditions (48 per cent), economic recession (12 per cent) and currency crisis (7 per cent). Next came a group of neutrally phrased internal causes, including high costs (41 per cent), and a wrong product or service formula (9 per cent). Only 3 per cent of the respondents confessed that failure as an entrepreneur was one of the primary causes.

Weggeman and Berendsen also asked about the proposed solutions. In tone with the preceding explanations, they found that only 1 per cent of the senior managers interviewed thought about changing the corporate leaders. Offensive methods were also scarcely cited. Only 4.6 per cent intended to penetrate new markets or start with other market-oriented innovations. More then half of the indicated solutions were defensive. This covers measures such as cost reduction (9 per cent), outsourcement and reduction of commercial activities (10 per cent) and reduction of personnel (35 per cent).

4.5 Inference 2: entrepreneurial performance and public accountability

This section relates entrepreneurial performance to the moral accountability of business by showing that total quality management (TQM) has a hidden potential for producing a clear response to moral demands. Specific moral requirements from the public are already being met within quality management, in an unselfconscious and oblique way. Our aim is to point to TQM's potential as a relatively independent, highly sophisticated response to demands of the moral community.

4.5.1 A normative idea of entrepreneurial performance

Entrepreneurship consists of personal skills as a leader, especially the ability to implement strategic marketing decisions. We refuse to admit that being an entrepreneur always implies ruthless behaviour. Basically, a highly performing entrepreneur thinks along situationalist lines. He or she does not always see marketing activities as a matter of a competitive struggle, with one side emerging the winner and the other side the loser. More specifically, besides competitive warfare for the survival of the fittest, there are other business games that allow for proper exchange of views and real partnerships. Also, morally involved entrepreneurs have great skills in convincing and motivating interlocutors, first of all by setting a coherent and appealing example.

Our idea of entrepreneurial performance accepts that market demands oblige companies to implement cost reductions, re-engineering, and outsourcing, and to lay off employees. But while proactively anticipating market pressures, a manager also has to give moral considerations a higher profile. Business managers can achieve a *higher* performance by personally integrating moral demands in corporate policies.

Here, the term 'higher' refers to a balance between three different moral requirements:

1. Meeting corporate goals, especially medium- and long-term profitability.
2. Ethically motivated job satisfaction.
3. The fostering of durable partnerships.

Ethically valid performance is produced by preventing unnecessary harm and by the ability to build constructive and durable partnerships with employees, consumers and suppliers. The basic objective of ethical entrepreneurial performance is articulated by the corporate mission statement. This mission statement should define the balance between two constituents: (a) the strategic vocation of the corporation; and (b) its commitment to specific corporate responsibilities.

4.5.2 Quality programmes respond to moral demands in their own way

The basic fact we start with is a broadening of consumer requirements, obliging companies to redefine quality. Quality no longer refers just to the proper functioning of a product.

The *safe and satisfactory functioning of a product or service* is still the basic objective, and it will remain very important. Reducing health risks and providing customers with reliable products is the perennial moral corporate responsibility. Here especially, non-moral legal talk and one-sided strategic concerns often obscure the moral basis of this responsibility.

For the moment, many corporations are unable to formulate their quality commitments in moral terms. Though many of their performances may be morally quite respectable, a huge potential for creating commitment remains unexplored by not using moral language. Instead of seeing quality as a means to obtain a certificate that may help the company to survive competition, a broader and less defensive attitude is needed. Before that, it is important to explain in more detail in what sense consumer requirements have increased and developed.

We start by defining the general meaning of 'quality': 'Quality is fully satisfying agreed customer requirements at the lowest internal costs' (Banks, 1992). Now, how do we perceive the development of agreed consumer requirements? It has to be seen as part of a much deeper change in consumer mentality and public concern, which no longer just refers to the performance of the product itself. Opinion makers, like consumer organizations, are no longer concerned only about personal satisfaction, they propose new requirements which include claims of a different kind. This broadening of the quality requirements may have drastic consequences on corporate sales and on the product portfolio.

Above all, the greening of business is spurred by a shift in customer requirements which stretches beyond the old hedonistic specifications. Ease of use is no longer the benchmark. Many consumers are becoming more and more willing to pay for a product that stands for environmental values. They prefer environmentally safe production, materials with a natural and non-depletable appearance, and they will boycott products that endanger our common future. These new requirements combine a mix of environmental and social concern. Not living up to these demands may trigger powerful reactions and consumer sanctions.

Even if many uninformed consumers remain unaware of real environmental threats and seem an easy victim of sentimental green marketing, it can be argued that private concerns face a big public appeal here. Already many private corporations have committed themselves to elaborate environmental care programmes, often outperforming what the market and the law require.

The moral concern for our natural environment and our common future makes whole branches of business endorse voluntary norms for environmental care. They may cover various aspects of production and distribution processes. In German-speaking countries, for instance, the norms corresponding to the 'Grüner Punkt' label are being applied widely.

Besides the environmental requirements, other requirements have developed in addition to the basic demand for functional quality. These extra demands vary according to the type of product or service. They often go beyond the standards of private consumer satisfaction. An example of these emerging new requirements is the resurgence of a classic labour rights topic, but now on a worldwide scale: the fight against child labour and slavery. Nowadays, activists of high reputation express concern about the use of child labour and bonded labour for the production of goods exported to the rich countries.

So, a group of the additional requirements have to do with *minimal labour conditions*. Many consumers are ready to pay a higher price for recognizing employees' rights. National and European Community legislation have an important role to play here, for they can impose minimum requirements for the humane labour quality of *imported* goods. Wholesaler organizations might commit themselves to participatory ethics, by creating a quality hallmark indicating minimum labour conditions free from torture, slavery and severe exploitation. In the end, such action defends the reputation and interests of those corporations that do maintain more than a minimum of decent labour conditions.

In summary, additional consumer demands going beyond consumer satisfaction and individual safety have been accepted as quality goals. These demands cannot easily be treated as non-moral consumer expectations, as they refer to public goods.

The ethical profile expressed by present agreed consumer requirements clearly transcends the continuous effort of business to satisfy private needs, and calls for a positive corporate commitment to the promotion of common welfare.

The common practice of certified quality corporations is non-moral. Spurred on by a narrow non-moral concept of strategic corporate objectives, they abide by ISO 9000 regulations. It seems as if it is only by accident that quality regulations force corporations to produce in ways that do not damage human wellbeing and do not jeopardize our common future. The link between quality and agreed moral demands is still not properly appreciated.

One notable reason for this inability to understand and communicate properly the need for responsible product and environmental care in moral terms may be due to inadequate skills in this respect: that is, moral muteness.

4.5.3 Moral muteness is predominant in total quality management programmes

Even in the midst of the 1990s, corporate managers seem unwilling or unable to communicate their efforts to produce safely and care about the environment in moral terms.

Surveys reveal that senior managers rarely express any voluntary commitment to moral demands when they discuss the reasons for implementing quality care. Business people seem unable or unwilling to state publicly how their integrative quality norms actually are corporate commitments that redefine moral concerns in operational requirements and controls. Even environmental care is simply profiled as complying with legal duties or created by market demands, not as a moral obligation which also happens to be profitable in many instances.

We begin with one example that may illustrate this point. A partner of KPMG, G. C. Molenkamp, explains his work on environmental care schedules in a Dutch newspaper article by T. Westerwoudt. Dr Molenkamp works for KPMG environmental consultancy group. He gives advice on environmental care programmes, mainly as part of larger TQM pro-grammes. He explains that in the end corporations often become more competitive and save money through environmental care. The following examples illustrate how he sells the implementation of environmental care by referring to that precept of business rationality, 'reduce costs, increase profits':

> People often talk about the costs of environmental care, but a more careful study reveals quick returns on environmental investments. One good example is the food industry, where they deal with huge quantities of waste and waste water, requiring expensive treatment. By implement-ing integrative environmental care schedules and by changing the production process you can cut costs drastically. We know examples of factories where they only had started to mind about the water logistics and paid little attention to the quantities of chemicals used or waste

discharge. If you look at these things carefully and implement changes, you discover great opportunities for making money. In Ireland we screened a soft drink plant that planned to invest millions in extending its waste water treatment system. A closer look revealed that this was superfluous. By taking relatively simple measures the plant limited the volumes of water input drastically and reduced the dosage of chemicals. (NRC Handelsblad, 1994c)

The general point Molenkamp makes is stated in the same newspaper article:

We assist to a silent green revolution. Environmental issues are no longer hot items as they used to be in the 1970s. Things no longer happen under pressure of ideological yelling, but behind the curtains corporations work hard on improvements. And by going along with the process of quality improvement they learn new things every day. (Ibid.)

The NRC Handelsblad newspaper article also refers to a KPMG survey, showing that corporations start the race towards ISO 9000 certificates out of a defensive need. First, they do not see any real benefits in starting quality programmes. Many companies rally to quality management simply because clients demand it; in other words, they respond to market pressures. According to a KPMG survey directed by J. Kok in 1993, from the 63 corporations which responded, the large majority had just one single objective in implementing total quality controls in accordance to the ISO 9000 regulations: they wanted to have the certificate, nothing more.

In an earlier chapter we discussed Bird and Waters' article on moral muteness, explaining why, in business, moral behaviour often occurs in the absence of moral talk. The above-mentioned arguments for environmental care match well with their definition of moral muteness. In the case of the race towards ISO 9000 certificates, managers apply environmental care because it helps them to gain a competitive edge. By accident they achieve financial gains. Thus this positive feedback is a powerful, but external, reinforcer.

What remains is the inability of senior managers to express moral concern when referring to quality performances. This makes one wonder about the explanation for moral muteness.

4.5.4 Possible explanations for the absence of moral talk in TQM

Our general impression about the underlying standards of TQM programmes and books is quite positive, yet even authors like John Banks (1992) rarely dwell upon the way quality management responds to moral demands. This author mainly uses such reference in the beginning and end of his book; in between moral talk is absent from the discourse on TQM. Thus the moral concern shines through in the opening paragraphs of his preface: 'Events leading up to "the major malfunction" of Challenger provide the raw material of a case study on how *not* to manage a complex technological project' (Banks, 1992, p. xi). At the very end of his book John Banks then quotes from a powerful case study on the causes for the Challenger disaster: 'In reality, as Challenger's crew smiled down from the launch pad catwalk at the massive white columns of the solid rocket boosters, they were looking at the final product of flawed policy and political corruption' (McConnel, 1987, p. 7). In order to give more detailed explanations for the absence of moral talk in TQM, we refer once more to the three explanations provided by Bird and Waters.

Threat to harmony
Moral talk is said to be intrusive and confrontational and to invite cycles of mutual recrimination.

As business people often have a poor impression of the interpersonal confrontation and accusatory tactics used by early environmental activists, smaller entrepreneurs especially will avoid confrontation. They are willing to act, but do not seek public debate with perfectionists always insisting that there are still shortcomings.

Threat to efficiency
Moral talk is said to assume distracting moralistic forms (praising, blaming, ideologic profiling) and is held to be simplistic, inflexible, soft and inexact.

Business entrepreneurs still believe moral talk to be a matter of voicing some abstract absolute duty, of proposing some holy obligation, whenever an issue is raised. Due to this unsophisticated image, the very idea of moral talk is shunned. It is felt that showing real care about public demands only leads to futile debate with people who are never satisfied. They fear that they will simply waste time and energy in useless debate with environmental fundamentalists.

Threat to image of power and effectiveness
Moral talk is said to be too esoteric and idealistic; morally mute managers think that moral talk lacks rigour and force.

Whenever they have an opportunity for environmental debate, some entrepreneurs may indeed feel their professional authority weakened since they have to talk about issues on which their opponents are experts and they are not. Entrepreneurs excel in discussions on organizational politics, technical qualifications, and competitive advantages, but they have little knowledge of the different ethical theories as expressed in Chapters 5, 6 and 7.

4.5.5 Dangers of not articulating implicit moral commitments

Instead of simply describing the potential for TQM of moral talk in positive terms, we prefer now to comment on the five long-term consequences of moral muteness formulated by Bird and Waters. Little by little the hidden potential for gold, which too often still remains implicit, will start shining through.

1. Creation of moral amnesia

Quality management is presented as a technical performance, not as a moral activity. Corporate communications are slow in recognizing the degree to which the implementation of integrative quality management is in fact a wonderful example of how business handles moral demands in a truly responsible way. By imposing quality procedures on itself, business has constantly to work on what one might call the *intentions and actions of the corporation*: its schedules and logistic planning and their execution during production and distribution processes. Corporate planning and production according to integrative quality requirements do respond to moral demands. Yet most business people do not comprehend that quality responds to moral expectations.

> It is characteristic of this moral amnesia that business people only feel themselves moved by moral obligations and ideals and find no way to refer explicitly to these pushes and pulls except indirectly by invoking personal preferences, common sense and long-term benefits. They remain inarticulate and unselfconscious of their convictions. (Bird and Waters, 1989, p. 80)

2. Inappropriate narrowness in conceptions of morality

In Chapter 1 we defined ethics as the critical study of moral convictions, and we identified distinct features of moral standards. Above all, moral standards can be characterized as dealing with matters of serious consequence for human, animal and environmental wellbeing and as expressing some impartial ideal of equity and justice.

Bird and Waters (1989) formulate a common experience of ethicists concerning the narrow idea of morality used by persons in business. Corporate managers tend to block moral issues. They obstruct moral debates by presenting issues in the non-moral terms of operational management. Managers present morally respectable policies as strategic choices, and only speak about morality when they refer to extraordinary and urgent items, that is, blatantly immoral activities with very harmful consequences. Managers are often unwilling and unable to state positively that they *do* act morally:

> They 'stonewall' moral questions by arguing that the issues involved are ones of feasibility, practicality and the impersonal balancing of costs and benefits and that the decisions on these matters are appropriately made by relevant managers and directors without public discussion. . . . These managers attempted to treat issues that had been questioned as if they were not publicly debatable. . . . Moral muteness in the form of stonewalling thus perpetuates a narrow conception of morality, i.e. as only concerned with blatant deviance from moral standards. (Bird and Waters, 1989, p. 81)

This very last citation is immediately followed by a statement on the positive value of moral talk for entrepreneurs: 'Most importantly, moral muteness in this case prevents creative exploration of action alternatives that might enable the organization to balance better conflicting demands or to approximate better the highest ideals.' In 1994, many TQM programmes provided good examples of the blocking of moral references.

3. Moral stress for individual managers

The inability to articulate moral expectations in a more balanced and open way finally rebounds on the personal wellbeing of managers. Bird and Waters (1989) insist that the absence of moral human talk exacerbates moral stress.

In the case of our topic – the moral muteness in TQM – the levels of stress most probably remain tolerable because the purpose of TQM is often so implicitly moral. Whenever personal stress becomes unbearable for the manager during the implementation and improvement of quality management, this is probably due more to other causes, such as inability to communicate directly about moral concerns, or perhaps uptight behaviour. The individual managers of the KPMG survey mentioned in section 4.5.3 may have felt that they were being coerced by some external market demand to obtain the quality certificate, and consequently they were not really committed to this quality programme and had to force themselves to comply with it.

4. Neglect of moral abuses

This consequence of moral muteness may seem less relevant, as quality involves controls. Nevertheless, the sheer ignorance about what are the specific moral issues to which the organization commits itself by implementing an integrative quality programme may lead to setting wrong priorities. Moreover the inability to articulate the underlying moral demands has immediate consequences for the motivation of employees. The manager will often resort to bullying employees instead of presenting legitimate moral reasons for the planned new procedures and controls.

Bird and Waters indicate a more general point:

> Just as norms of confrontation contribute to moral muteness, in circular fashion that muteness reinforces those norms and leads to a culture of neglect. Organizational silence on moral issues makes it more difficult for members to raise questions and debate issues. What could and should be ordinary practice – i.e. questioning the propriety of specific decisions and actions – tends to require an act of human heroism and is thus less likely to occur. (Bird and Waters, 1989, p. 82)

5. Decreased authority of moral standards

The fact that moral talk and moral standards are not used explicitly for the formulation of corporate commitments has another consequence. As people are not committing themselves to moral objectives, so these objectives lose their influence in the business community.

Sustained moral muteness in TQM might lead to the mockery of persons who insist on the presence of moral standards in quality requirements, since they are regarded as external interference:

> Moral arguments possess compelling authority only if the discourse in which these arguments are stated is socially rooted. It is an idealistic misconception to suppose that moral reasons by virtue of their own logic alone inspire the feelings of obligation and desire that make people willingly adhere to moral standards. (Bird and Waters, 1989, p. 82)

This consequence also prevents companies from developing a corporate culture fostering co-operative self-ruled behaviour. Here lies the great opportunity for inside communications on the basis of moral commitments expressed in the corporate statement. It should focus on screening the quality requirements by caring about their alignment with these core corporate responsibilities.

For the first time in the history of modern industrial production the requirements for quality production are expressed in a system of comprehensive procedures and controls. The public does not ask for details on these programmes, but they might appreciate it if corporate communicators would express the business response to moral concerns in ordinary language. The communicators should show how quality relates to basic moral commitments, and should achieve this by insisting on moral concerns being incorporated through quality production and service. A tidal wave of public satisfaction might then occur as a consequence.

4.5.6 *Moral core responsibilities of entrepreneurial performance*

Great opportunities are available to business entrepreneurs with existing quality programmes. Quality care can be seen as serious, constant and practical attention to specific moral demands. The corporate image can be communicated in a coherent and convincing way, that is, as a morally outspoken acceptance of corporate responsibilities. While being frank about the fact that it also takes care of private interests, the corporation can explain clearly that it promotes specific public concerns, especially concerning consumer satisfaction and environmental care.

By contrast, let us state briefly an example of corporate promotion which does not fit in with this idea. We do not consider that Benetton behaves like a morally responsible agent. Their publicity campaign shows contempt and disregard for existing beliefs by associating the private Benetton label to some publicity campaign 'presenting' moral tragedies. It does not educate people or provide responsible and appropriate help, but mainly exploits cheap sensationalism. The black and white opposition campaign pays lip service to silly moralistic ideals of sloppy permissiveness and non-discrimination.

Worst of all, it is my personal conviction that these campaigns mix two types of discourse in an unethical way, using public ideals for private promotion. If Benetton wanted to promote public concern in an ethical way it should remove its label from these posters, and instead sponsor proper charity work. They do the contrary, using a photo with a dying AIDS patient to promote a private label. Benetton's 1993 and 1994 campaigns made many people sick and angry and we believe that the basic value they felt had something to do with the moral difference between charitable promotion of public goods and private publicity campaigns. In our view, the Benetton publicity director Mr Toscani prostitutes honourable public issues to the private interest of brand promotion. Even if Benetton has strategic reasons for being happy with bad publicity – because, after all, it is still publicity – not everything is morally acceptable.

Let us now return to the general issue of defining core moral responsibilities at a minimal level. By accepting an outspoken commitment to these responsibilities TQM can gain a lot. The core moral responsibilities are threefold (see Table 4.1). First of all, the corporation is committed to its original and basic moral core responsibility: that is, *producing goods and services that are functional and safe for the individual consumer*. On top of this perennial cornerstone of business, other core activities now have to be added. The second moral commitment therefore concerns the larger environment: *environmental care and reduction of resource depletion*. Finally, the third accepted responsibility refers to *the quality of the corporation itself*

Table 4.1 The three core moral responsibilities

Moral responsibility	Objective	Content
Labour conditions	Minimum standard of labour conditions.	No torture. No child labour. Minimum standards of job health care and safety precautions.
	Minimum standard of fair retribution of risks and profits.	No slavery. Clearly defined employee payment and bonus systems.
Natural environment	Output-oriented environmental care. Limit harmful waste.	Norms for waste discharge. Phasing-out programmes. Use of filters. Design for disassembly.
	Input-oriented environmental care. Reduce the depletion of natural resources.	Waste minimalization programmes. Recycling.
Functional	Consumer satisfaction.	Meeting agreed consumer requirements. Screening of ease of use for consumer.
	Consumer safety.	Design. Production controls. Usage instructions.

as a moral community. At a minimum level this implies the absence of certain abuses. These three core moral responsibilities for business organizations aim at guaranteeing a minimum of moral excellence. They are linked with an idea of normative entrepreneurial performance and encapsulate what the public may at least expect from an entrepreneur committed to quality management.

Our three entrepreneurial responsibilities also imply a redefinition of corporate objectives. It pushes the meaning of the famous separatist expression 'mind your own business' in a quite opposite direction. Corporate mission statements that include these moral responsibilities enlarge the matters for which the public may hold business accountable for by insisting on safe and reliable customer relationships, environmental care and humane working conditions.

The entrepreneur should gain this broader perspective as the corporation commits itself to wider human objectives, especially in relation to our common future. Although industry will go through even more stringent reductions of employee numbers in the future, certain minimum standards of working conditions should be agreed upon by all those committed to quality goods. This statement is a moral appeal for legal means and voluntary covenants to enforce respect for minimum labour rights.

4.6 Inference 3: groupthink in coping with technological innovation

A third consequence refers to new techniques or new applications of existing techniques. Innovating is a decisive part of entrepreneurial performance. The history of modern industry really started with the introduction of steam engine power, allowing corporations to produce without depending on the vagaries of natural windmill energy.

Innovation is an important factor in competition, but here too ethical decision-making is important, often requiring a capacity to deal with new, unfamiliar and hazardous potentials. Many famous cases in business ethics relate to this type of failure of control: The senior managers' inability to assess risks of new products and technologies, the wrong choices that are made, and the subsequent tragedies this provokes – employees had often pointed out the risks, but those at the top did not want to listen.

Several major catastrophes can be explained as management failures in assessing incorrectly the risks of innovation and in not taking adequate precautions.

For example, the tragedy of *The Herald of Free Enterprise* at Zeebrugge on 6 March 1987 can be linked with the failure of senior management. The capsizing of this top-heavy ferryboat caused the death of 193 persons. It was due primarily to an omission: the bow doors on the roll-on-roll-off deck were not shut properly. Right after the accident the public could see on television an experiment with an existing scale model of this modern ferry boat, which revealed that after only a small inflow of water onto the lower decks the scale model simply toppled over and fell on its side. Although the crew and the captain were aware of the imminent danger, commercial pressures from the board of directors created a state of negligence in staff performance. Tasks were overlapping, personnel was cut to the minimum, and requested safety devices such as control lamps for the shutting of bow doors were not installed – all due to the board's short-term financial priorities. Senior management drastically underestimated the safety risks of this new boat design.

Murphy's law, which states that whatever can go wrong will go wrong, was tragically proven for a second time when the catastrophe of the *Estonia* in October 1994 again revealed the risks inherent in this type of ferry. Modern roll-on-roll-off ferries have bow doors, and they may break off at their hinges. Completed designs for much safer ferries exist already. Yet it is mainly due to short-term commercial pressure and to lack of public legislation to actively promote the construction of these new designs that more accidents remain possible for decades ahead. The presence of bow doors on many ferries with a top-heavy construction remains a major security risk.

Another example is the Ford Pinto car, the first small car produced by Ford in the United States. For Ford producing a small car required new technology, and it was this that led them to create a car with a high potential for catching fire. This feature was created by accident not by purpose, but Ford retained the design error even after it was revealed in crash tests. Although the design error could be repaired by putting rubber shock absorbers around the petrol tank in the rear, senior management wanted to keep the selling price low. The absorbers did cost $12, which unfortunately raised the car price above the sacred target of $2,000.

We will demonstrate one practical explanation for errors in innovation risk assessment – *groupthink*. The Pinto case will serve as an example.

Originally, the word 'groupthink' was invented by George Orwell in his novel *1984*. John Donaldson (1989) later defined groupthink as follows:

> it refers to what are called group norms, though usually referring to those norms which do not admit challenge or amendment. Individuals are required to believe what the group thinks, suppressing or exchanging their own views in favour of the official view of the group. Very widespread. (p. xiv)

In business environments groupthink is imposed by coercive hard-headed entrepreneurs, who do not allow for moral autonomy or neglect warning. A famous study on groupthink was made by Janis (1972), who attributed errors in foreign policy decisions and fiascos to eight key characteristics of groupthink. In his textbook on corporate responsibility Tom Cannon (1994) refers to these eight key characteristics in his comment on the Pinto case. He uses them in particular to explain the failure of Mr Lee Iacocca to assess the true impact of neglecting safety precautions on the Ford Pinto. What Mr Iacocca still presents as a feat of achievement is most probably the greatest blemish on his reputation as a frank and concerned top entrepreneur:

> Group think is perhaps the biggest barrier to positive change in attitudes to risk and hazard management. . . . The Pinto was an important but not vital element in Ford's efforts during the early 1970s to reposition its operations in the face of growing competition especially from overseas. It was, however, closely identified with the egos of several key executives at Ford notably Henry Ford II and Lee Iacocca. The latter was battling to become the leader of the company when Henry Ford II eventually retired. Iacocca had promised to produce the 2,000: 2,000 quickly and under budget. This was achieved. The car weighed just over 2,030 lb and sold for $2,000. It took six months to develop and was well under budget. *Ego identification* became linked to a sense of *invulnerability*, the first reports of problems added to this sense of invul-

nerability. Henry Ford II rejected Nader's criticisms arguing that people wanted 'good cars, good looking cars, fast cars, cars with power and styling'.

Reading the accounts of the principles, there is powerful sense of *collective rationalization* – people were getting the cars they wanted. Critics were *stereotyped* as ignorant and hostile. This reinforced the sense of *inherent morality* which prompted the firm to ask the national Highway Traffic Safety Administration to put a price on Auto Safety. The figure produced was $200,725 [for each mortal accident]. This was then used to calculate the cost per vehicle of improvements needed to solve the problem. The internal report virtually concluded that it was cheaper to pay the accident claims [the calculation did not contain any budget allowing for the costs of bad will due to neglect of safety precautions, which later turned out to be at least 100 million dollars]. This symbolized the *pressure* on group members to rationalize decisions, repress doubts and keep members in line. (Cannon, 1994, pp. 182–3)

Immediately after this passage, Tom Cannon adds a comment indicating that self-serving bias is also a widespread phenomenon, also to be found in the writings of the respected American entrepreneur who a while later put Chrysler back on the track again.

Even in his autobiography, Lee Iacocca gives a clear impression of self-justification. Although he admits 'we resisted making any changes and that hurt us badly', he argues that 'the Pinto was not the only car with this problem' of fire breaking out if hit from the rear. At no point does he comment on the deaths or injuries caused by the problem. His argument seemed to centre on the notion that no one 'deliberately [tried] to make this car unsafe'. No critics had made this assumption but had argued that no one put enough effort for making it SAFE. (Ibid., p. 183)

In contrast, a quote from John Banks that indicates the need to allow employees to express moral concern:

Engineers or shop floor workers who discover flawed design should be encouraged to 'blow the whistle' by their company's own commitment to continuous improvement and to quality processes, rather than wait to play dramatic parts as witnesses in an inquiry. (Banks, 1992, p. xiii)

4.7 Three classical theories of product responsibility

This section contains a brief outline of three well-known theories: contract theory; due care theory; and social costs theory. The discussion stresses the specific moral concerns articulated by each of these theories. Also, it identifies the kind of issues connected with each of them. We will maintain that they serve specific purposes: that each theory can best be applied to a range of specific stakeholder settings. Some philosophical comments on each theory point towards our next two chapters.

Before revealing these theories, it is important to state a practical issue: the rise and overheating of consumer claims. We will ask for a more philosophical understanding of liability, based upon our second definition of individual responsibility (see section 3.7).

4.7.1 Plea for redressment of balance in liability jurisprudence

Over the last ten years consumers in Europe have discovered and extended the use of liability claims. Above all, the discovery of unknown risks with retroactive value has fuelled these demands. Examples of such retroactive claims relate to soil pollution from the 1950s and 1960s, to employee diseases due to working with dangerous products like asbestos and, finally, to consumer products connected with the DES hormone, that later proved to be dangerous or fatal to human health.

In The Netherlands, liability insurances now make heavy losses due to a combination of factors. Until 1993 the 100 insurance companies still made a profit on their services in third-party insurances. In 1992, business entrepreneurs, medical professionals and accountants paid almost DFl 600 million in insurance premiums. This was the last year that the insurance companies made a small profit on this insurance business (*NRC Handelsblad*, 1994d).

The rise of retroactive valid claims poses several unforeseen problems. The insurance companies have never made reservations for this type of claim, and Dutch laws prohibited doing so. Moreover some of the risks like soil pollution are subject to public legislation. Whereas soil pollution was a neglected issue until the middle of the 1960s, the Dutch authorities started a draconian clean-up programme in the late 1980s that bankrupted several respectable companies who had been unlucky enough to take over building ground from the original polluters. Dutch law simply obliged the present owners to pay, not allowing them to make retroactive claims. However, about a year ago, new and cheaper methods of soil cleaning were accepted by public authorities, which gave some relief to many corporations.

Other risks pertaining to old custom and practice have recently been discovered, inciting former employees and consumers to claim. In the United States, for example, there is currently a glut of lawsuits concerning past use of lead-containing paints. The sum of the claims for this health damage is estimated at $100 billion (NRC, 1994d). According to Professor J. Wansink, a specialist in insurance legislation at the Erasmus University, Rotterdam, the liability jurisdiction is now out of control. American jurisprudence is already recognizing the dangers of one-sided consumer protection (NRC, 1994d). Until recently, unlimited care for damage to the consumer often had top priority, and a more balanced concept of responsibility was ignored.

The jurisdiction on the consumer claim about the poodle that exploded in the microwave oven is probably a good example. A housewife used to dry her wet pet in the oven, and she continued to do so after buying a new type of oven, with unfortunate results. The manufacturer had to pay out on the claim as the user instructions did not warn against this extraordinary use of microwave ovens. Other judges might have paid more attention to the housewife's responsibilities in the matter. Do consumers have to be protected in all circumstances, even if they use goods for extraordinary purposes?

We accept the possibility of corporations going bankrupt because of liability fines based upon harm they knowingly and willingly inflicted. However, we are much more hesitant about crediting retroactive claims, especially when the legal authorities use legislation in order to put all the burden on innocent new owners.

Corporations should pay for failures and damage directly linked to straightforward failures of their products and services. The alleged damage is clear in those cases where it is directly caused, beyond control of the victim, durable, overt and of great impact on personal wellbeing. Nevertheless when more complicated liability claims are involved, one has to be more attentive. Circumspection and prudence are required most of all in cases of employee claims for injury at work.

In order to determine the degree of human suffering, it is necessary to see things in proportion. For instance, the problems of persons who put their own pets in the microwave oven should be valued less than the hurt and humiliation of women violated and made pregnant due to military 'policies' executed by soldiers.

4.7.2 Contract theory

Comment on the philosophical assumptions of the contract theory
The contract view holds responsibility to be the result of the mutual obligations accepted by partners in a deal. Both partners are regarded as fully responsible for their own individual engagements, and are capable of taking care of their own interests (see Table 4.2).

Table 4.2 An outline of contract theory

Item	Relevant content
Creed	Let the buyer beware!
Assumed duties of producer/supplier	To provide consumer with product/good according to the sales contract. This includes the contractual duties for quality of design, production and delivery; nothing more.
Assumed power balance	Both parties are equal, they both know what they are doing when they make this deal.
Scope of valid application	Those business-to-business relationships and other commercial relationships and deals where: (a) both parties may be expected to have equal expertise about the qualities of the bought product or service; and (b) in which each party has strong means for punishing breach of contract by the opponent, especially due to market pressure possibilities.
Dangers and inadequacies	Failures that cause harm and damage, but are not directly stipulated in the contract, remain the buyer's risk.
Main uses	In regular deals of a buying department. For the bulk of the consumer shopping activities for food and clothing (regular needs with low risks that may be assumed to be known).

CASE STUDY

You buy jeans and a few shirts in a big town shop near your home. As you are told the cost, you realize that the salesperson has forgotten to count one T-shirt, which is 10 per cent of the whole sum owed. All magnetic labels have been removed, and all items are nicely put in a bag. Once more you ask for the amount, and again you hear the salesperson confirm the lower sum.

1. What happens if you strictly apply the contract view here?
2. How do you feel about using the contract view to your advantage in this way?

Please note that this case points to an omission in our presentation of the contract view. The contract view obliges us to present the intended deal fairly, but does not ask us to be overly considerate, especially when the other partner is a professional.

The two most obvious solutions are as follows:

1. You do not say anything, but start to walk out hoping to get away with it. If you get caught you already know you will claim innocence and pay. As you are a tough but fair person, you accept others to behave likewise towards you in comparable situations. On the other hand, you would get angry if a salesperson overcharged you; it is their job to calculate the right amount. Basically, you are transactionalist, adhering to the contract view.
2. You ask the salesperson to count again. After running through the items the mistake is discovered. You now have to pay the full amount. You feel good about your honesty, and the salesperson has thanked you and explained that finding this mistake would save a lot of trouble at closing time. Basically, you are an absolutist. You would like other persons to apply the rules as you do, for it would make the world a better place.

This does not imply that contractors have to run through all the clauses of their deals each time they do business. In ordinary business transactions, many conventions exist defining responsibilities. Whenever difficult issues arise, it is possible to formulate additional clauses.

These philosophical assumptions align with *transaction ethics* as formulated by Henk van Luijk (see section 2.6), which regards moral interaction as a defence of private interests and bargaining whenever there is a conflict of interest. This does not mean that we recognize others interests in an altruistic way, and does not allow for feelings of solidarity and loyalty. Sacrificing individual interests goes much too far according to this outlook, as the moral agents are seen as egocentric rational individuals seeking to optimalize their private profits. This approach may have positive results in win-win situations, where arrangements can benefit participants.

It is a view that assumes both agents to be rational and aware of what they are doing. In simple situations where the gains on both sides are easy to see, this view may work. As soon as the deals are about more complicated products common sense may prove to be insufficient, and one side may prove weaker due to a lack of knowledge.

Most owners of Pinto cars thought they had bought a fine and cheap car; they did not expect that they were exposing themselves to a risk – relatively minor in percentage terms – of car burns. Neither did they know that the manufacturer knew about this risk and could prevent it at a low cost per car, but chose to leave things as they were. Indignant public feelings concerning Fords' voluntary negligence are not really catered for by the contract view. The contract view does not contain general obligations, as it only allows for contractual obligations. This view leads to absolute respect for contractual clauses, but it may also lead to acceptance of the most immoral clauses, simply because they are in the contract. Shylock adhered to this view, according to Shakespeare.

The most dangerous consequence of a legal façade can be inadvertent subscription to risk disclaimers. Extreme risk disclaimers are acceptable in the contract view because both contractors agreed to them. In The Netherlands a famous case of risk disclaiming was the contract of a plastic surgeon with a patient suffering from a skin disease in the 1950s. Their contract exonerated the surgeon from all liabilities, even due to professional incompetence. The specialist then used the patient as a guinea pig for an experimental 'therapy' with X-rays, which resulted in the disappearance of the patient's lower jaw. Although in court the specialist pointed to his exoneration clause, he still had to pay indemnities. So jurisdiction here protected the weaker party against irregular abuse, even though the weaker party had first consented in writing to absolve the specialist. The point is that this type of damage was out of all proportion and resulted directly from applied methods. It was a clear case of bad service, causing great and unexpected injuries.

Table 4.3 An outline of due care theory

Item	Relevant content
Creed	Let the seller beware!
Assumed duties of producer/supplier	On top of the existing contractual duties, the seller has unconditional responsibilities. The seller should repair all regular failures due to mistakes in design and production. Due care responsibilities cannot be overruled by contract. These responsibilities concern:
	■ safe and careful design;
	■ reliable production; and
	■ appropriate delivery.
Assumed power balance	The seller/producer is the stronger party, having knowledge and expertise that one cannot expect from the purchaser.
Scope of valid application	All commercial deals involving goods and services where severe damage appears during regular use due to production defects that fall beyond the written clauses of the contract. It can be applied more often than the other two theories, without causing great injustices.
Dangers and inadequacies	Imputing irregularities to the producer beyond the due care responsibility. Inability to get smart money in case of accidents produced by several causes.
Major examples	Manufacturers selling their lemonade in glass bottles are responsible for eye damage caused by explosions, especially if this happens before any shaking has occurred. The victims of the aeroplane crash on the Amsterdam flats might not obtain smart money, if this tragedy was seen as caused by a combination of various activities, neglects and fatalities.

4.7.3 Due care theory

Comment on the philosophical assumptions of the due care theory

The due care view states that the consumer or end user has certain unconditional rights. Whatever clause the supplier may insert in his contract, from a moral point of view this theory maintains that the supplier always has to provide due care (see Table 4.3). Such absolute obligations fit in with a position called 'duty ethics', the archetypal theory of what most people hold to be a moral obligation. As we shall see in Chapter 6, duty ethics formulates unconditional moral obligations, moral claims that remain valid whatever the consequences.

If we only use the concepts already explained the due care theory fits best with recognition ethics, as formulated by Henk van Luijk (see section 2.6). In the case of due care, the consumer has rights, and positive claims on a fair share. These rights and the corresponding obligations are not

CASE STUDY

You work at the counter of a big city bank. A new client comes in. A few months previously he had opened an account at your bank, but had not used it so far. Now he walks in, after leaving two heavy-shouldered persons outside. He puts his suitcase on your counter, and says he wants to deposit a large amount of cash in his account ($100,000). A few weeks ago, you had heard a rumour about this new client. He was said to be the brains behind a big hold-up, which had left some innocent victims slightly injured. For the time being these are just rumours; nothing has been proved yet. It is still the early 1980s, and national legislation does not prohibit the handling of money for clients who are possible criminal suspects. Also, your bank is reluctant about defining guidelines in cases of possible money laundering. Earlier this week the local bank director had insisted on being 'customer-minded', that is, accept all cash deposits that do not create scandals, because 'business is business'.

1. What do you do about this client's request?
2. What do you do with the information you now receive from this client?

based on an individual contract, but on the idea that commercial deals are social actions. As members of the moral community, individuals have to respect reciprocal rights and duties. The due care obligations and rights are seen as part of a tacit social contract, valid for every member of civilized society. According to this view, due care requirements override individual interests and contractual clauses. Moral agents are bound to the whole of society by this tacit social contract.

The due care theory also fits in with another feature of recognition ethics: the asymmetry in human duties and obligation. Due care theory perceives product responsibility as the result of the asymmetrical relationship between a weaker party (consumers) and a stronger party (suppliers). The theory is imposed by society in order to redress the dangers of this asymmetrical relation. The duties are mainly on the side of the supplier or producer; due care theory protects the rights of the weaker side.

Thus this theory endorses the idea of being a member of a moral community that practises compensatory justice. It stipulates unconditional rights and duties that override possible egocentric calculations based on the private interests of the stronger party.

This, basically honourable, concern may, however, lead to various excesses, such as imposing too heavy demands on suppliers. In their turn the suppliers may then become the weaker party, as we tried to point out in the beginning of this section. Thus, for instance, in the case of due care claims concerning clean soil, this may lead to new kinds of injustice. Certain corporations were obliged to clean up at high cost, although they had not caused the original pollution and were not aware themselves of this risk when they bought the property. This has caused bankruptcy amongst innocent corporations, who have become the naive victims of the original polluters.

Table 4.4 An outline of social costs theory

Item	Relevant content
Creed	In all cases manufacturers have to pay for the damage inflicted by the products they made!
Assumed duties of producer/supplier	The producer/supplier has all the duties, and no rights. Manufacturers have to pay for all accidents and damage, even if they have exercised due care when they designed and manufactured the product, and gave appropriate product information to the consumer. It does not matter if the consumer showed gross carelessness when using the product or that he or she might have been aware of the risks.
Assumed power balance	The manufacturer's activities are regarded as such a powerful cause in producing the damage that the consumer/victim is completely excused from any guilt.
Scope of valid application	Big catastrophes like aeroplane crashes, and mass deaths and severe health damage due to pollution in which several causes interact in a way that makes the attribution of guilt difficult. As attaching blame to a main agent is difficult and cannot be proved by using due care theory, stronger assumptions have to be accepted here in order to incriminate those held responsible.
Dangers and inadequacies	Abuse in case of minor catastrophes (e.g. the poodle in the microwave). Incrimination of only one minor responsible agent, often because this agent can be identified and caught most easily, while the main responsible agent stays clear.
Major examples	The plane crash in Amsterdam. Asbestos in industry and building (until the health risks of this product were known, since when claims can be based on due care). The DES daughters claims, accusing the manufacturers of the DES hormone of legal responsibility for their health problems. Current lawsuits in the United States against the manufacturers of leaded paint, or most recently, against the tobacco industry for selling products that were known to be dangerous for health.

4.7.4 Social costs theory

Comment on the philosophical assumptions of the social costs theory
The social cost view expresses various social concerns and moral demands.
A primary concern is the protection of victims of accidents where an
unfortunate combination of several causes makes it impossible to in-
criminate just one main agent. There is a strong tendency towards
attributing all injuries to one specific agent – the manufacturer (see Table
4.4). In almost all cases where social cost arguments are applied, the
manufacturer is incriminated as the chief cause of health risks and

CASE STUDY

You are a parent of a 3-year-old child. While you were busy elsewhere in the house, your child goes into the kitchen, opens a bottle of liquid detergent, and starts to drink. After the first screams, you rush in, give the child a drink of water, and call right away for an ambulance. After the child's stomach is pumped out at the hospital, the child can go home. First, you think about sending the hospital bill to the manufacturer, claiming that the bottle was not child-proof. A closer look at the bottle, however, shows that it is a plastic bottle originally used for mineral water, and you now remember that your wife decanted the detergent in order to have a separate supply in the kitchen. Then a careful study of the text on the original bottle reveals that it does not contain a warning against decanting into other bottles. Is it *moral* to go to court now?

---

consumer deaths because it is considered most probable that technical mistakes in the product design were somehow at the root of a fatal chain of events.

Another motive can be the fact that even though it was an individual corporate executive who committed a serious error, the injuries inflicted as a result of that irresponsible behaviour have to be compensated by someone who can pay. As the executive worked for a corporation, the corporation is responsible, even if their procedures guarantee due care. A disputed case was the *Exxon Valdez* shipwreck in Alaska. Exxon blamed the captain for drunkenness, although other sources deny this and claim that the ship's rudder mechanism was defective. Anyhow, the outcome was that Exxon had to pay for the clean-up costs.

From a malicious point of view, it could be said that this theory is a legal construction to place the blame on only partly responsible agents, because they are strong enough to carry the whole burden. This imputes a strong motive of revenge against the most powerful: somebody has to pay, then let it be the richest.

More respectable ethical principles are also expressed in the social care theory. The manufacturers of mass products like asbestos or CFCs were at first often unaware of the risks of these products. Yet definite damage has been inflicted. Especially when manufacturers like Johns Manville are slow or even criminally negligent about health warnings and refuse to phase out their high-risk products after these risks are proved to exist, they merit moral contempt. Johns Manville's negligence and refusal to do their utmost in earlier stages to make their products safe, make many conclude that they should pay. Reports dating from before the Second World War had already mentioned the risk of asbestos in industry (Velasquez, 1992, pp. 121–31), yet Johns Manville did little to prevent further harm, except to put a friendly warning on asbestos packages.

Whereas due care is an adequate theory in cases where the risks are consciously neglected, many new products have unknown health risks that only appear later. The social care theory does provide arguments against the manufacturers of products that may carry possible serious risks. It tells these companies that in such cases, where subsequent risk is proved, initial ignorance will be no defence.

One way to perceive this aspect of the social costs theory is to consider this as a version of *recognition ethics*. By manufacturing new products moral agents choose to involve themselves in moral obligation towards the larger community. They provide goods which they believe will not harm consumers and other third parties. When later the contrary turns out to be true, they can be obliged to pay for the damage. They took a chance voluntarily, and it is one of the rules of the game that private business should not only have the financial benefits, but also accept the specific accountability which belongs to taking risks. Paying for real injuries caused by these risks is one of these burdens.

4.8 Examples of liability issues

4.8.1 Halamid residues in Olvarit baby food

Although opinion makers used words like 'environmental concerns' when referring to the following case its basic issues are health risks for humans, satisfaction of consumer expectations, and a certain type of overcommitment to recalls by corporations in the 1990s.

In 1993 and spring 1994 the Dutch consumer was involved in a variety of cases of product recalls. One involved a cleaning chemical, and some people felt that this issue had something to do with poisoning. Now, one of the most popular beliefs is that chemicals have an adverse environmental impact. Here is an example of the contrary.

In the summer of 1993 residues of the cleaning chemical with the brand name Halamid were detected by one of the two Dutch administrative agencies for food control. They raised big publicity in newspapers by presenting their findings under headings like 'Forbidden chemical found in Olvarit baby food'. Olvarit is a brand owned by the Dutch-based corporation Nutricia, which has a great reputation and a near-monopoly position on baby food in The Netherlands. They soon detected the source of the Halamid residues.

This sulphonamide is used as a bactericide in human medicines, drinking-water and in butcheries. In this case, Halamid had been used by an industrial butcher supplying the meat chunks, HVV, in Gorinchem in The Netherlands. This butcher pleaded guilty saying that they must have been careless with the use of Halamid during the cleaning of their cutting-boards. Other sources indicate the widespread use of Halamid as a bactericide by butchers. It is an effective and not dangerous disinfectant, although national legislation forbids this application.

The legal norms for the concentrations of Halamid date from 1962. They are based on animal laboratory experiments, probably using its predecessor chloramine-T. The doses proven to be slightly dangerous for rats were divided by a factor of 100 in order to give norms for adult maximum consumption, in milligrams of Halamid per kilo of food. For baby foods, the doses were once more divided by a factor of 10, resulting in the norm of 1 mg/kg. The outcome was that Olvarit with meat might contain 4 mg/kg. In this case, each 200 gram pot had about 0.8 mg of Halamid in it; the equal amount can be found in two glasses of Rotterdam drinking-water. The actual risk of poisoning was non-existent.

The only valid argument referring to a moral concern here was the satisfaction of consumer expectations. Parents that buy this product expect it to correspond to health care regulations. Whenever the product does not meet these requirements, this may be regarded as abusing consumer confidence.

Later articles pointed to strategic motives for the Dutch food control agency KvW urging newspapers to publish findings that might have been detrimental to Olvarit's market position. The agency's actions were said to be part of their own rivalry with another government agency, RVV, the primary agency responsible for monitoring serious health risks. By publicizing this news, KvW hoped to expose their competitors, RVV, as incompetent. They believed this might help them to stop government plans to merge the two agencies. Also, this incident pointed to the danger of the government's intention of having their activities financed by those they had to control, namely, the food industry.

We call the Olvarit case a non-issue concerning environmental care. It may serve, however, to exemplify the extended use of recalls in modern business, inspired mainly by strategic concerns of 'issue management' without any serious communication about the underlying moral concerns. The expression 'overdose of a cleaning chemical' may have made some consumers afraid of poisoning, but in this case this danger was absent.

Moreover not all synthetic chemicals should be treated as environmental threats. Even if certain toxic substances like cyanide kill people, they are not automatically environmental threats from an ecological point of view.

4.8.2 An environmental issue: DuPont and CFC production

A case study in the textbook of M. Velasquez (1992, pp. 258–67) relates at length the slowly increasing concern about the CFC environmental risks. Although laboratory experiments proved in 1974 that CFC could devastate the ozone layers, it took 13 years for DuPont to change its policies. In the meantime, until 1987, the corporation had started up various new production facilities, maintaining its position as a worldwide leader in CFC production. In 1987 DuPont senior management were finally convinced by the arguments of their technical staff to start a phasing-out policy that aimed at a total reduction of all CFC production by DuPont by the year 2000. These statements may overlook the most important issue faced by DuPont, that is, the uncertainty about the actual risks to the ozone layer. Academic research was not at first firmly convinced about the CFC effects on the ozone layer. Nonetheless, it is true that in 1975 DuPont lobbied to prevent banning legislation and started a pro-CFC advertising campaign. Nor did they proactively apply the April 1980 agreement, in which all the large CFC-producing countries convened to decrease CFC production.

DuPont is not the only corporation that practised self-protecting groupthink here. Even after the September 1987 meeting in Montreal, where CFC reduction targets were set by 65 nations, some corporations regarded their short-term priorities to be more important than our global future: 'Officials of KaiserTech and other CFC producers argued that the Montreal agreement would be "catastrophic" for their business' (Velasquez, 1992, p. 264). Just before, on 24 March 1987, DuPont had announced a significant change in their policy. They opted to phase out CFC production, leading to a complete cessation of production around the turn of the century.

According to many scientists the depletion of the ozone layer will now increase for at least twenty more years. The main cause of this depletion is the ongoing emission of fluorocarbons like CFCs, released from scrapped refrigerators, air conditioners and rigid insulating foams. These gases float up into the stratosphere and act there as a very stable and effective catalyst. One single CFC molecule helps to break down tens of thousands of ozone molecules into simple oxygen molecules.

Due to the deterioration of the ozone layer harmful ultraviolet rays can get through, especially at places where the ozone has virtually disappeared from the stratosphere – the 'holes' in the ozone layer. Until the mid-1990s its effects were mainly felt in Australia and New Zealand. For humans it may result in skin cancer and cataract. For the other species in our natural environment the devastating effects of ultraviolet rays start right at the bottom of the food chain. In the southern oceans, plankton growth is damaged, decreasing the world's oxygen production and causing lower food supplies for all other beings, especially fish and whales.

In the early 1990s the prognosis is quite alarming. If on a global scale CFC production is stopped in 2000, the presence of this gas in refrigerators and other products will guarantee that until 2020 more of this substance can get into the air. This prognosis foresees maximum CFC concentrations in the ozone layer near 2010, followed by a very slow process of natural breakdown.

More recently, during the scientific conference 'Scientific Assessment of Ozone Depletion: 1994', the outlook was more optimistic. The reduction of the ozone layer in the northern hemisphere will still diminish about a further 2.5 per cent and be at its lowest in 1998. This level will be 13 per cent less than in the early 1960s. This revised optimistic scenario holds that after 2040 the ozone concentrations may return to a level nearer to the assumed concentration in 1960, when the layer was still intact (*NRC Handelsblad*, 1994d). Until then, thousands of humans will have become victims of skin cancer, especially in the southern hemisphere, not to mention the environmental injuries caused by increased ultraviolet penetration.

One final comment. The apparent success of the campaign for the protection of the ozone layer might make people optimistic about all environmental issues. One must understand, however, that only a few big corporations produced CFCs and halones. By means of public debate, political pressure, scientific reports and covenants these few big players could be made to adopt an effective phasing-out policy. Other environmental issues are originated by a multitude of individual players who can less easily be made to revise their habits. The best example of this is the destruction of the tropical rain forest, in which millions of small landless farmers play significant roles.

Thus in the 1990s DuPont de Nemours became a leading example of environmental management. They now have several proactive environmental policies. One of the first was DuPont's decision to phase out CFC production, introduced before legislation obliged them to do so. This is called pre-emption. However, whereas this decision was forced upon them, their more recent policies have been voluntary, and in general they have now regained a good reputation: 'It is clear that DuPont matched or outperformed the market at the time of the announcement of their environmental spending performance' (Plesse, 1992).

4.8.3 Colliding concerns of chicken industry and consumer safety

While the bulk of the larger multinationals have now started more active quality care policies, the smaller food industries especially are still lagging behind. One example to illustrate this general statement is the Dutch chicken industry.

While recalls for minor contaminations happen for various other food products, the salmonella epidemic amongst chicken products remains overlooked. Insiders like Dr E. H. Kampelmacher have proved that the salmonella epidemic that now probably contaminates 50 to 60 per cent of all Dutch industrial chickens has become endemic since the Second World War (*NRC*, 1994b). The main reason why the statistics only reveal some few deaths amongst mainly elderly and sick people is because Dutch consumers tend to cook chicken and boil eggs thoroughly. Until 1993 Dutch newspapers reported incidents involving complete football teams that had to be hospitalized after eating bavarois made from raw eggs. Fortunately, professional restaurants now use screened eggs, of which only 4 per cent is contaminated.

This whole problem could have been eradicated easily, and to the great satisfaction of the chicken industry, by X-raying chicken products, but this was prevented by consumer organizations that urged politicians not to vote in laws permitting this harmless method. The danger to public health from the salmonella epidemic has been reported officially twice, on both occasions by the national health council in 1962 and 1978. Both reports indicated the cause of this epidemic. After the Second World War the Dutch started an animal feed industry on an industrial basis, using cheap ingredients from abroad – fish meal, tapioca, cotton seed scraps and maize scraps were used instead of cereals. Nowadays, about 15 million tons of animal feed arrive each year at Rotterdam harbour, and quality control on such amounts is said to be unfeasible. Some of these cheap chicken food ingredients are contaminated, and they are the main cause of the continuing epidemic.

Another danger has been added. Towards the end of the 1980s the less dangerous Salmonella typhimurium was being supplanted by the more aggressive Salmonella enteritides, which can penetrate the egg yolk. Recent reports indicate that further progress of this bacteria has been stopped, but in 1994 it remains dangerous to use raw Dutch eggs in, for instance, mayonnaise. Cooking for a few minutes will prevent this health risk.

What measures have been taken to stop this public danger? At present, most chickens are fed with granular pressed ingredients that were heated during production. This does considerably reduce the amount of contaminated food. According to the Dutch branch organization this is the best they can do, since X-raying eggs and chicken meat is still forbidden. However, a comparative study in the summer of 1994 revealed striking differences between the quality of European poultry and eggs. It indicated that a country like Sweden had a quality performance for both stocks, with almost 100 per cent clean, fresh and healthy products. Improvement on a large scale is quite possible in the Dutch poultry industry – as soon as public pressure makes it happen.

This example points to a substantial injustice. While other products with benign salmonella contaminations have been recalled immediately, the chicken industry has not made much effort so far to produce salmonella-free poultry and eggs. The financial and commercial influence of their branch organization have prevented the public health control agencies from starting a test case on poultry contamination. And it was stated that the financial interest of two thousand poultry farmers should not be jeopardized in an effort to reduce the tens of deaths that happen each year because of salmonella infections (*NRC*, 1994a). Self-serving groupthink flourishes here too.

4.8.4 Heineken beer crates

Until the mid-1980s the Dutch home base of Heineken Breweries used their bright yellow beer crates without any public agitation. The corporate marketeers were very attached to this bright cadmium yellow colour which they considered to be an essential part of the Heineken beer brand image. It was only in later years that the use of cadmium in hard plastic crates became an environmental issue.

The new crate bank of 1985
In 1984 the beverage distributors' request for uniform beer bottles called Eurobottles was granted by the big Dutch beer producers. Amongst them, Heineken was the most prominent. Consequently, Heineken also had to design a new beer crate that could be stacked with crates from other producers. The resulting uniform beer crate dimensions had great logistic advantages for the distributors.

The required number of new yellow crates for the Heineken A-brand Heineken and red crates for their B-brand Amstel was 10 million. They were to be introduced on the consumer market early in 1986. In 1985 Heineken decided upon the colour and the ingredients for this new crate bank. Because of the strategic importance they attached to the bright yellow colour and because of the technical quality cadmium has as a durable and constant colorant, Heineken again used cadmium as a colorant and stabilizer in all crates. Moreover, at that time they considered the environmental risks of cadmium in hard plastic crates to be negligible, as this heavy metal could not leach or evaporate. Also, virtually all crates were returned periodically to Heineken, and even in the few broken crates that might exist cadmium would remain non-toxic as long as it was not burned.

Cadmium in hard plastics at first a non-issue
In 1985 the technicians at Heineken did not consider the use of cadmium to be a serious environmental issue. Since the very first use of hard plastic

crates, cadmium had always been used without any mention of the environmental dangers, and, trapped in plastic, cadmium was inoffensive. They added cadmium to plastics because of its two great advantages. First, it considerably improved resistance to ultraviolet sunlight, preventing the crate becoming brittle and breaking. This resulted in extremely long life cycles for their crate bank. Secondly, it served as a colorant, giving the clear red and bright yellow colours to their beer crates.

Heineken marketeers also used the argument of consumer ease. Clients either picked separate bottles from a crate or took a whole crate with them, and consumer behaviour in the market was shifting towards taking whole crates. The aesthetic quality and recognizability of these crates were therefore becoming more important. The bright yellow of Heineken crates was regarded as a very distinguishing feature, and so Heineken marketeers thought that the use of cadmium yellow must continue.

One other argument relevant for environmental waste management might have been stressed more by Heineken in 1985 and 1986 in their opposition to the environmental activists. Heineken already used existing plastic crates containing cadmium; the bulk of the ingredients for their new crates could be found by recycling the chips made from withdrawn old crates.

Moreover for these crates a deposit of Dfl5 is charged when you buy a crate of beer. This deposit, and the thrifty mentality of the Dutch, guaranteed virtually a 100 per cent return of crates. It still is a remarkable example of operational environmentally friendly beverage packing. On average, each Heineken crate goes through more than 150 distribution cycles and lasts between 10 and 12 years before it has to be withdrawn by Heineken.

Finally, the continued use of cadmium might have been backed by views that only later became part of environmental policies. Cadmium exists as a by-product of zinc production; mined zincblende contains cadmium and arsenic by nature. So, the production of 'natural' zinc gutters is in fact more polluting than making grey plastic gutters, as it also creates concentrations of cadmium and arsenic waste. As an analogy, Greenpeace would improve environmental wellbeing more by ripping off the zinc rain pipes at Norwegian embassies, than by caring about the controlled killing of a non-endangered species (the minke whale).

The new crates with cadmium raise the waste disposal issue

Heineken decided to order a new bank of 10 million plastic crates with cadmium. The crate manufacturer first used fresh ingredients for the initial series of new crates, but later on, only old chips from shredded crates were used. At the end of the project, this manufacturer still had left over a few tons of plastic chips containing cadmium colorant, which they recycled in a more dangerous way: the material was used for consumer products like plastic flowerpots. Here the environmental risk is apparent, as broken pots soon end up in garbage incinerators. In that event, pure volatile cadmium can come out of the incinerator chimneys. Though in nature infinitely small quantities of cadmium are all around us, a higher concentration can be quite dangerous to life forms.

Coping with environmental activism

Several organizations of environmental activists started a public campaign criticizing the use of cadmium in the 10 million new crates. In 1986 reports reached Heineken about activists picketing in front of large self-service shops and trying to stir up the Dutch beer consumer who carried these crates in and out the shop. They also started rather spirited discussions with Heineken management.

Soon the discussions became more constructive. Spurred by this external pressure, Heineken itself recognized that there was a real environmental issue involved, especially when cadmium plastics are recycled for use in consumer products. Until then manufacturers and professional users of crates had not appreciated this point, but now they started to acknowledge the risk. Also the dangers of cadmium consumption were being better documented by that time. Just like two other heavy metals, mercury and lead, cadmium is a highly toxic substance. Small concentrations of these metals can cause infertility, diseases and death amongst many animals. Their first victims are found amongst the water mammals and birds of prey at the top of the food pyramid. The slow extinction of seals, otters and water birds like sea eagles is a sign of this type of pollution. Similarly, humans suffered from metal poisoning in Myamata (Japan) and near a few other fishing towns.

The specific danger of low cadmium poisoning is kidney disease, but there are indications that it also starts prostate cancer and contributes to several congenital defects. The word 'congenital' is appropriate here, for human DNA may be affected by this heavy-metal poisoning.

An alarming argument for the environmentalist cause was provided by calculating the quality of cadmium required for these 10 million Heineken crates: 25,000 kilo of this highly poisonous substance. It should, however, be noted that Heineken mainly recycled plastic chips from old crates.

In the face of activist pressure, which was covered by national newspapers, Heineken first took a defensive attitude. In 1985, promised to ensure that from now on the withdrawn crates would no longer be used in consumer products that might end up in incineration ovens. In reply, the Dutch green movements argued that Heineken could hardly guarantee this, since what happened to products made from recycled plastic was beyond the control of Heineken.

Then in December 1986 Heineken finally reached a full compromise. It publicly announced that they would no longer use cadmium in future new crate banks. Both parties shook hands and signed a covenant. According to the manager of the Heineken environmental affairs section, Mr P. van Oeveren, Heineken committed itself to two commandments: '(a) Thou shalt not use cadmium as a colorant in the future. (b) Thou shalt see to it that withdrawn crates with cadmium additives do not pollute the environment.' On their side, the activists promised in this contract to stop all public agitation against the newly made Heineken crates.

In 1995 Heineken is still using the extremely durable crates made in 1985. Heineken soon has to commission the renewal of its crate bank, and for this project it has found environmentally friendly pigments that have already been accepted by the environmentalist groups. So Heineken can live up to its promise not to use cadmium any more.

The present issue

The second obligation poses serious problems, however. In the next two to five years, huge quantities of bright yellow and deep red plastic chips have to be treated in an environmentally friendly way. The issue raised by the environmentalists is not yet resolved. Heineken has researched methods of cadmium disposal, and one treatment is seen to be the most promising: in laboratory tests pure cadmium sulphide has been produced after dissolving the hard plastic crates. The current issue now is what to do with the tons of toxic cadmium sulphide that might be produced this way.

A second option in conflict with the first commandment

One other distinct possibility appears: Why not choose a different solution for the cadmium problem with a possibly higher potential for environmental care; that is, recycle the plastic chips in the old crates once more? The first series of new crates can be produced according to the new recipe, the following series can be made from recycled old chips. As recycling requires a heightened concentration of some additives, a larger volume of old chips is needed to produce a smaller volume of new plastic. In this process cadmium remains trapped in new crates. This solution guarantees that no significant quantities of cadmium-coloured crates would end up in incinerators. It might provide a perfect example of making the best out of a potential waste.

Another suggestion might be to go for a bank of new crates without any cadmium, and use the tons of cadmium sulphide that will hopefully be produced as a strategic metal reserve. However, as the number of applications of cadmium becomes less, offer exceeds demand. Also, due to inflexible government philosophies on the treatment of purified heavy-metal waste, this option is still taboo.

For legal reasons, however, the Dutch environmental movements still prefer to force Heineken into using huge amounts of new plastic. Soon after the December 1986 covenant between Heineken and the Dutch environmental activist groups, another covenant was signed between the Dutch government and the crate-using producers of beer and soft drinks. This second covenant is called the 'cadmium crate covenant' of 1987. It states that no more cadmium-containing crates will be produced after 2006, and that in 2010 all such crates have to be withdrawn from the market. The director of Heineken public affairs, Mr Hugo Byrnes, is trying to open this debate now.

Both covenants seem to exemplify participatory ethics. Different parties co-operate in order to achieve public goods. Here, in order to protect the environment from toxic cadmium gases, certain solutions were adopted. However, new insights might make it worthwhile to reconsider the target fixed in the cadmium crate covenant. In this debate both environmentalists and government authorities are important stakeholders.

The ideologic arguments of the environmentalists fit in with a duty-ethical approach. In 1986 they were mainly obsessed by the one overall target of stopping the use of cadmium as an additive in plastics. Now they will have to reconsider certain targets in order to agree again upon the very best environmental policy. This may be something different from the earlier covenant as the current circumstances might recommend another solution that serves the overall goal of environmental care better.

4.9 Corporate responsibility

4.9.1 Attributing responsibilities for the Bijlmer catastrophe

In Chapter 3 we indicated that our second definition of responsibility is a valid guideline. Yet one point referring to the first definition should be kept in mind. Reasonable people are 100 per cent accountable only for the things they can really do something about, and the main things they can improve on are their intentions and actions. Responsible behaviour consists basically of wise planning and showing the utmost care and skill in our actions. It is often too simple to attribute later events to one unique agent, blaming this agent although a whole chain of events caused the dramatic outcome.

One example may illustrate this. The 1992 El Al plane crash in Amsterdam could not have been imagined by a writer of even a Hollywood horror scenario. On 4 October 1992 a Boeing 747 freight plane flown by El Al lost one engine while it still was climbing slowly after departure from Schiphol airport. The engine that fell off hit the neighbouring engine, tearing it off also. The crew knew something was wrong, but sight control was impossible, so they guessed the two right-wing engines had stopped functioning. We will not relate the fatal events that followed in the next few minutes. Ultimately a heavy cargo plane with more than half its maximum load of kerosene fuel crashed into a block of flats in the Amsterdam suburb of Bijlmer, killing and incinerating the plane crew and about fifty flat-dwellers.

This catastrophe was caused by the interaction of several unfortunate events, actions and circumstances. However, the crash reports reveal that the chief contributory factor was a mistake in a bolt design (*Leeuwarder Courant*, 1994). Boeing, the aeroplane manufacturer, can rightly be blamed for this design error and for the time it took to discover this mistake. But it would be an overreaction to blame Boeing for the whole train of events that finally resulted in the tragedy. What we should blame Boeing for are mainly design mistakes and serious negligence in quality control, as their shortcomings in this field caused the first engine to tear loose. All the subsequent events cannot simply be blamed on the manufacturer alone, although the crash would never have happened if the fatal chain of events had not been triggered by an important failure on Boeing's part. At the heart of the matter lies this one lesson that can be learned by a business corporation as a result of this catastrophe: it is vital for corporations to improve designs and to be very responsive to feedback about the product. In the case of the bolt design, Boeing did know about this problem a long time beforehand (*Vrij Nederland*, 1993).

Besides reports indicating defects in these bolts, there had been an accident with a cargo plane of the Boeing 747 type in Taiwan. In December 1991 an older 747 freight carrier of China International crashed in a mountain area. Boeing argued then that in such cases not only they should be blamed for bolt defects. Often cargo planes are old and are not scrupulously maintained, allowing for negligence in the bolt control procedures. Also, cargo planes are often very heavily loaded, and in these circumstances bad engine tuning may then result in abnormal vibrations which will cause damage to the bolts. However, some months after the Bijlmer accident a more solid construction was finally adopted, providing a safe technical solution for this design problem.

4.9.2 *General conclusions on entrepreneurial accountability*

This point brings us back to the main thesis of the second inference drawn from the responsibility definition: corporations willing to take a lead at the beginning of the third millennium should implement policies that really keep them ahead of ever-shifting consumer requirements. Morally concerned entrepreneurs should lead their corporations into active moral commitments to consumer safety, environmental care and working conditions.

The parallel with coping well with personal responsibility is evident here. The individual has to improve and adapt skills during a process of iterative doing and learning. Nobody will perform perfectly in a constantly changing environment, yet individuals can make huge progress in the way they learn to achieve their objectives in life. What a person can master first and foremost are individual skills. Better behaviour is never inspired merely by the fear of repercussions after mishaps: it should also be motivated by well-informed objectives and targets and should result from the quality of trained craftsmanship in a specific area.

Likewise, the company management should not focus on repression and on inspiring awe in their staff, but rather act as the organizational force that expresses mutually felt objectives. Their primary role is to foster responsible behaviour on the shop floor and to ensure that all details and progress are in line with the corporate targets. The core tasks of a business lie in creating excellence in the areas it can master itself, not in subsequent events and injuries. Focus must therefore be maintained on the constant improvement of the inner production process in order to meet a broader concept of quality.

Corporate communications may often be triggered by external events with great negative publicity, but in the long run they should be based on a corporate philosophy with a broader view of its relationship with the public. This does not mean that corporations should not prepare themselves for crisis management – preparing a scenario, informing personnel, faxing invitations to the press, and so on. Here also, one will be held accountable for one's actions and for expressed willingness to enter into open dialogue. Above all, one must give top priority to displaying total commitment to the satisfaction of vital consumer demands.

Staying ahead of rising consumer requirements for health and safety, and for environmental and social care, often requires making choices that may hurt one's self-image. The challenge for the Dutch chicken industry in the 1990s may illustrate this, although their present moral muteness is not very promising. For the time being the egg industry can boast about an alleged success in green marketing. They have introduced a 'free-range chicken' egg ('Scharrelei'), which has become a notable marketing success. The free range consists of allowing five or six hens to walk about in an indoor hen run, with clipped beaks and shortened wings. The outcome seems 'green', as free-range eggs have a brown shell. They are *not* guaranteed to be free from salmonella. These so-called free-range eggs are a brilliant example of a short-term moral sales proposition, which satisfies the cosmetic environmental needs of consumers.

When we talk about moral entrepreneurship we mean something else. Moral entrepreneurship means that corporations operate in partnership networks, with the aim of satisfying authentic consumer requirements, and not just reinterpreting demands to suit the purpose of some supplier. It means constant efforts in TQM, covering the whole chain of purchase, production and delivery. Only then does business do its moral duty best. Such clean companies can make a stand in front of the public, as they truly reply to the limited moral demands corporations should accept.

In the field of corporate communications the result may be a more mature and less episodic understanding between public opinion leaders and private business. Companies may evolve to become partners in the dialogue with public interests, accepting a clearly delimited responsibility, but also refusing to accept all blame for the entire burden of our world's misfortunes.

4.10 Synopsis

1. The corporation producing quality products and services accepts specific moral responsibilities. At a minimum level, there are three such corporate responsibilities:

   (a) consumer care, expressed by satisfying demands for ease of use and product safety;
   (b) environmental care; and
   (c) care for minimum working conditions.

2. Corporations should not remain mute about their moral performances and commitments. A balanced presentation of one's corporate response in face of specific moral concerns can create a basis of understanding with one's own employees as well as with the concerned public. Communicate the priorities you have in your commitment to quality management by a sophisticated use of moral talk.

4.11 References

Banks, J. (1992) *The Essence of Total Quality Management*, Hemel Hempstead: Prentice Hall.

Bird, T. and Waters, J. A. (1989) 'The moral muteness of managers', *California Management Review*, **32**, 1.

Cannon, T. (1994) *Corporate Responsibility. A textbook on business ethics, governance, environment: roles and responsibilities*, London: Pitman, reprinted by permission of Pitman Publishing.

Donaldson, J. (1989) *Key Issues in Business Ethics*, London: Academic Press.

Hoffman, W. (1986) 'What is necessary for corporate moral excellence?', *Journal of Business Ethics*, **5**, 223. Reprinted by permission of Kluwer Academic Publishers.

Janis, I. I. (1972) *Victims of Group Think: A psychological study of foreign policy decisions and fiascos*, Boston: Houghton Mifflin.

Leeuwarder Courant (1994) 'Niks was normaal bij rampvlucht El Al' (Nothing was normal during the disastrous flight of the El Al Boeing), 25 February.

McConnel, M. (1987) *Challenger: A major malfunction*, London: Unwin.

NRC Handelsblad (1994a) 'Geen gebrek aan produkten die met salmonella zijn verontreinigd' (No lack of products contaminated by salmonella bacteria), 25 March.

NRC Handelsblad (1994b) 'Claims mogelijk doodsteek bedrijven' (Claims might kill corporations), 31 May.

NRC Handelsblad (1994c) 'De stille groene revolutie van de kwaliteitszorg' (The silent green revolution of quality care), 25 July.

NRC Handelsblad (1994d), 'Nasa overschatte aantasting ozonlaag: herstel ozonlaag begint rond 2000' (Nasa overestimated the reduction of the ozone layer: restoration ozone layer begins around 2000), 6 September.

Plesse, J. (1992) *Business Strategy and the Environment*, Bradford: European Research Press, Vol. 1, pt 1.

Velasquez, M. (1983) 'Why corporations are not morally responsible for anything they do', *Business and Professional Ethics Journal*, **2**, 1.

Velasquez, M. (1992) *Business Ethics, Concepts and Cases*, Englewood Cliffs: Prentice Hall.

Vrij Nederland (1993) 'Boeing wist het allang' (Boeing knew it already for a long time), 6 February.

5

What is in it for all parties concerned?

God loves from whole to parts; but human soul
Must rise from individual to the whole.
Self-love but serves the virtuous mind to wake,
As the small pebble stirs the peaceful lake;
The centre moved, a circle strait succeeds,
Another still, and still another spreads;
Friend, parent, neighbour, first will it embrace;
His country next; and next all human race.

(Alexander Pope, *An Essay on Man*)

5.1 An outlook based on interests

In this chapter we study stakeholder interests in business deals and arrangements. Our subject-matter is morally relevant *outcomes*, the possible benefits and injuries resulting from transactions.

Our main question is how the pursuit of interest can be transformed into a morally valid goal. If strategic concerns and the moral demands could be combined without oversimplifying the issue and without causing severe damage, a powerful and useful guideline might be defined.

In order to study the possibility of a match between moral demands and strategic concerns, we adopt in this chapter a mainly transactional approach (see section 2.7 above). This approach is concerned with which moral standards ought to guide human relations when moral behaviour is seen as a negotiation about interests. Transaction ethics considers all issues involved to be a matter of stakes or interests and holds that these concrete interests can be traded off against each other.

Interests are often associated with the objective of egocentric satisfaction. By studying one modern example of a business organization based on shared interests it can be shown that such a conception is too narrow. Moreover, by calling upon simple insights into human psychology and human history, it is possible to conceive a more realistic and co-operative idea of interest. Therefore, the motives for business transactions are interest; transactions do not only aim at egocentric satisfaction.

Transactionalists in fact do admit this point. In general, one can distinguish three moral goals in business transactions:

1. Self-centred interest (actor-directed blatant egoism).
2. Enlightened self-interest (recognizing others' interests).
3. Public utility (pursuit of social welfare).

5.2 Interests combine moral goals and moral principles

5.2.1 Restating goals and duties as interests

Some interests or stakes can be described as external goals, others are based upon relational guidelines. In most books on ethics these two categories are treated separately; traditional ethics often simply uncovered two basic standards of normative ethics, one outcome-based, the other duty-based. We will use transactionalist ideas in a liberal manner, allowing for a mix of both.

An initial idea of such transactionalist trade-offs between both standards consists of four steps:

1. Analyze which outcomes and duties are at stake.
2. Reformulate both standards in terms of interests at stake.
3. Proceed with mediating between these interests.
4. Conclude how they should be balanced and applied in given circumstances.

5.2.2 Traditional outcome-based and duty-based ethics

It may be useful to explain in more detail what is traditionally meant by outcome-based and duty-based ethics.

Another general expression for this distinction is the opposition between *goals* (outcomes) and *procedures* (duties). Some ethical theories maintain that a certain end or ultimate purpose justifies all moral behaviour. Others insist on ultimate rules, obligations or procedures for judging moral quality. Moral standards formulating goals are called *teleological* standards, while those that identify values as based on motives, rules, procedures or duties are called *deontological* standards. Let us briefly expand on this dichotomy, which can be found in the ethical theory of the last two centuries.

Goals that justify our actions provide the moral standards for the teleological ethicists. The Greek word *telos* means target, objective or achievable optimum. 'Teleological' refers to an ultimate goal that should be pursued or obtained in order to call the action good. The teleological approach points to a result in order to justify a policy. Some teleological theories take a reductionalist stand, maintaining that all human behaviour ought to be judged according to just one ultimate moral objective, like self-interest, profit, or pleasure. Thus, the theory that holds the pursuit of self-interest to be the highest aim of moral action is called egoism. Likewise, the teleology that holds lust to be the ultimate good is called hedonism, after the Greek word for lust, *hédonè*.

Ethicists who are inclined towards general values like duties and right procedures maintain a deontological position. 'Deontological' is derived from the Greek substantive *deon*: that which ought to be done, the duty. They insist on checking whether our conduct is in line with moral guidelines.

5.2.3 Making deals: negotiating on both aspects

People trained in commercial negotiations know that effective and satisfactory deals depend both on each party's goals and on the quality of the mutual relationship. In the eyes of transactionalists both the duties and the teleological goals can be reformulated in terms of concrete interests. Conversely, behind vital human interests we always find a combination of duty-based moral guidelines and outcome-oriented moral goals.

Many operational targets in business are positively related to the more strategic goals of corporations like profit, growth and continuity. However, when achieving these goals inflicts damage on others, they may be called immoral. When harmful acts can only be explained by the unrestrained pursuit of a commercial target, one has to make such judgements. Examples are the target of selling unsafe Pinto cars under $2,000 or the absolute priority given to profit-making on *The Herald of Free Enterprise*.

Just as in private relationships, business partners usually reach a morally acceptable balance. This balance not only grants stakes to each party, but also imposes relational obligations. Our idea of transactional ethics considers these relational duties and rights – such as values like trust, loyalty and mutual respect – to be a vital part of any transaction.

5.3 A practical business philosophy based on interest

Before examining ethical theories that allow for interests, we will first cite a practical example of the innovative use of interests in a Brazilian corporation. Ricardo Semler's use of concrete human interests sheds an interesting light on our topic, which transcends the basically egoistic associations attached to 'interest'. On the basis of mutual transparent self-interest he has organized his corporations in a way that satisfies most participants, and gives high profits and job satisfaction.

Ricardo Semler wrote *Turning the Tables*. He owns a Brazilian organization consisting of five fast-growing corporations. Corporate employees decide about their own working schedules and have a say in all corporation matters, and many company professionals even fix the amount of their own salary. Vacancies are not announced in newspapers, yet for each vacancy there are some 300 applicants. All this Semler has achieved by applying three principles: employee participation, profit-sharing, and good communication.

Semler applies what we would call egalitarian tribalism. He maintains that humans have survived already for many thousands of years by just co-operating within a restricted circle. He uses this idea in his business organizations, dividing his factories into relatively small units. The outcome is a far better employee commitment and important productivity gains.

The corporate hierarchy is almost horizontal, with very few hierarchical levels. People are promoted only with the consent of subordinates, and twice a year anonymous questionnaires are used to assess the qualities of the foremen and senior management. Semler puts into practice the idea that it is of utmost importance that employees are content and satisfied. As one example, the employees chose the new location of their factory. As a direct result of this approach, productivity has tripled over a period of four years.

Semler has developed his approach even further. Small expenses are not checked for fraud. The time clock could be abandoned, because whoever arrives late gets a proper dressing down from his direct colleagues. There is job rotation, that is, every couple of years each employee has to move to another job within the organization. Newcomers are not assigned to a specific task. They are allowed to try out a dozen or so activities and only then have to make a choice.

The comments on Semler's ideas made by a Dutch professor in psychology, Dr P. Vroon, are particularly illuminating:

> Semler's ideas are derived from the evolution theory. Humans carry a very long cultural history within them; for 99.9 percent of human history we operated as hunters in small groups. When you saw a mammoth, you did not have the time to elect a leader, to draw up an organization schedule, not to mention starting up with relational group therapy. The hunters did not want to dispute amongst each other who had the right to kill the beast, everybody was going to eat it anyway. Analogous to this idea of common purpose cooperation, Semler made his corporations consist out of small departments. After a few days leaders appear naturally, and the profits are shared equally amongst members. . . . It has been said before. We are age-old creatures that are thought of in the twentieth century as if they should *not* obey very old laws. Because of such expectations a lot of things go wrong unnecessarily. (Vroon, 1990)

5.4 Distinguish interests from egocentric materialism

By referring to three quite different sources we will try to show that interests do not necessarily serve egocentric goals of survival.

5.4.1 Sahlins' Stone Age economics

According to Sahlins, traditional 'primitive' tribes divided their human environment into three concentric circles. The inner circle was their own greater family group. Here the non-calculated gift is the natural way of dealing with one and another. In family relations *altruism* and sacrifice of private efforts were highly valued. The intermediate circle covers the relations with the clan, the neighbours and eventually a part of the tribe. Here the basis of relationships is the exchange of gifts, which has to be balanced in a precisely equal way. Sahlins calls this *balanced reciprocity*: 'The gift is the primitive way of achieving the peace that in civil society is secured by the State' (Sahlins, 1974, p. 169). The exterior circle contains the people that do not really matter, one can cheat and twist them as much as possible. Towards these outsiders one applies *negative reciprocity*.

Primitive economies were autarkic; they consisted of a multitude of small self-sufficient family groups. Division of labour, specialization and innovation were very limited. Above all, people had very few needs. Sahlins called such societies original affluent societies.

We use Sahlins' view of Stone Age economics as a mirror. Our economies are quite different. Still, the presence of corporate groupthink and the modern practices of negative reciprocity indicate that the negative moral features of the Stone Age mentality are not obsolete.

A more constructive use of our human heritage is feasible. Many studies point to the fact that humans operate best in small teams sharing common goals. The Semler way provides a good indication that our ancient tribal mentality can be used for constructive and mutually profitable purposes by modern business.

5.4.2 Excellent negotiation

A vast amount of transactional and stakeholder theories have appeared over the last decade. One of the most influential books at the origin of this movement is Roger Fisher *et al.*'s (1991) *Getting to Yes*. Their theory of excellent negotiation uses the insights of Thomas Gordon in a powerful theory of negotiation. Some of their most significant statements on interests, taken from their chapter on 'Focus on interests, not positions', speak for themselves:

For a wise solution reconcile interests, not positions.

The difference between positions and interests is crucial. *Interests define the problem.* The basic problem in a negotiation lies not in conflicting positions, but in the conflict between each side's needs, desires, concerns, and fears.

Reconciling interests rather than compromising between positions also works because behind opposed positions lie many more interests than conflicting ones. *Behind opposed positions lie shared and compatible interests, as well as conflicting ones.*

In many negotiations, however, a close examination of the underlying interests will reveal the existence of many more interests that are shared or compatible than ones that are opposed.

Shared interests and differing but complementary interests can both serve as the building-blocks for a wise agreement.

How do you go about understanding the interests involved in a negotiation, remembering that figuring out **their** interests will be at least as important as figuring out **yours**?

Ask 'why?' One basic technique is to put yourself in their shoes.

Ask 'why not?' Think about their choice.

Only rarely will you deal with a decision-maker who writes down and weighs the pros and cons. You are trying to understand a very human choice, not making a mathematical calculation. *Realize that each side has multiple interests.*

A common error in diagnosing a negotiating situation is to assume that each person on the other side has the same interests.

The most powerful interests are basic human needs.

Basic human needs include: security, economic well-being, a sense of belonging, recognition, control over one's life. As fundamental as they are, basic human needs are easy to overlook.

Negotiating hard for your interests does not mean being closed to the other side's point of view. Quite the contrary. (Fisher *et al.*, 1991, ch. 3) [emphasis added]

5.4.3 Jean-Jacques on the first mutual exchanges

Modern Western philosophy is based on a more egocentric idea of man. In these theories we find some brilliant observations on how mutual interests may create a task force, but even then authors, like Rousseau, insist on the self-sufficient and individualistic nature of man. This is quite contrary to the insights of anthropologists like Sahlins. Still, the myths created by Hobbes, Locke and Rousseau are dominantly present in received business ideas of man:

> When they had to hunt a deer, everybody was well aware that he had to stick to his assigned task; but when a hare turned up in front of one of them, one must not doubt that he would chase it without any scruples, and that after catching his prey, he did not care about his mates missing their bigger one. (Rousseau, 1964/1755, pp. 166–7; my translation)

The idea that some interest can be better taken care of by individuals, might help to amend the one-sided attention to group work that some may find in the Semler organization. Allow for tasks that call for individual hunting while organizing the unit around the hunt for bigger game, be it a deer or a mammoth.

5.5 Unethical attitudes on moral issues

5.5.1 Blatant egoism

This attitude may cover two different positions:

1. Everybody always does pursue self-interest disregarding others (descriptive egoism or *psychological* egoism).
2. Everybody ought to pursue only self-interest, disregarding the interest of others (*normative* egoism).

Normative blatant egoism is the position of most interest here. It refers to one ultimate goal, self-centred interest, that ought to be pursued without restraint. It does not allow for any moral obligation based on a relational duty. Normative egoism holds that the psychological motive for behaviour is identical to the intended goal, a strange mixed-up conception that will be refuted under subsection (f) below.

(a) The blatant egoist idea of man
A blatant egoist only recognizes a very limited scope of human motivations. A more general classification of human motives may recognize:

1. Self-interest, without the intention of harming anybody.
2. Self-interest, accepting harm to others.
3. Calculated altruism, based on self-interest.
4. True altruism or selfless care for others.
5. Sense of duty, overriding personal preferences.

The blatant egoist does not want to consider any moral guidelines or duties. So the motives of innocent self-interest (1), true altruism (4) and sense of duty (5) drop off. In short, self-interest overrides all other considerations, especially paying attention to the avoidance of harm.

(b) It is an ineffective reductionalist stand
A blatant egoist is only interested in his or her own interests; breaking promises as soon as his or her interests tell him or her to do so. It is an ineffective and counterproductive attitude because of the absence of impartial moral guidelines, that is, rules about how other parties' interests and attitudes should be taken into account. It cannot guide us when we want to obtain durable outcomes, because it totally overlooks the primary principle of transactions, which is accounting for others' interests.

(c) Blatant egoism relies on a false idea of free choice

Blatant egoism is an unrealistic attitude related to the popular definition of freedom as 'being free to do as I please'. It maintains an abstract stand, which does not consider the given situation and the need to reckon with the present conditions, especially others' interests at stake.

(d) Against descriptive blatant egoism: descriptions of behaviour inspired by altruism and sense of duty

There are many examples of heroic efforts to help strangers, showing evidence for the claim that people are sometimes motivated by true altruism or by a sense of duty, putting their own lives at peril. It seems hardly proper to pretend that people are never motivated by altruistic motives overruling personal comfort and security.

(e) Both positions are self-contradictory

Affirming that I either ought or actually do pursue my self-interest without restraints leads to a paradox when I try to generalize this statement. What about accepting this line of conduct from others? Do I have to accept that others will do the same, thus accepting that they will violate my claim for an unrestricted pursuit of my self-interest?

(f) Blatant egoism is a confused theory

A strange feature of this false ethical theory based on interests is its inability to distinguish between goals, motives, methods and consequences. Together with hedonism, blatant egoism is the best example of such a mix-up. They put motives and goals for human behaviour together in one basket, while neglecting consequences. In both theories the goal is also the motive of 'moral' behaviour: that is, egoism holds that the self-centred pursuit of interest is both the motive and the goal of morality, whereas hedonism states this about lust. Moreover both contain the common human fallacy of excusing harmful behaviour by pointing to 'good intentions'. One example may illustrate the fatal consequences of this fallacy. In the 1980s, modern yuppies took the motive of personal lust to be an all-excusing interest, which was both the goal and the motive of their actions. The Canadian homosexual purser who made an important contribution to the spreading of the AIDS virus in Europe and Northern America was a nice, beautiful and friendly gay man. He thought it was a matter of his own free choice to have sex with many others. In this particular setting his hedonistic attitude had mortal consequences for himself and many others. Even after the reports on the HIV virus identification and the spreading of the news of the symptoms, this sero-positive and sick man continued with his way of life. Pursuit of personal lust had become his idol.

5.5.2 *Amoral business egoism*

The unrestrained pursuit of self-interest is rejected by conventional morality and by ethicists. Nevertheless there exists an 'implicit' theory on business morals which refuses to apply moral criteria in business. Business amoralists simply state that business has nothing to do with any moral consideration. 'The myth of amoral business' (De George, 1990) claims that the pursuit of profit in a business environment is a goal lying beyond any moral considerations (amoral means non-moral). It maintains that conventional moral judgements do not apply to business. Success in free market competition relies upon a tough target-oriented attitude that should not be hampered by moral predications.

This myth relies on two fundamental ideas:

1. Taking care of one's own interests in business should not be disqualified when it clashes with conventional morality (isolating statement).
2. In business the unrestrained pursuit of one's own interests ought to be the ultimate goal (normative claim).

This position may be illustrated by many examples of people with the ideal of *getting rich quick, no matter how*; this cynical ideal is very questionable from a moral point of view, especially when we consider the damage done to other parties.

The idea behind this myth can be quite close to the blatant egoist's praise of the unrestrained pursuit of self-interest. It is also a reductionist stand, not accepting other standards that might moderate the unique quest for private profits. We have already criticized one basic assumption of this myth, the separation view concerning business and society (see section 2.2 above). Corporate interests do not exist in splendid isolation from the larger moral community.

Here, we will briefly mention some further objections.

(a) Amoral business egoism is a self-contradictory position
The trouble is that the amoralist no longer has the right to say that personal profit *ought* to be pursued, as it does not allow for moral normative goals.

(b) It refers to an inconsistent concept of self-interest
This is a tempting stand. The prosperous part of mankind may indeed seem to behave like amoral business egoists, ready to bargain about everything. Yet amoralists are often inconsistent when they refer to pursuing one's interests. They may start off with a normative concept of blatant egoism ('In business we should only consider our own interest'),

then shift to some vague kind of enlightened egoism ('Success in business depends on making deals that also satisfy other parties'), and finally conclude with the refusal of any moral standard ('Moral standards hamper doing good business').

(c) The normative claim in amoralism glorifies capitalist abuse

Most arguments against blatant egoism mentioned above can be applied against the normative claim of the unrestrained pursuit of profit. For instance, one may study the arguments used in favour of maintaining child labour, slave trading, or bad working conditions in new capitalist enterprises. The old arguments in favour of labour conditions in nineteenth-century England may overlap with the arguments in favour of present labour abuses in countries like Mexico, the Philippines, India or Malaysia.

(d) Amorality in business companies abuses the idea of profit maximalization

Macroeconomic theories of profit maximalization maintain an ethical criterion: economic government policies should stimulate free markets based on profit maximalization. Careful reading of these theories shows that they advocate government policies for utilitarian reasons; it also becomes quite clear that they accept many moral guidelines, like bans on bribery, cartels and protectionalism.

Accepting the normative statement on amoral business has dangerous consequences. It leads to the acceptance of socially unproductive transactions like price cartels, but it may also lead us to accept behaviour we would ordinarily consider to be immoral, such as female slavery or child labour.

5.5.3 In-group egoism or closed tribalism

This position is based upon a combination of a moral objective, self-interest, and a moral guideline, the recognition of *certain* in-group interests. It implies a willingness to restrain initial claims as an individual stakeholder, in order to reach a deal that optimizes the outcome for one's own party.

It can be very harmful, especially to outsiders. It accepts at least two persons as mutual interlocutors, but it can ignore the interests of other parties concerned. This may lead to unfair trade policies or even to criminal activities. It should be noticed that in-group egoists do not agree on moral guidelines concerning the rights of excluded parties.

When the Escobar family in Medellín, Colombia, agreed to liquidate competitors from other drug cartels and create their cocaine monopoly, they respected the self-interest of some other members of their family. But they did not count the murders amongst competing drug cartels, police, judges, journalists and politicians. In July 1993 their reign of terror had weakened to such a degree, that even in their home country the deputy editor of *El Tiempo*, Enrique Santos Calderón, could write an article on the blood and sorrow they had shed, with the title 'The family that nobody wants'.

This minimalist position is important in game theory but has to be amended in order to provide an acceptable standard for business ethics.

Anthropological studies have revealed the existence of identical expressions for 'outsiders' and 'edible'. In the Stone Age mentality, closed tribalism seemed to be dominant, yet it must not be overlooked that in the exchange and mutual visits between other tribes elaborate codes of hospitality existed. By using the expression 'closed tribalism' we refer to a type of in-group morality which does not allow for hospitality and generosity towards outsiders. A closed ethnic-minded tribal mentality looks upon foreigners as non-human, that is, as beings that do not have equal civil rights and should not be taken into consideration.

5.5.4 Distinguishing features of unethical interests

Blatant egoism, the myth of amoral business and in-group egoism share features in common. These features are characteristic of ethically unacceptable and immoral attitudes. We will review some of them briefly.

(a) Partial rules
This feature is most evident in the case of egoists. It consists of not accepting a basic principle of moral exchange – reciprocity. Reciprocity implies the acceptance of common guidelines, equally valid for all parties involved. Contrary to this, these immoral attitudes give absolute priority to the interests of one party.

(b) Abuse of power
The high priority for some self-centred or group-centred interest may cause great suffering amongst others. Here personal skills are only used to promote one's own position, which often violates the liberties of other persons.

(c) Absence of altruism
From a psychological point of view, all the above-mentioned attitudes have difficulties in accepting and respecting others. Some might even go as far as to say that these attitudes show a lack of self-acceptance, making it impossible to relate openly to others on an equal basis.

(d) Instrumental reason

Actions are mostly seen as aiming towards external goals like success, money or peer esteem. These external ends develop out of deeply held beliefs that serve to rationalize highly damaging activities.

(e) Lack of concern for weaker parties

The consequences of immoral attitudes often have a serious impact on the wellbeing of others. The interests of outsiders and respect for their right to participate are overlooked and ignored.

(f) Creation of a competitive fighting atmosphere

Pushing bargains too hard often creates animosity amongst the losers, and they may want to pay you back in the same fashion.

5.5.5 The four requisites of ethical communication

The Dutch business ethicist Jan de Leeuw (1994) states that moral communication and exchange have to meet four conditions. We have amended his wording, especially in (d) below, to fit our purpose.

(a) Openness

All participants have a right to have their say. In the literature on business ethics we observe this in respect for the moral autonomy of employees and in open relationships with the corporate environment.

(b) Mutual respect

De Leeuw used 'equality' here; we prefer 'equal rights' or 'mutual acceptance'. The moral minimum people have to be capable of is 'other-including self-interest', i.e. self-interest that includes empathic understanding of others' needs. This does not mean neglecting one's own interests, but does involve comprehension of other participants' stakes. This also has a relational aspect. Both sides must accept the other party's right to have interests and must be willing to look beyond self-centred concerns. Basically, they should be willing to formulate propositions that seek mutual gain.

(c) Logical coherence

Recently various scholars started to apply argumentation theory to business ethics. Argumentation theory can help to denounce *invalid* arguments. Two significant groups of fallacies are the unfounded statements and ambiguous concepts. Amongst the unfounded statements one type of fallacy is particularly linked to normative ethics: the naturalistic fallacy. Many unethical theories, like blatant egoism and hedonism, commit this fallacy. From an alleged fact, 'People do in fact pursue X', they jump to the conclusion 'People *should* pursue X'. In the case of the blatant egoist, X is 'self-centred interest', whereas in the case of hedonism 'lust/immediate pleasure' becomes the goal.

Here, do not forget what has been mentioned in 1.7.4, that is, in order to draw normative conclusions one always refers to an (implicit) normative standard. Judgements are never the simple result of facts alone.

(d) Changing and relating various points of view

One may distinguish three perspectives that participants in moral debate may have concerning their own and their opponent's position: the I-perspective – the agents' own view; the you-perspective – one's perception of the interlocutor's view; and the it-perspective, referring to a neutral observer's view. Especially, the empathic understanding of the opponent's point of view is important here.

A basic assumption of our argument in this chapter is that in business ethics interests should be handled in a way which combines my interests and a true understanding of my interlocutor's interests. In a one-liner this axiom can be formulated as follows: in order to become ethically respectable, the process of defining all the interests at stake has to be permeated by an other-including mentality.

Already we pointed to the presence of self-interested and yet altruistic behaviour in the theories of Semler and Sahlins. We may also add here some lessons one may learn from the theory of excellent negotiation, especially the following essential points:

☐ Separate the people from the problem, remain respectful.

☐ Focus on interest, go beyond initial positions.

☐ Stress co-operative goals by aiming for win-win.

☐ Do not play the game of powerful 'dirty' players, insist on rational agreement based on mutual understanding instead of merely giving in to coercion.

5.6 The overdone business ethics required by utilitarianism

5.6.1 Defining utilitarianism

Utilitarians hold public welfare or *utility* to be the ultimate criterion for moral quality. Utility is often presented as outcome-based ethics.

Nevertheless all versions of utilitarianism contain at least *one unconditional rule*. This deontological guideline tells us to take the interests of all concerned human beings into account. Every person counts, so for all participants costs and benefits have to be weighed.

There are many different theories that fall under the heading of utilitarianism. The following discussion outlines some aspects of two important positions: the hedonistic and eudaemonistic versions of act utilitarianism. Rule utilitarianism is not mentioned here; our reasons for discarding utilitarianism from business ethics apply equally to this more complicated theory.

5.6.2 *Act utilitarianism*

This theory checks whether concrete individual acts meet the chosen criterion for utility.

A general definition of act utilitarianism runs as follows: Act utilitarianism is the ethical theory that one should adopt the course of action which produces, or tends to produce, the greatest amount of beneficial consequences for the greatest number of people affected by the action. Good equates with providing the highest aggregated outcome of calculated individual benefits and individual costs.

The main question here is: What is our criterion for utility? In other words, which beneficial consequences should be seen as good for their own sake? Two answers will be discussed: the criterion of pleasure, and that of happiness.

Pleasure
The first reply may be *pleasure*. The Greek word for lust or sensual pleasure, *hédonè*, provides the root word for this version of utilitarianism. The theory maintaining that the ultimate outcome should be individual pleasure or absence of pain, is called *hedonistic utilitarianism*. It stems from Jeremy Bentham who wrote his *Introduction to the Principles of Morals and Legislation* in 1789. According to Bentham, every interest can be reduced to pleasure or avoidance of pain. To each sensation of pleasure and pain we can then attribute a value. After reducing every human interest to corresponding units of pleasure and pain, a cost-benefit calculation may follow, which finally leads to the choice of the action that rates highest.

Bentham's theory was one of the first to introduce quantitive methods of cost-benefit analysis. He believed that the pursuit of self-interest would indirectly be beneficial to society. Some of Bentham's basic assumptions were quite weak and had to be seriously amended by later adherents.

One assumption is that people are mainly motivated by some kind of self-interest. But it is not evident how egoistic pursuits produce public utility, even if this may sometimes occur as a non-intended side-effect. Bentham's theory did not allow for a quite different motive, the active pursuit of social welfare.

Later utilitarians tried to explain how the motive of public utility transcends a self-centred attitude, although they too started by perceiving man as an independent self-conscious individual driven by self-interest. On such a basis it remains difficult to find overruling social values.

To solve this issue, later utilitarian theories had to accept implicitly a *second deontological obligation*. They had to assume that moral behaviour includes a second duty: to ask humans to override private interests. This second moral duty can be formulated thus: one should implement the option with the highest public utility, even if it is contrary to one's own private interests.

Happiness

A second criterion for utility identifies a more durable state of individual wellbeing as the desirable outcome: *happiness*. The theory of *eudaemonistic utilitarianism* was invented by John Stuart Mill in his book *Utilitarianism*, published in 1861. He assumed that the pursuit of public utility was the goal of individual moral activities. He also tried to solve a second big weakness in Bentham's approach, that is, the reduction of all intrinsically valuable goods to a one-dimensional scale of pleasure and pain. Mill postulated an ultimate value, happiness, allowing for heterogeneous pleasures in various areas of life. Mill claimed that comparisons between the different pleasures in life were feasible by giving more value to durable satisfaction.

Eudaemonistic utilitarianism claims that all options can be evaluated by reducing the interests at stake in terms of their contribution to durable individual happiness. The best option is the one that produces the highest aggregated amount of happiness amongst the concerned individuals over a longer period. A practical example may illustrate that this can be a quite demanding, but responsible, attitude for the individual: utilitarians with various sexual relationships should always use condoms.

Mill redefined the Greek concept of *eudaemonia*, assuming that the durable pleasure or happiness produced by an action may be measured objectively. His concept of happiness claims that one can assess separate options or policies by means of a cost-benefit analysis. Whereas Aristotle and the ancient Greek moralists believed that definitive opinions on someone's happiness can only be stated after death, John Stuart Mill changed the meaning of *eudaemonia* to the aggregated sum of calculable 'higher' and 'lower' pleasure.

5.6.3 *Unfounded objections against utilitarianism*

One should not underestimate the way utilitarianism counts the benefits and injuries for all stakeholders. Two unfounded objections (A and B) are related to this misunderstanding.

Objection A

Utilitarianism is a kind of egoism because it claims that the right action is the one which produces most utility for the person performing the action.

Reply to A: As mentioned above, every concerned party has an equal right to put forward his or her claim. An action is right if it produces the highest amount of utility for all parties concerned, which implies the obligation to override opposite personal preferences.

Objection B

Utilitarianism only takes into account human utilities; it cannot be applied to animals or nature.

Reply to B: Bentham already speaks of the greatest happiness of all those whose interest is in question. The parties concerned may be only one person, other human beings, all sentient animals, and nowadays even environmental interests. Traditionally, utilitarianism mainly calculated the common good of a human political society. This interpretation often had a nationalist bias, overlooking for instance the welfare of colonized nations.

Recently, other interpretations have arisen, accounting for severe injuries to all social agents and even the natural environment. Utility calculations have been used to prove the truth of various causes. For example, it has been calculated that not cutting tropical rain forests is more profitable than continuing deforestation policies. Also, manufacturers of milk cartons have 'proved' that the use of carton packages produces less pollution than recycling glass milk bottles.

The second misunderstanding assumes that utility is only concerned with short-term and clearly measurable consequences. We will now discuss two objections based on this assumption.

Objection C

Utilitarianism holds an action to be right so long as its measurable benefits outweigh its costs.

Reply to C: Utilitarianism holds that in the final analysis, if we knew all relevant data, one option is right. Even if many data are not available, still the need remains to make the utmost effort to approach as close as possible a final analysis. This implies that when relevant data are non-existent, one has to make the best possible approximations.

Objection D
Utilitarianism only accounts for immediate costs and benefits.

Reply to D: Utilitarianism claims that both the immediate and all foreseeable future costs and benefits should be taken into account. Again, there is a need to use approximate estimations in order to assess future outcomes that are not easily measurable now.

5.6.4 Four true problems

1. The problem of measuring utility: one-dimensional pleasure is a false concept

Bentham was criticized for his claim that all interests can be reduced to a one-dimensional search for pleasure and avoidance of pain. If it is true that all pleasures and pain are at the same level, Bentham would have to admit that a well-nursed idiot or a well-fed pig is morally superior to an unsatisfied Socrates. Mill refuses simply to reduce everything to one dimension of pain and pleasure; he tries to compare different kinds of pleasures and interests. At this point we meet a second problem of measurement, which contains a terminal objection to applying utilitarianism in business ethics.

2. The problem of comparing utilities: radically different pleasures and pains cannot be compared, at least not in reference to the false concept of general happiness

Both modern and ancient philosophers maintained that the concepts of pleasure or happiness do not refer to one homogeneous state of wellbeing. One of the most famous criticisms may be found in *After Virtue* by Alisdair MacIntyre (1985):

> Human happiness is *not* a unitary, simple notion and cannot provide us with a criterion for making our key choices. . . . there are too many different kinds of enjoyable activity, too many different modes in which happiness is achieved. And pleasure or happiness are not states of mind for the production of which these activities are merely alternative means. The pleasure-of-drinking-Guiness is not the pleasure-of-swimming-at-Crane's-Beach, and the swimming and the drinking are not two different means for providing the same end-state. The happiness which belongs peculiarly to the way of life of the cloister is not the same happiness as that which belongs peculiarly to the military life. For different

pleasures and different happinesses are to a large degree incommensurable: there are no scales of quality or quantity on which to weigh them. Consequently appeal to the criteria of pleasure will not tell me whether to drink or swim, and appeal to those of happiness cannot decide for me between the life of a monk and that of a soldier. (pp. 64–5)

This criticism can also be applied to the economic sphere. What if governments really start taxing companies in order to clean polluted ground, especially if that would cause many industries to go bankrupt? Bankruptcies would lead to indirect costs like unemployment, and advantages for competitors from countries with no waste disposal legislation. There are also many questions concerning the cost-benefit ratio of the various methods of soil cleaning. How can we compare the benefit of less pollution to the indirect costs of a 99 per cent effective, but extremely expensive, method?

3. Problems with justice

It may happen that an option seems to be most profitable for the large majority, while at the same time we feel that it is morally totally improper from the point of view of distributive justice. Whereas most receive a relatively minor benefit, a small number have to cope with outrageous costs.

One example might be a clause in a contract between a Western constructor and an Arabian country, stating that no Zionists should be employed. From a utilitarian point of view it may be beneficial to accept such a contract, but for a minority of Jewish employees it may mean that they have to quit their jobs. In this situation other ethical guidelines (employee rights) should suggest a less harmful solution for the small minority.

The feelings of anger some people have when hearing about the decisions made in the Pinto case also have to do with injustice. They criticize Ford because of the way Ford management sacrificed the lives of a small minority (possibly 200 persons) in order to save $11 for each Pinto owner (potentially 10 million persons).

4. Problems with rights and duties

Utility calculations, especially when they serve as an ideological mask for unrestrained partial interests, may lead to the recommendation of solutions that are opposite to accepted moral obligations.

The best-known example in business ethics is the famous Pinto case. In 1968 Ford Motor Company decided to develop the first cheap subcompact car made in the United States. The Ford president, Lee Iacocca, wanted to rush the product development, in order to produce a small car in 1970 costing less than $2,000. Car styling here preceded engineering, and one result of this policy was a serious safety problem with the position of the gas tank. Between the rear axle and the rear bumper there was just ten inches of crush space for the gas tank. A differential housing was fitted on the rear axle with an exposed flange and a line of exposed bolt heads. Rear-end crash tests revealed that impacts from behind by a moving barrier at 21 miles per hour pushed the fuel tank forward, causing fuel leakage. A small spark would then be sufficient to set the car on fire.

Other tests concluded that supplementary safety measures were possible by improving the design. The estimated cost of the measures was $11 dollars per vehicle. However, Ford put forward several reasons for not adapting the design. It would make the car cost more than $2,000 dollars, thus failing to meet an important marketing target. Also, the design already met all the applicable federal safety standards of those days (further legalization was approved later as a result of this case). Furthermore, Ford was in a hurry to come up with a car able to fight the growing market share and popularity of the Volkswagen 'beetle'. Therefore, ultimately approved by Ford president Mr Iacocca, the decision was made to go ahead with producing the unchanged model.

In 1971 Ford USA published a cost-benefit analysis aimed at convincing federal authorities that the $11 safety improvement was not cost-effective for society. It should be noted that this analysis was made after the management decision to produce the Pinto without modification to prevent the reported dangers of the tank design.

Tables 5.1 and 5.2 show the costs and benefits calculated by Ford's lawyers in order to produce a shrewd argument for not improving the car. Table 5.3 explains how an American public institution calculated the estimated social costs of a death; this estimation was used in the Ford calculations.

Table 5.2 indicates the 'social costs' of introducing the $11 per car safety improvement. The conclusion of the lawyers was clear: improving the car safety would cost society three times more money than leaving the design as it was. It should be noticed that this calculus did not mention the item badwill.

Table 5.1 Estimated costs of not improving the safety of the Pinto

Item	Numbers	Cost/item ($)	Total costs ($m.)
Burn deaths	180	200,000	36.00
Serious burn injuries	180	67,000	12.06
Burned vehicles	2,100	700	1.47
Total sum			49.53

Table 5.2 Estimated social costs of design improvement

Item	Numbers (m.)	Cost/item ($)	Total cost ($m.)
Pinto car	11.0	11.0	121.0
Light truck	1.5	11.0	16.5
Total sum			137.5

Table 5.3 NHTSA estimation of the utility cost of one lost life

Item	1971 costs (US$)
Future productivity losses:	
direct	132,000
indirect	41,300
Medical costs:	
hospital	700
other	425
Property damage	1,500
Insurance administration	4,700
Legal and court	3,000
Employer losses	1,000
Victim's pain and suffering	10,000
Funeral	900
Assets (lost consumption)	5,000
Miscellaneous accident costs	200
Total cost per fatality	200,725

The value attributed to the loss of life was based on the estimation made by National Highway Traffic Safety Administration, shown in Table 5.3.

At least one detail was overlooked here in all these calculations. The cost-benefit calculation forgot to estimate the costs of bad publicity as a result of infuriated consumers claiming that Ford should have applied due care. For almost 10 years Ford USA did not design another small car, because of the resulting bad reputation of the Pinto. This neglect of risk and hazard management did indeed cost a lot of money; some estimations go up to $250 million including badwill (Cannon, 1994). It should be noticed that this amount largely depends on uncontrollable consequences, like amount of lawsuits, amount of involved smart money claims, reaction of consumer organizations, and general bad publicity in the newspapers.

Continuing with this line of calculation does not seem particularly promising. The application of non-utilitarian rights and duties corresponding to the due care theory seems much more appropriate. The real issue in the Ford Pinto case is the effort of the manufacturer to do the utmost in making a safe car or, more negatively, in not being negligent about overt risks.

5.6.5 Why is utilitarianism not fit for our purpose?

As a general ethical theory utilitarianism may be criticized following the above-mentioned arguments. If one keeps these objections in mind, utilitarianism can quite well be applied in the ethics of public policy and public administration.

For our purpose – defining valid moral guidelines for separate corporations in the economic sphere – utility is an inadequate criterion. Our main argument for this conclusion follows now.

1. Main thesis
Private corporations do not have to promote general public wellbeing; not damaging certain minimal rights and respecting certain minimal obligations are sufficient.

Applying utilitarian guidelines continually is impossible, even for private corporations with noble humanitarian intentions like The Body Shop; it is often too expensive to fully implement high moral standards concerning environmental and global wellbeing. Utility asks too much from individual private businesses.

If each time decisions were made corporations adopted only the utilitarian most perfect solution, many would have to close down, especially if they had to pay for the environmental damage they do. Hardliners may reply, so what? What they do not see, however, is that they sometimes take an inadequate unitarian stand. In fact this attitude may be counterproductive. For instance, when national legislation forces corporations into compliance with utility standards, this may lead to competitive advantages for foreign companies with a very bad record.

The positive argument for a different moral guideline can be found elsewhere. Corporate mission statements do not have to state complete adherence to public wellbeing. Business is about optimalizing transactions with a more limited scope. As part of a larger society and as economic agents, separate corporations have to respond to certain requirements. In section 4.5 we saw that these demands can be formulated as specific moral demands, especially those concerning consumer satisfaction and safety, environmental protection, and labour rights. Only in these fields, and then only up to a certain degree, should corporations meet moral demands.

2. Circumstantial argument
Applying utility standards is used by powerful participants as a sophisticated means for exploiting others.

The abuse of utilitarian arguments in order to present partial propositions can be illustrated by the Pinto case. In fact, the lawyers' cost-benefit calculation served to provide a moral wrapping around a decision that neglected due care obligations and simply omitted to question a sacred groupthink target (here, the $2,000 car price).

Now, existence of abuses is not a really valid argument against a moral theory. The very best moral principles have been called upon to cover up immoral practices. Such abuses alone do not invalidate those principles, especially when informed persons can perceive the bigoted and partial position behind some harmful practice. For example, principles of religion are often highly respectable even to non-believers, but some religious fanatics distort these principles in order to achieve political or private goals, or to nourish negative emotions of hatred, jealousy and blame.

Yet in the case of utility guidelines, one often finds that not all the stakes have been accounted for. In particular, parties that were in a weaker bargaining position due to existing power relationships often have to carry the burden of harsh and inhumane solutions. Most such abuses of utilitarian arguments are found in the modern bureaucratic and economic spheres, especially where cartels and monopolies exist.

Public wellbeing has been referred to by Thatcherist privatization policies. The following example may illustrate the abusive use of utility arguments in such situations. It illustrates that utility arguments are not in themselves a guarantee for equitable solutions, especially when public service monopolies become profit oriented. The example also indicates a tendency towards ruthlessness in such policies, imposing heavy burdens on the weak parties involved.

Example: Thatcherist privatization of water authorities

It seems evident that the best interests of customers need to be backed up in face of the privately owned monopolies distributing water. This support was not given by the public authorities due to a separatist dogmatism that probably assumed the mere fact of privatization would create market competition.

The recently privatized water companies in England and Wales in fact still have a monopoly, created under Mrs Thatcher's government. This causes two big problems for customers. First, since the privatization in 1989 water prices have gone up 55 per cent (above inflation). Secondly, the number of households that had their water supply cut off multiplied dramatically. While in 1989 only 480 cut-offs per year were registered, in 1992 21,282 households were cut off. Of course, water cut-offs are preceded by warnings to people who do not pay their bills, and so, from a contract point of view, these companies seem to function adequately. However, from the monopolist viewpoint, the benefits might allow for rather more consideration towards the financial situation of individual households. Also one should consider the indirect costs that result from cutting off the water supply, and the public nuisance caused by the stench of waste products in apartment blocks like Hamilton House, Birmingham in 1992. On their side, the benefits for these monopolists were quite interesting: an average 12 per cent net profit in 1991 and 1992. Moreover, while amongst their customers almost 25 per cent has to live with less than half of an average income due to the recession, suffering poverty and distress, the presidents of these new private companies have been allowed to increase their own salaries to sometimes well over £200,000 per annum. Is this an echo of the 'get rich quick, no matter how' ideology, dressed in the cloak of a Thatcherist commitment to public utility? (*NRC Handelsblad*, 1993b).

5.7 A view fit for moral commerce: enlightened egoism

Enlightened normative egoism provides for adequate and optimal exchanges with relevant partners while respecting minimum rights for outside stakeholders. It does so by defining ethical guidelines in terms of negotiations based on personal interest; only the requirement to respect weak outsiders can be seen as a duty. Thus it has higher standards than in-group egoism, but is less demanding than utilitarianism, as it primarily takes into account the interests of persons making the deal. It does not positively aim at public welfare.

This position can easily be understood and is directly applicable to business practice. Although very promising, this idea also has some serious problems. Some of them will be stated at the end of this chapter. Chapters 6 and 7 will then study outlooks that can also reply to these problems.

5.7.1 Defining enlightened egoism

We propose to apply one moral attitude when looking at the interests of all parties concerned. In business, therefore, we should follow *enlightened egoism*, an attitude that recognizes every stakeholder's right to pursue other interests, including self-interest.

A general idea of enlightened egoism can be given by the following description. Enlightened normative egoism claims that in business people ought to follow moral standards based upon the pursuit of other-including self-interest. These moral standards express a willingness to restrain one's initial claims as an individual stakeholder, applying methods of negotiation aiming at mutual gain. More specifically, a morally acceptable deal not only optimizes the outcome for all directly negotiating parties, but also takes into account a minimal number of moral obligations towards outside stakeholders. This has to be done in order to prevent severe injuries.

In other words, enlightened egoism accepts as a valid motive that everybody pursues his or her interest, as long as one allows the others to do the same. While being inspired by such motives, one has to meet two supplementary conditions, or objectives:

1. Reaching an optimal deal between the parties that actually achieves, if possible, a win-win solution (strategic goal).
2. Guaranteeing a minimum of rights for relevant outside stakeholders (moral goal, stating a duty towards outsiders).

This description outlines a procedure for making morally acceptable deals, according to a transactional view.

What is a moral optimum when positions are unequal?

Considering the first condition, many vital ethical issues are already at stake. In business, parties have often *unequal* resources of knowledge, skill, market position, or money. The party that is stronger at that moment may often easily get the best part out of the deal, but has to moderate his or her claims for several, mainly strategic, reasons.

The first reason is the presence of competitors. The second reason stems from the consideration that market positions change. Another time the same parties might meet in quite different circumstances, so it's better to create some sense of obligation and respect.

Other reasons are more strictly moral. Corporations have subscribed to moral obligations when they supply services or products. These corporate duties are often codified by law. Many issues described in Chapter 4 can be redefined in transactional terms. Our example in section 4.7.2 of the mistaken bill is quite illuminating for the room to manoeuvre that this position allows. Though in principle both suggested positions may fit with enlightened egoism, the strict application of the above-mentioned guideline does not allow us to walk out unnoticed, as we then set the burden to one side and do not look for a more equitable win-win solution. Only enlightened egoists still attached to primary self-interest might argue that one may leave things as they are, as it is the salesperson's responsibility to do his or her job well. But this sounds more like in-group egoism, regarding the salesperson as an outsider on whom you may push a hard bargain.

At this point we hit upon a key question when applying enlightened egoism. It is of utmost importance not to overlook customers and contractors, treating them as outlawed outsiders. Thus the question is: Did the transaction involve unfair risks for the weaker party?

One example of an unfair risk imposed upon clients in a service contract may illustrate this question. Passengers buying a ticket for the ferry *The Herald of Free Enterprise* expected the ferry company, Townsend Thoresen, to bring them safely from Zeebrugge to Dover. The company did not fulfil this part of the transaction on 6 March 1987, when 193 people were killed in the biggest North Sea ferry disaster of this century. Later reports revealed several weaknesses in safety precautions – not only on that day, and in respect of several procedures – and in the hiring of sufficient personnel. Above all there was the danger of the top-heavy ship design, causing the vessel to capsize after only a relatively small volume of water had come in. In several ways, the passengers' interest in a safe transportation from A to B was neglected here.

Which rights of outside stakeholders should be considered and what duties do they imply?

Several important topics in business ethics are related to this question.

One topic is to what extent parties should endorse third-party liabilities, and which responsibilities this includes. In section 4.5, we mentioned that engineers often feel pressure from their superiors obliging them to ignore their misgivings. The consequences of this groupthink pressure can be most tragic. A good example of this is contained in Kipnis (1992).

Another primary topic concerns methods for protecting the rights of outside parties. Analogous to the idea that donkeys may be persuaded to go forward either by waving a stick at them from behind or by holding a carrot in front of them, it is possible to outline two stratagems concerning moral codes in respect of outside customers. One code focuses on the sticks consumers have for use when their rights are not respected. Most prominent amongst the institutions defending the rights of consumers are public legislation, consumer organizations, activist groups, newspaper articles and consumer programmes on television. Conversely, the carrot stratagem fosters a proactive and responsible approach inside the business company. The goal is constantly to improve on client-oriented and communicative performances in such a way that customers are not only satisfied, but feel really well treated. Various articles on marketing have indicated that not simple satisfaction, but being 'very satisfied' makes the customers come back. One reference here is in a recent survey for Xerox: 'Customers who said they were "very satisfied" bought six times more of a Xerox product than customers who only said they were "satisfied"' (Verwey, 1994).

5.7.2 On tribal roots and respect for outsiders

Enlightened egoism is not an abstract type of humanism, as it can evaluate moral codes present in concrete commercial agreements. Corporations are part of various networks of relationships with suppliers, clients and competitors. This existing corporate culture and the related branch practices can be evaluated by applying enlightened egoism.

When referring to what was said in section 5.5.3 on closed and open tribalism, it is possible to relate the present attitude to open tribalism. Enlightened egoism is ready to take some interests of relevant others into account. Following the tribe image, one might say enlightened egoists are relatively open-minded and hospitable; they have a taboo on the murdering and eating of outsiders.

Through enlightened egoism people may create an environment where they can take care of their own interests, while at the same time aiming at mutual gains with direct relations and respecting the minimum rights of outsiders. This attitude therefore acknowledges the fact that businesses have a home base and promote their corporate interests, without idolizing this motive. If commercial deals have to be established on a more durable basis it is in each partner's strategic interest to create a win-win solution. Besides this consideration, one has the moral right to show a minimum respect to non-participating stakeholders. The main reason for this can be explained in a negative way: when great injuries are inflicted on outsiders, corporations should accept accountability for their part in it.

It should be noted, however, that this attitude has its own limits. Enlightened egoism does not necessarily go beyond calculated altruism. Doing things out of a sense of duty, or just to please dear friends, is not part of an enlightened egoist's emotional repertoire.

5.7.3 A conditional pro: enlightened egoism stirs one tender cord

By insisting on interests, it is possible to create a basis of understanding with people from other cultures and backgrounds. It is a basic approach, especially when frontiers have to be crossed – geographical, cultural or otherwise.

This approach creates space for transcultural bargains on an equal basis. This basis is provided by the fact that the deals are regarded as consisting of at least two different elements: one element is the interests, while the other is the human part. Regarding the communication between humans this attitude remains rather blind, but it has one strong asset: the bargaining element. Provided that the partners learn to respect each other (which is in fact a considerable problem that cannot be resolved with this attitude alone), they can fruitfully work towards mutual gain.

5.7.4 Con: colonization by strategic concerns

Especially cross-cultural commerce illustrates that although the interest motive may be a potent incentive, the sole presence of mutual gain prospects does not guarantee successful deals. Pretending that decision-making in business depends on interests alone has often been disproved by studies on cultural misunderstanding.

Enlightened egoism is a normative attitude for business ethics which mainly focuses on interests. It carries the risk of becoming a manipulative bargaining method. To counterbalance this danger, one will need some insight into why people have to be respected even if they act strangely at first sight. This calls for some additional guidelines referring to human respect and to human rights and duties, which go beyond commercially interested exchange.

If one becomes obsessed by 'What is in it for me?', the stakes may turn into the dominant issue, and you no longer have a clear perspective of yourself and the people on the other side. The other parties often sense this manipulative attitude quite easily. For example, when dealing with foreigners some people show a lack of tact and empathy which is not very comforting. In an earlier age and in another place, such primitive hard bargaining would make the foreigner think they were talking about how to prepare him for supper.

Enlightened egoism is a useful and valid tool, but it is not a complete treatment that can do without supplementary assistance.

5.7.5 Con: no sense of common purpose

Professor Mark Pastin (1986) has made a powerful comment on the importance of a clear sense of corporate purpose for employee commit-ment. An illuminating example he uses is a story about woodcutting.

The story starts with the head forester setting targets, isolated objectives, without any further explanation. He orders his team of woodcutters to cut down 50 per cent of the trees in six months. The team starts and goes on chopping and wielding axes for three months. Then the momentum starts to falter and a suspicion arises. What happens if they achieve this target? Will they then simply be moved to other forests, each time obliged by command to cut down 50 per cent of the trees? They begin to feel that something is missing: the head forester has not explained to them why it is important to chop down 50 per cent of the trees. The team therefore has no sense of common purpose.

A risk of perfunctory agreements is that they do not call upon powerful commitments – that is, gut feelings combined with insight about what really matters here. Although the comments by Professor Pastin were primarily aimed at building and developing strong inner corporate culture, they also have a bearing on commercial exchanges.

In his article 'Ethics as an integrating force in management', Pastin (1985) indicates three principal questions to determine corporate purpose, or 'what is valuable for the company':

1. Who counts (relevant stakeholders for each choice)?
2. When counts (relevant time period)?
3. How do you count (relevant criteria, goals and methods)?

In his comment on the first question, he indicates that stakeholder concern should go beyond the inside of the corporation:

> Participatory approaches currently in favour emphasize participation by *internal* constituencies. Some of these approaches, such as those purportedly rooted in Japanese management practices, are based on the belief that internally directed participation builds team and organizational identity. But a value-informed decision process must also take account of significantly affected external constituencies, including customers, suppliers, competitors and regulators. (Pastin, 1985)

Two sentences later comes the empirical evidence of the importance of commitment to external stakeholders:

> An ongoing study of successful companies [New York Stock Exchange industrial corporations that have paid a dividend for at least 100 years consecutively] shows that a key factor in these companies' success comes from their view of themselves as an intermediary between suppliers and customers. The chief executives also believe that to be successful in the long run, a company must be in dialogue with society at large on every topic of mutual concern to the two entities. (Ibid.)

We believe that this indicates more than just the procedural willingness to be in dialogue with outside stakeholders. The best-performing corporations show moral commitment to certain issues; they express a sense of common purpose that cannot be understood by means of the transactional view. Purpose hooks on to what we call the fostering of desirable skills, desirable because they help us to attain a common purpose.

5.8 Synopsis

1. Moral standards in business ethics can be seen as the outcome of transactions between different parties with often unequal resources.

2. Some transactional standards insist on the ethical quality of the produced results and identify goals ('moral objectives'); others stress the importance of the means and procedures by formulating duties and rights ('moral guidelines'). The first are called teleological criteria, the second deontological.

3. In all transactions both aspects play a role. Parties have expectations about their mutual relation which are often expressed by the methods they apply. Regarding their mutual duties and rights they apply moral guidelines like confidence, honesty and compliance to deals. Also, parties have goals at stake, and they seek to realize them by obtaining certain concrete consequences.

4. Not all goals are coherent and clear, and they may imply unacceptable moral standards; more general moral criteria have to be defined that may provide ethical checks for the quality of goals.

5. At a descriptive level three moral objectives are of great importance for business transactions:
   (a) self-centred interest (actor-directed blatant egoism);
   (b) enlightened self-interest (recognizing other people's right to pursue self-interest, other-including self-interest; and
   (c) public utility (pursuit of social welfare).

6. Blatant egoism reduces all morality to self-centred interest; this moral attitude is not accepted in transactional ethics as it is self-contradictory and ineffective. Furthermore it relies on a false idea of man; it rationalizes the unrestrained pursuit of private desires by presenting this goal and motive as something respectable in itself, whatever the methods and consequences.

7. Enlightened egoism is based upon a combination of a moral goal (i.e. the defence and care of self-interest) and a moral guideline (i.e. the recognition of everybody's right to pursue their own interests as long as they do likewise with you and others). To this other-including pursuit of self-interest it adds two conditions. The first condition is strategic (i.e. individual claims have to be mediated and restrained in order to arrive at an optimum for the stakeholders that participate in the deal). The second condition is a moral value: only those deals are acceptable which at least admit certain moral obligations towards outside stakeholders. These minimum obligations towards outsiders are nega-

tive rights such as the interdiction of torture, murder, useless hardships and exploitation.

8. Utilitarianism goes two steps further than enlightened self-egoism. It postulates a moral goal transcending separate individual interests – public utility – and it poses the duty-based guideline that every human being has a claim on the right to pursue happiness and to avoid pain. The concept of utility, however, is notoriously vague, and it often leads to biased interpretations covering up some partial interest.

9. Only one primarily teleological standard for judging actions and policies is acceptable in business ethics: enlightened egoism. The position that only accepts minimum obligations towards outsiders will be called enlightened egoism-1. At the end of the next chapter we define enlightened egoism-2.

5.9 Examples and questions

5.9.1 Example 1: cheap charter flights to more unsafe airports

Following MacIntyre (1985) we cannot compare the pleasure of taking a cheap charter flight to the avoidance of pain due to a heightened risk from sloppy safety procedures. The latter risk refers to death or injury. The costs of the ticket are measured in money and will be considerably less. What criterion should we adopt in order to compare (a) a slightly higher risk of getting killed with (b) the evident financial gain?

Task
Carry out a cost-benefit analysis comparing these quite heterogeneous stakes, based on a reduced model for ethical audit.

Remember
The example of the charter flight normally leads up to the conclusion that it is more in my 'enlightened self-interest' to gain financially by buying a cheap charter ticket. Psychologists can explain why customers accept the possibly higher risk of accidental death.

5.9.2 Example 2

Which attitude described in this chapter fits best with the following concept of societal marketing: 'the organization should determine the needs, wants, and interests of target markets and deliver the desired satisfactions more effectively than competitors in a way that improves *the consumer's and the society's well-being'* (Kotler and Armstrong, 1989, p. 15).

5.9.3 Example 3

The prominent Dutch economist Sweder van Wijnbergen often attacks Western European protectionism and puts forward arguments in favour of free trade. The following more practical argument may easily be interpreted in terms of standards based on enlightened egoism:

☐ It identifies (some of the) different parties concerned.
☐ It criticizes a kind of corrupt 'in-group egoism'.
☐ It is the beginning of a wider argument in favour of a more 'nourishing' economic policy in Western Europe, supporting technological innovation which will be the key to economic success in the future.
☐ It criticizes our lack of defence for 'outside' stakeholders, not only the new technologies, but also Eastern Europe.

> From a theoretical point of view it is not so clear at all that free trade improves economic growth, nobody has really shown that. But there is another way to find an argument in favour of free trade. To do this, one has to analyze the mechanism behind protectionism: conservative lobbies. New entrepreneurs do not yet have a capital at stake, so when they meet a trade barrier at one place, they simply divert their effort to another market. The old entrepreneurs are interested in maintaining the status quo. They already have written off the investments they made and have built something that they wish to defend. Now Western Europe is a perfect example of a trade policy made by lobbies from traditional industries, fostering a preference for old declining industries. The EEC once began as the European Community for Coal and Steel, with the original purpose of making production more efficient. Yet the whole EEC policy never went beyond relief regulations. This subvention policy and the protectionist lobbies lead to institutionalized corruption. (*NRC Handelsblad*, 1993a)

5.9.4 Example 4: the legalized cartel for public notaries

General remarks
Over the last ten years a debate has started on the following question: Are the Dutch notary fees for house sales and mortgage deeds too high? It has

not been settled yet, and is still being fiercely argued. The reports on this topic are divided. One position leads to an affirmative answer on this question by indicating profit rates up to 50 per cent, while the second view denies this accusation and raises queries about the quality of the reports that back the former view.

We will quickly look at both sides of the argument. The view denouncing the present tariffs is outlined below under 'Thesis'; the second point of view can be found under 'Antithesis'. As a synthesis is not available, we end with some further questions. First, however, some basic facts on rear estate deeds and on the legal function of a public notary.

Historical facts on deeds of sale and mortgage deeds

On 25 July 1994 the Dutch public notaries reduced their fees for deeds of sale and mortgage deeds. Since 1991 the fixed notary fees for both forms of deeds on the average Dutch house costing DFl 231,000 have dropped by DFl 573. These fees are based on the price of the house, and are still not directly related to the actual costs of the service activities. The fees for deeds on small transactions have been slightly raised, while some fee reductions are found in the bigger sales. Compared to 1991, the rates for houses valued at above DFl 100,000 have remained the same or, in some cases, have even decreased by up to 18 per cent.

Mortgage deeds also have a tariff system which is based on the amount of the mortgage. Generally speaking these fees are 10 to 25 per cent lower than the fees charged for deeds of a sale of the same value.

All in all the net profits made by public notaries have risen greatly over the last ten years. Even more so than in 1985 real estate deeds are now the biggest cash cow for notaries, yet this increase is not caused by an increase in the tariffs for each separate deed. The fact that real estate deeds have become more and more profitable is due to the rising volume of house sales and the rising prices for houses. Also in this period, notaries' productivity increased considerably. The notary services did not become more complicated, but the introduction of word processing allowed their offices to handle much larger volumes of transactions with the same staff.

A legal monopoly

In 1847 the Dutch parliament voted in a law that attributed such deeds to notaries, establishing a legal monopoly and fixing minimum tariffs. The number of public notaries was also restricted by this law. Other regulations and nationwide tariff agreements also exclude price competition.

The law obliges Dutch citizens and corporations to register their deeds in the office of public notaries, that is, with members of the Royal Dutch Brotherhood of Notaries (KNB: Koninklijke Notariële Broederschap). The fees for such deeds are fixed by the Brotherhood.

Dutch notaries do not regard their job as a purely commercial service for just one of the parties concerned. They provide a public service comparable to other public offices, and insist on the importance of the *impartiality* of their services.

Continental deeds of sale are never negotiated by each parties' notaries, as this function is not within the responsibilities of the public notary. The contract is drafted first by the parties concerned. The role of the public notary comes in later as a public check and guarantee. This idea of notary services is called the Latin notary system, which is quite different from the Anglo-Saxon system in Great Britain, Ireland or Denmark. The Dutch public notary is an independent impartial official, invested by law with the duty of checking the contract. This also is done as a public service for general interest: the notary has to verify that the proposed deal falls within the limits of general ideas of contractual decency.

The above-mentioned tariffs have only to be paid once in every deed of sale, usually by the purchasing party. Conversely, under the Anglo-Saxon system in Great Britain, Ireland and Denmark both parties have to pay a fee when they hire solicitors to defend their interests. These persons are also called notaries in these countries, although they each look after the interests of only one of the parties involved in a deal or dispute.

The Anglo-Saxon notary services can easily be evaluated by the standards, for example, of blatant egoism or enlightened egoism, as they primarily represent private interests. Contrary to this, the Dutch public notaries would not want to be classified along these lines, because their independent position and their duties are concerned with the general public interest. Most probably they would align with the standards that acknowledge the normative respect of general wellbeing, that is, either utilitarianism or a version of duty ethics. Continental notaries regard themselves as public officials, and indeed most services they perform look a lot like those of a civil officer. Due to their legal position, they are impartial authorities bestowed with a public mandate for checking, registering and guaranteeing the authenticity of deeds.

Thesis: this cartel charges disproportionate fees

The unilateral decision of the Royal Brotherhood of Notaries (KNB) to reduce their fees can best be understood by studying the critical view first, especially the reports made by a customer organization and by the Dutch government.

The actual debate on the tariffs was started in 1988 when a Dutch house-owners' organization published a report on the actual costs and benefits made by notaries. They concluded that the mortgage deeds and the deeds for house sales were a cash cow for notaries, estimating that on the total net amount of the real estate deeds profits were made of at least 40 per cent.

Table 5.4 Annual turnover and profits on real estate deeds (DFl m.)

	1984–86	1987–91	1993
Average annual turnover on real estate deeds	351	479	710
Total annual profit	226	313	340

These profit margins were based on detailed estimates over the period 1984–86. It refers to the annual average output of nearly 145,000 mortgage deeds, 100,000 deeds of sale on existing houses and 45,000 deeds of sale on newly built houses. It should be noticed that in The Netherlands about 97 per cent of house sales are financed by a mortgage loan. In latter years the number of deeds of sale and mortgage deeds have increased considerably, reaching a total of about 182,000 deeds of sale and 178,172 mortgage deeds in 1993.

In Table 5.4 we list the annual turnover and the overall net profits calculated by three reports. Two of the reports were prepared for the Dutch organization of house-owners, while the last one is a more comprehensive study made by KPMG accountants for the Dutch government. All data mentioned in the first two reports are estimates, and they only refer to the deeds on private houses. The third report prepared by KPMG in 1994 is based on more elaborate research which included a study of the notary books for 1992. They came up with a higher volume of turnover, which is due partly to a higher volume in the private house market and partly to the fact that this report also takes into account the deeds on business real estate. On basis of the data for 1992 they prepared an estimate for 1993.

The 1994 KPMG report is the first to give an overall idea of all the notary costs and services. It estimates that in 1993 all fees for all deeds related to real estate produced a net profit of DFl 359 million on a total turnover of about DFl 1 billion for all services, including the family practice. As there are 1,100 public notaries in The Netherlands, this annual profit margin generates about DFl 323,000 average income – of this sum, about DFl 300,000 comes from the real estate deeds. This income may be added to the standard annual income of DFl 180,000 that is already included in the cost of the deeds.

One of those responsible for running the Dutch consumer organization, Mr van Loon, comments as follows: 'This is a comfortable top manager salary which only requires the skills of a higher public official. It does not involve the risks of market competition, nor the strenuous fight of the corporate entrepreneur' [my translation].

It should be noted that during this study KPMG received active co-operation from the KNB, including the mentioned 1992 account books.

If this side of the story is true and complete, we are dealing with a notable example of in-group egoism. The normative conclusion should therefore be that notaries abuse their cartel position. A policy suggestion would then be to put the KNB under strong pressure, applauding the Dutch government's new tariff law based on EC anticartel legislation.

On 25 March 1994 the government refused to grant the notaries' request for continuation of their tariff agreements, and in early April 1994, the government announced new proposals to change the law on notary tariffs, which would impose drastic cuts in the tariff rates and tear down cartel privileges. This initiative, however, has not been carried out, and the notaries themselves have proposed new 'more realistic' tariffs.

Antithesis: notaries are independent authorities with a public mission
The notaries claim that they charge reasonable fees. Also, they emphasize their independent public obligations invested in them by law. Moreover they admit that the tariffs for more expensive houses and the larger mortgages are indeed quite profitable, but maintain that these benefits are at least 15 per cent lower than estimated by the KPMG report. To substantiate this idea they refer to a report by Moret, Ernst & Young which criticizes the KPMG report. Finally, they explain that the Moret report clearly shows that the benefits on real estate deeds serve to subsidize other activities making heavy losses, especially the family practice which involves the drafting of wills and marriage contracts.

It should be noted that whereas the KPMG report has been made public, the Moret report has only been sent to the Ministry and to KPMG. After reading the Moret report KPMG has stood by all its initial statements. Information on the Moret report can only be found by means of KNB newsletters. (This indicates, therefore, that KNB does not yet accept the idea of a level playing-field.)

Now, some additional remarks on the real estate fees. In a newsletter of 18 July 1994 the KNB announced its new fee policy:

> The tariffs for deeds of sale and deeds of mortgage will be drastically reduced for deeds between Fl 100,000 and Fl 1,000,000, with cuts amounting up to 18% of the previous fees. Thus 9 out of 10 deeds will become cheaper for the new owners. Up to Fl 100,000, the tariffs remain at the present level, which does not cover costs. The notaries thus see to it that the costs for that part of the housing market remain low. Over a period of three years the notary fees for simultaneous deeds of sale and mortgage on the present average house of Fl 231,000 will thus be reduced by Fl 573.

To emphasize that the house-owners and the government have been pushing too hard, the KNB adds some less pleasant news on fees for wills: 'Last wills, marriage contracts and cohabitation contracts will cost more money from 25 July onwards.' Yet they still claim that they do not make money on these deeds: 'We have not reached the break-even point on these items. The notaries find the principle that such services are available to everyone more important than arriving at a completely cost-covering tariff. Even after the present change in tariffs the family practice (last wills, marriage contracts, etc.) is subsidized by the real estate practice.'

This newsletter also disagrees with the KPMG report, claiming that this report underestimated the notary costs on the family practice by about 30 per cent. Whereas KPMG states that the notaries break even on these services, the notaries maintain that they lose money and have to cross-subsidize the services internally. They substantiate this point by referring to details in the KPMG report on the actual costs and benefits in 1992 which fit quite well with the notaries' point of view. According to the Moret report, the notaries incur DFl 79 million loss on the family practice on a gross turnover of DFl 158 million in those services.

Remaining questions of moral philosophy

The Moret report was commissioned by the KNB. Both the two opposing accountant reports – Moret and KPMG – and the notary tariffs raise technical and philosophical issues. Here we will first mention briefly the remaining technical issues and then consider the basic principles.

Several technical points were already hinted at before. So far we do not yet have one study of the actual costs and benefits on real estate deeds that is accepted by both sides. As the notaries claim that they use the profits on real estate deeds to subsidize family practice deeds, it is important to obtain an authoritative assessment of the costs and benefits of the family practice also.

A new technical point has been raised by the recent KPMG report, pointing to possible cost reductions by the implementation of more efficient procedures. The KPMG report criticizes the inefficiency of the present notary work methods, and calculates an annual productivity of 50 to 57 per cent. The productivity loss in excess of 40 per cent seems to remain unnoticed because of the fixed high tariffs.

The philosophical issues are related to and influenced by the outcome of the technical reports. If it is proved that notaries do make a net profit of 40 per cent on their real estate deeds, and if it is also shown that the family practice is cost neutral and needs virtually no subsidizing, then the normative conclusion leads to an affirmative answer to our initial question.

Yet even here an additional question should be answered first, referring to the moral acceptability of a certain professional income. The KPMG report indicates that the average public notary makes DFl 300,000 in addition to his DFl 180,000 standard annual income. By which standards should we decide whether such an income is excessive or improper?

In the fees they charge, public notaries take into account that they should have an income at least equal to the DFl 117,000 salary for cantonal judges. This in fact mounts up to the DFl 180,000 gross allowance for notaries, as the KNB adds pension money and other insurances. Compared with other high public officials it does seem that notaries make a disproportionately large amount of money: almost half a million Dutch florins in 1993.

The KNB contests this view, mainly by making rather general objections that do not seem very applicable in this case. First of all, they claim that the annual income of a judge is guaranteed, whereas the annual income of the notary depends on his or her annual turnover. This argument, however, is not a valid excuse for the considerable difference, according to the records, between annual notary incomes over the last ten years and the much lower incomes of highly qualified judges. Another of the notaries' objections claims that the notary has invested in his office and equipment and that the interests on these investments should at least be covered by his income. This second general argument may also sound valid at first hearing, but it is not sufficient to explain why a legalized cartel on relatively simple deeds should yield at least twice the income of other public officials.

From the question of fair fees, we have thus arrived at the question of fair income or fair reward for services. Two additional matters should not be forgotten here.

The notaries claim to be impartial people with a public mission. It should be made clear, then, what advantages the Continental system really provides for house sales. According to the house-owners' organization these advantages are so low and charged at such a high price that they would prefer to introduce the Anglo-Saxon system. The public notaries have already warned against this move, indicating that the general expectation that such a change would reduce fees by some 50 per cent is totally unrealistic. They point out that in the present Anglo-Saxon system, *both* parties hire a lawyer, broker or private notary, which results in a total cost over 60 per cent higher than the Continental system for an average transaction.

The principle of a fixed tariff system is closely related to the principle of an independent public notary. The KNB maintains that there are virtually no lawsuits concerning sales in The Netherlands, whereas the attitude of the Anglo-Saxon notaries, who act for only one of the parties in a deal, is a significant reason for the existence of many expensive and tiresome lawsuits. To this the house-owners' organization replies that in The Netherlands, already more than 90 per cent of house sales are done using a model contract, which gives little reason for lawsuits anyhow. In The Netherlands people mainly use brokers to negotiate and advise them. The house-owners' organization says that in more than 90 per cent of all estate deeds the public notary services mainly function as an obligatory legal ritual, which adds little value to the actual quality of the deal.

5.10 References

Cannon, T. (1994) *Corporate Responsibility. A textbook on business ethics, governance, environment: roles and responsibilities*, London: Pitman.

De George, R. T. (1990) *Business Ethics*, New York: Macmillan.

de Leeuw, J. and Kannekens, J. (1994) *Bedrijfsethiek voor HBO*, Best: Damon.

Fischer, R., Ury, W. and Patton, B. (1991) *Getting to Yes: Negotiating agreement without giving in*, 2nd edn, New York: Viking Penguin.

Kipnis, K. (1992) 'Engineers who kill: professional ethics and the paramountcy of public safety', in J. H. Fielder and D. Birsch (eds), *The DC-10 Case*, New York: SUNY.

Kotler, P. and Armstrong, G. (1989) *Principles of Marketing*, Englewood Cliffs: Prentice Hall.

MacIntyre, A. (1985) *After Virtue: A study in moral theory*, 2nd edn, London: Duckworth.

NRC Handelsblad (1993a) 'Van Wijnbergen: Polen staat dichter bij de vrije markt dan Nederland' (Van Wijnbergen: Poland comes closer to the free market system than the Netherlands), 24 July.

NRC Handelsblad (1993b) 'Geprivatiseerde water bezorgt Engelsen kommer en kwel' (Privatized water hassles the English), 5 August.

Pastin, M. (1985) 'Ethics as an integrating force in management', *New Jersey Bell Journal*, 8(2), 1–15.

Pastin, M. (1986) *Hard Problems of Mangement*, San Francisco: Jossey-Bass.

Rousseau, J.-J. (1964/1755), *Discours sur l'origine de l'inégalité parmi les hommes*, in *Oeuvres Complètes*, tome III, Paris: Gallimard, Bibliothèque de la Pléiade, 166–7.

Sahlins, M. (1974) *Stone Age Economics*, London: Tavistock.

Verwey, W. (1994) 'Het laatste duwtje' (The last push in the right direction), *NRC Handelsblad*, 27 August.

Vroon, P. (1990) 'Signalement', *De Volkskrant*, 29 December.

6

Is this policy decent, right and just?

6.1 Introduction

In this chapter we study duty ethics in the business environment. Having a sense of urgent moral obligations is part of basic human decency. In business practice, however, it is difficult to mediate between common-sense moral duties and interests.

After explaining the necessity and specific approach of duty-based ethics, we will discuss deontological theories that have been applied to business ethics, that is, theories establishing duty-based moral standards for the business environment. Finally we define balanced and applicable ethical concepts that take into account the relative autonomy of business issues while maintaining a strong commitment to basic values of human decency. To meet this requirement we will have to amend enlightened egoism, allowing for more stringent rights of outside stakeholders.

Duty-based theories have often been applied to business ethics according to unitarian views (see section 2.2). However, caution is needed against overstating moral claims.

6.2 Manipulative and non-manipulative relations

Most of the transactional standards in the previous chapter looked upon moral actions as manipulative relationships with other people and with nature. The transactionalist concept of interest may stop at this point, perceiving every issue as something useful for individual self-interest. Transactionalist theories seem to lack the idea of inviolable values; it seems as if all interests and values are exchangeable. Every stake might be sacrificed whenever other interests offer more gain. The core criticism against this manipulative outlook is that it does not acknowledge the proper or intrinsic value of objects, animals or people. Also transactionalism may exclude other-directed action for the benefit of other individuals. Conversely, many claims in this chapter are based on altruism and respect for others, imposing duties that override self-interest. The strongest claims even set aside other-including self-interest with short-term definitions of win-win situations. A modern example of such strong claims would be the decision of a private corporation to stop producing cigarettes, sacrificing a core business for a strong commitment to public health values, although such strong appeals have not yet been heard concerning the topic of tobacco addiction. Yet other taboos limiting self-interested pursuits are embedded in modern culture. For instance, the prohibition of slavery imposes accepted duties; employing slaves is not done and falls beyond basic principles of modern human decency.

Enlightened egoism does allow for inviolable rights and duties, as it respects minimum rights. As yet, however, we have not defined well enough what type of duties are meant. This chapter will clarify the deontological guidelines that restrain the scope of other-including self-interest. This point is vital, and to overlook it may create great misunderstandings. Enlightened egoism does not see transactions only as a game of reciprocal manipulation.

Not allowing for any moral duties, value creation, mutual obligations or moral commitments indicates a situation in which individuals only use one another. They perceive deals only as a part of economic rationality. Due to the underlying separatist outlook, they are unable to see direct links between commercial behaviour and moral obligation.

A similar manipulative attitude is expressed in many utilitarian cost-benefit calculations concerning natural goods, like those proving the greater utility of preserving tropical rainforests. The value of the rainforest is defined by its use as an object that can be exploited by man. As Charles Taylor (1991) said, when explaining his concept of instrumental reason: 'Once the creatures that surround us lose the significance that accrued to their place in the chain of being, they are open to being treated as raw materials or instruments for our projects' (p. 5).

On the other hand, one may argue that both humans and nature have a value of their own. This intrinsic purpose should not be expressed only by instrumental concepts like its promises, as a source for new palliatives. The basic notion of a purpose for itself, something that cannot be traded off against another value, is expressed in many modern duty-based ethical theories.

6.3 The need for duty ethics in modern societies

Industrial society gives rise to a plurality of moral codes. Modernity creates an unstable social environment where various cultures co-exist under constantly changing conditions. In this context normative ethics has to insist on the values of tolerance and the acceptance of pluralism. Modern open societies ought to prevent both extremes that we encounter nowadays – on one side cynical permissiveness and on the other side nationalistic or fundamentalist cruelty.

In modern open societies we have to cope with the diminished pride for our proper cultural values and face the need to achieve a genuine understanding of other cultures. Business people have to cross cultural borders, and trading with people from other cultural backgrounds requires that we should relate to them as human beings, perceiving them as embedded in a moral community with customs of their own.

Many social groups have to evolve a way of life that is capable of incorporating features that are foreign to their previous autarkic culture. These new social identities arise under the pressure of globalization: (post)-industrial people participate in the expanding commercial network that distributes a growing variety of knowledge, material goods and other services all over the globe. Another factor is the general rise of literacy, which for the first time in human history even involves the lower classes. School and professional training may open minds. We are no longer only educated by our local community when public education is introduced. Finally, it should be noted that the messages that go around the globe are not morally neutral, and one dominant message is the ethical ideal of equal human rights for all.

Humanitarian ambitions mean that modern citizens no longer identify only with the ideals of the nation state: in some ambivalent and vague way they are committed to the welfare of humanity. An example of priority given to human rights before national loyalty is present in the modern German legislation: it recognizes the recruit's right not to enrol in the national army. If his or her moral concerns are accepted, the postwar German citizen can perform non-military public services.

Different forces destabilize our local lifeworld, though not always with positive consequences. In reaction to social changes, all kinds of violent xenophobic feelings may flourish. At the same time as we advocate universal rights, so we assist in the large-scale slaughter of nations and tribes. Whereas Herodotus mainly reported genocides in entire cities in the third century before Christ, modern historians can now study the phenomenon of genocides of entire peoples (Jews, Zingari, Tutsis) or entire social classes like farmers (Ukraine in the 1930s) or literate people (Cambodia). The degrading and dangerous effects of xenophobia, and the bigoted cultivation of these feelings by nationalist politicians, seem to flourish in the 1990s. In Western Europe and the United States, the jubilation of human rights idealists after the defeat of Communism soon ceased, when belligerent politicians triggered ethnic hatred in former Yugoslavia.

The brutalities in Bosnia and Croatia partly result from the organized resurrection of in-group moralities full of hatred towards 'others'. Politicians like Mr Milosevic claim the right to avenge past injustices done to their ethnic group by causing havoc amongst outcasts. Though in Bosnia almost 25 per cent of the marriages were mixed, indicating a large degree of integration and mutual understanding, a combination of several unfavourable factors stirred up a process of blaming 'others'. People now define themselves as members of opposed ethnic parties, perceiving former neighbours as uncompromising enemies.

The opposite extreme of permissive consumerism is equally dangerous. Those who propound superficial theories requiring the obliteration of traditional cultures by globalized groupthink do not understand that they may destroy human civilization. What alternative do they offer in the end? The 'infotainment' culture now spreading over the world may easily lead to petty consumer individualism, paying lip service to abstract values, while actually promoting a self-centred pursuit of private profit, personal comfort, brainless fads and narcissistic posturing.

Contrary to Allan Bloom in his *The Closing of the American Mind*, the directional shift in our modern culture can also be viewed more positively. Other authors are more positive about the modern citizen's search for personal and psychological wellbeing.

> The moral ideal behind self-fulfilment is that of being true to oneself, in a specifically modern understanding. . . . I am going to use the term 'authenticity' for the contemporary ideal. . . . It's not just that people sacrifice their love relationships, and the care for their children, to pursue their careers. Something like this has perhaps always existed. The point is that today many people feel *called* to do this, feel their lives would be somehow wasted or unfulfilled if they didn't do it. (Taylor, 1991, pp. 15–17)

In Chapter 1, we noticed that cultural traditions are attached to human values like truthfulness, mutual respect and not killing or torturing equals. As values they may inspire hope, although the concrete norms and behaviours show that in practice humans may have very narrow definitions of who is 'equal'.

We will end this plea for the recognition of inviolable moral values with an aphorism, an insight pointing to education: people can only treat others with respect, if they have been educated to respect themselves in an affirmative and other-including way.

6.4 The pluralistic duty-based view of human rights

6.4.1 Classical human rights and social rights

A first concrete idea of duty ethics can be exposed by referring to legal rights. Many rights are based on accepted moral obligations; thus, the laws of civilized nations can be seen as a codification of moral rights that are backed by moral duties. Such rights and duties can be divided in two groups.

Classical human rights
Classical human rights were first advocated by philosophers like John Locke, defending every gentleman's right to enjoy the fruits of private property. Basic values are privacy, respect for personal property, life and physical security, freedom of speech and conscience, due process, informed consent and participation in one's social groups. The concrete norms that are codified as human rights go together with stringent duties that are imposed upon public institutions and on the other citizens. All have to show unconditional respect for these individual liberties; others may not infringe them. These rights are *negative rights* insofar as they carve out a sphere of private independence which obliges others, both the state and individuals, to stay out. These ideas had a strong impact on an abstract concept of freedom called 'to be able to do what I want'.

These classical human rights or liberties were prominent values in the struggle of private enterprise against any kind of collectivist restriction – feudal (e.g. eighteenth-century England), corporatist (post-Franco Spain) or Communist (the present privatization policies in Eastern Europe).

Social rights
Social rights are based upon the more recent idea that institutions or other individuals have to guarantee a certain level of welfare for each citizen. These conditional rights stipulate demands made by citizens, to which the institutions addressed and private persons may respond by recognizing a conditional obligation. In the modern welfare state people often address public institutions, but nowadays private organizations also have missions allocated to them in the field of distributing public goods. An example of this is the privatized British water authorities. Individuals may also be urged to work for and give to charities.

Although the agents addressed do not have to satisfy these demands completely, conditional responsibilities are imposed on them: for example, social security has to provide for some income, health insurance has to guarantee payment of hospital bills to some extent, and so forth. The accepted obligations are conditional and not absolute, because much is left to the discretion of the addressees. Above all, the state must arrange the extent and cost of each service.

Social rights are also called *positive rights*, because they affirm the individual citizen's claims upon commodities. For the other contracting party, the institutions distributing specific public commodities and services, they entail less absolute commitments than the classical liberties.

Both categories of rights and duties have common features:

(1) They both put forward powerful moral claims. These claims can be most influential in moral debate, especially when they point to issues of overwhelming importance such as life-threatening risks. Notions of due care as well as public feelings of revolt about dangerous products or services refer to claims for consumer safety.

(2) Both amend claims made by calculative self-interest. They consider certain individual benefits and costs to be of higher priority than others, especially if they imply some unconditional claim. In business ethics especially, many issues relate to clashes between financial benefits and human rights.

(3) Together such rights may constitute a list of moral guidelines for responsible citizens, and have a direct impact on the obligations for corporate governance. They constitute some of the most important expressions of the moral community, and corporate decision-making has to take due account of them.

Here it is important to recall our theory of three moral corporate responsibilities, outlining the minimum commitments made by responsive entrepreneurs. These moral responsibilities can be seen as social duties that are fully accepted by private commercial institutions.

In business environments the classical human rights can give rise to important moral issues, especially those related to whistle-blowing, i.e. putting a stop to wrong practices by seeking publicity, and employee privacy. However, it is clear that not all claims based on negative rights remain absolute in the business environment. Freedom of speech in particular is a touchy issue in an environment where information can be worth lots of money; this negative right appears to be quite limited due to the constraints imposed by the job contract and the corporate culture.

6.4.2 A clash with Confucian powers?

In the early 1990s the Bush administration still was very critical about the civil rights conditions for Chinese citizens. The suppression of the Tiananmen Square revolt was widely covered by the world press agencies, and initially provoked many protests and sanctions. But in May 1994 the Clinton administration prolonged China's status as 'most favoured nation', while dropping the previous checks on human rights conditions in that country. Due to its experiences with Eastern Europe, the Western world no longer claims that democratic political reforms should precede economic development. Especially the Confucian nations in Taiwan and South Korea started by modernizing their economy, and only later introduced democracy.

In the short run the Chinese arguments seem to have gained consideration. At least for 1992 and 1993 it can be maintained that the bulk of the Chinese population were happier and better nourished than the majority of ex-Communist citizens in Rumania, Albania, Russia and Ukraine. The Chinese maintain that providing for economic and social rights takes priority, and that some civil liberties might eventually follow. William Overholt, banker and author of *China, An Awakening Giant*, also explains that the Confucian way starts with economic reforms. We are now starting to respect this approach: 'In the West we cherished Mikhail Gorbachev during his presidency and at the same time we despised Deng Xiaoping. But now there is famine, misery and war in the former Soviet Union. Contrary to that, China's economy flourishes' (*NRC*, 1994).

Most examples of efforts imposing political reforms ahead of serious economic modernization have collapsed. Democratic states build upon a strong, well-educated middle class. This middle class is created by economic modernization.

The 1994 yearbook *Human Rights in Developing Countries* composed by human rights institutions from Norway, Sweden, Denmark, Austria and The Netherlands is more critical about the Chinese policies. Chinese authorities, like Prime Minister Li Peng, have repeated that they give absolute priority to the right to subsistence. The observers contributing to the yearbook notice some severe problems concerning Chinese socio-economic welfare. Disparities are growing between the big economic centres near the sea coast and the inland countryside, while big inequalities also exist within the boom towns. In sum, although social rights are said to be the Chinese government's priority, this does not guarantee that these rights are well taken care of.

Moreover in the end it may turn out to be dangerous for a regime to cultivate a contempt towards the citizens' negative rights, as it may build up frustrations. The fact that public authorities do not create adequate institutions to cope with the legitimate demands of their rising middle class may create a latent civil war. The capitalist tigers in the Eastern Pacific seem to offer their population increasing political democracy, whereas blocking such a perspective is the biggest threat to the future of Communist policies.

6.4.3 How to choose between conflicting rights

The above-mentioned debate between Western human rights institutions and the Chinese regime reveals that these rights themselves offer little guidance when moral rights and duties are in conflict. What we need then is a criterion for giving priority to one right before the other.

> An appeal may be made to certain moral absolutes or various priorities and definitions may be voiced, but, either way, nothing within the deontologic viewpoints explains why these specific views and rankings are correct. . . . Proponents of free-enterprise capitalism, on the one hand, and defenders of forms of socialism or social democracy, on the other, tend to disagree vehemently about the relative priority to be given to the negative versus the positive rights of this list. Free-market theorists usually regard the high rates of taxation needed to fund social programs as unjust or confiscatory and as violations of the right to property, whereas socialists see basic programs of social justice as necessary to serve the basic and 'inalienable' rights of each citizen. These disputes go on within U.S. society and across national boarders with little prospect of agreement.[1] (Green, 1994, p. 71)

It remains true that the criteria for resolving such issues cannot be found within the plurality of concrete human rights. We need higher norms to set priorities. Ron Green (1994) considers that he has found such a criterion in his NORM method, which will be discussed later.

We now examine a classical method for verifying whether a rule or right is morally acceptable. Its author called it a litmus test for accepting moral guidelines, and remains one of the most powerful theories of general ethics. However, this theory does not contain any rules for choosing between conflicting guidelines. Its proper merit lies in defining the essence of a duty-based attitude. No more, no less.

---

[1]Reprinted with the permission of Prentice Hall, Inc. from *The Ethical Manager: A new method for business ethics*. Ronald M. Green. Copyright © 1994.

6.5 The deontological supernorm of Kant[2]

6.5.1 The litmus test for moral guidelines

The ethical theory of Immanuel Kant (1724–1804) is held to be the most clear-cut example of a duty-based theory, excluding any outcome-based criterion. He formulates a general test for the moral validity of concrete moral norms. His test does not prescribe what we have to do. It may still allow for a multitude of various rules, but it discards the clearly immoral ones. Kant claims it to be a universally valid test for moral rules, a supernorm. As mentioned before in Chapter 1, this supernorm can be seen as an improved version of the golden rule.

Here initially is a brief statement of the general idea behind this test. The supernorm can be worded by two main questions. First, a question checking moral guidelines for partiality: Would you like everybody to behave like that? Also, one may check for its respect of individual autonomy and human dignity. This leads to the second, negatively worded, question: Does this concrete guideline accept abuse of human decency, that is, does it only use yourself or others as a passive instrument, with no respect for human decency and disregarding individual free will?

More precisely, Kant's theory maintains that one should only follow guidelines that meet the following three criteria:

1. Reversibility.
2. Universalizability.
3. Respect for human beings as persons with their own will.

We will first discuss how the first and second of these criteria constitute the backbone of his first categorical imperative. This imperative runs as follows: *'An action is morally right if its maxim can become a general rule for everybody acting in a similar situation'* (Kant, 1965/1785; my translation). It checks whether the applied guidelines (norms or 'maxims') meet the criteria of reversibility (1) and universal acceptability (2). Though reversibility is in fact part of the second criterion, it deserves separate attention, especially for those applying enlightened egoism.

Reversibility is present in the question like 'What if others did to you, what you intend to do to them?' It verifies whether the reasons for applying the line of conduct in one way might also be applied the other way around.

---

[2]See also section 1.7.

It warrants against partial rules, by checking out unfair exceptions made on one's own behalf.

The second criterion, universalizability, is present in questions like, 'What if everybody behaved like this?' It checks out whether the line of conduct can be applied to every reasonable human being in similar circumstances. This also covers conduct that may harm the agent or inflict harm on non-humans, that is, animals or the physical environment.

In another formulation of the categorical imperative Kant introduces a third fundamental criterion: the idea that human beings may not treat themselves nor other human beings only as a means, because of the unconditional respect we owe to our rational nature and to each person's ability to behave as a moral agent with an autonomous will. Moral action implies respecting ourselves and others as moral agents. As we are autonomous individuals with our own will, humans are *ends in themselves*. We call this third criterion the idea of intrinsic human dignity (3).

Thus the second, amended version of the categorical imperative states: *'See to it that your actions respect the human dignity of yourself as well as of everybody else, by treating each person not merely as a means, but also as an end in itself'* (Kant, 1965/1785; my translation).

In various examples, Kant allowed for virtues here. He insisted on choosing actions that foster the further development of human autonomy, character and benevolence, and pointed to the importance of overcoming obstacles and depressions by personal strength and perseverance. This element indicates ideas that will be discussed in the next chapter.

For duty-based ethics it is more interesting to see what this moral principle of humans as ends in themselves means for human relations. Our contracts should respect each one's capacity to choose, and even foster it.

Some misunderstandings about the second formulation of the categorical imperative have to be mentioned. Above all, respecting the fact that other people have a will of their own does not imply that we may not call upon other people to serve our goals. In fact, commercial exchange is made up from this. For example, when we order something in a shop, we are using somebody's services as a means to obtain something for ourselves. Kant, however, insists that such services should be part of a (tacit) understanding between moral agents. Thus, when we call upon the services of the shop assistant, we do not simply use that person, because he or she has voluntarily accepted to do this job. Due to that contract, that person has chosen autonomously to provide those services that fall within the scope of the job. Both parties trade on the basis of this contract. When there is no coercion or abuse on one or the other side, there exists a mutual respect for everybody's will. Therefore commercial deals can be quite moral, providing that they also respect each person's ability to make autonomous choices.

This ethical theory claims that whatever our personal interest may be, we may never simply use other people, but should always show respect to ourselves and to others, thus living up to the idea that all humans are non-manipulable moral agents with a capacity for making autonomous choices.

The interdiction against using others *only* as a means implies that, according to this imperative, one may not overrun other people's interests completely. On the basis of this respect for human dignity, it is forbidden to murder, lie, steal or cheat.

6.5.2 Kantian duty ethics insists on pure intentions

In a recent book Tom Sorrell and John Hendry (1994) explain that Kant's theory is about the quality of the motives we have. As soon as our reasons for doing something depend on some external goal, they are of lower moral standing. Kant insisted on the purity of moral goodwill: that is, one should not do things because of the outcome, but because the action itself is right. According to Kant, moral action is not a matter of doing things which also comply to moral duties, but a matter of doing the right things out of a sense of moral obligation. The best motive is the will to do one's duty.

Here lies a difference of opinion with his followers, who stress the importance of respecting persons: 'The difference between Kant's theory and Kantian theories in general – theories inspired by Kant but different in formulation – is usually a matter of their dropping the emphasis on purity of moral motivation and laying weight instead on the concept of respect of persons' (Sorrell and Hendry, 1994, p. 37). It is important to see that Kantian theories insist on obeying certain rights, but that this obedience can quite well be motivated by strategic or even manipulative concerns. The purity of the intentions is no longer as important as it was in Kant's original theory.

Thus if one follows a unitarian view of the relationship between business and society, one may have to conclude: 'it may be that enlightened self-interest is one thing and morality another.' In the sentences that follow this passage, Sorrell and Hendry outline the distinction between complying with moral duty and actually being committed to one's moral duty:

Or again, it may be that the right way to classify most ventures in . . . business ethics is as Kant classifies right actions done from natural warmth and sympathy, namely as acts that are honourable, amiable and generally useful, but acts that are, nevertheless, not all they might be morally speaking – dutiful without being done from duty. This way of classifying acts would not necessarily undervalue partnership schemes in inner cities or training programmes for the disadvantaged; at the same, it would acknowledge the basis there is for supposing that morality is in tension with self-interest. (1994, p. 39)

This indicates the priority Kant gives to reasonable motivation. The ultimate check for moral quality consists in examining whether the individual wants to live up to the idea of behaving according to moral laws – that is, whether one does apply rule-guided behaviour, committed to the idea that one has to contribute to one's moral community by acting in an impartial and considerate way.

6.5.3 Problems with applying Kant

Duty ethics' insistence on personal moral commitment, on doing things because they can be universalized, is one of the most demanding criteria in ethics. It can be seen as an optimum, indicating that most actions are of lower moral standing as they include mixed motives and take outcomes into account. Our general problem with this position is comparable with our criticism of utilitarianism. Kant asks too much from morality in an abstract overrationalizing way. More specifically, it provides no guidelines for business morality.

Kant refuses to mediate between moral duty and self-interest or private benefits. Referring to our example in section 4.7.2, always doing one's duty means here that the true Kantian consumer would always have to tell the mistaken salesperson that the bill was too low, even if the salesperson's service is unfriendly and bad. This is the moral maximum, a position that imposes strict general duties.

On the other hand, many people, especially when educated in a permissive society that stresses the values of individual satisfaction and self-preservation, may incline towards other attitudes. They feel that other solutions are not as 'ethical', but are morally at least as acceptable and more rewarding. The risk of being too benign and nice is overt. In game theory tit-for-tat strategy was believed to be the best for a long time, but taking abuse from kind-hearted and slowly reacting idealists appears to be even more productive. This latter approach is called the Pavlov strategy. In a business environment, inflexible Kantians may lose easily against the first Pavlovian they come across.

A related problem is the issue of reacting towards violations. What should we do when confronted by people who violate moral duties? In The Netherlands, ethicists use this example: How do you behave in front of the Gestapo policemen who are asking you whether you know where Jews are hiding? American ethics teachers use the example of the axe-swinging man with bloodshot eyes who runs up to your doorstep asking, 'Did you see somebody run past here a few minutes ago?' According to Kant one should always tell the truth, as this is always part of one's duty. But how should we act in these cases when the questions come from criminals who are endangering innocent people? Kant's theory cannot cope with the issue of retaliation against such violations; his moral theory has little room for countervailing violence in order to protect potential victims.

More fundamentally, Kant has a rather abstract idea of free choice. He maintains that disregarding given circumstances and possible outcomes, people always have to live up to their moral duties, simply because a guideline meets the criterion of universalizability best. Conversely, our definition of free choice allows for the consideration of given circumstances and accepts that people have certain vital needs. This may even lead to the conclusion that eating one's dead friends is morally acceptable in the very specific context of the Andes aeroplane crash.

Concerning our subject, business ethics, we consider that Kant did have some inspiring ideas. In particular, he pointed to the merit of people who perform out of a sense of moral duty. Also, he portrayed morally responsible behaviour as adhering to generally acceptable, impartial and therefore reasonable rules.

The principal notions of Kant's deontology are present in Neutral Omnipartial Rule Making, a normative theory on moral decision-making by Ronald Green. Before outlining and criticizing this theory, we should first review some concrete topics of corporate duty ethics.

6.6 Standards of justice

6.6.1 Various purposes for justice principles

A general idea of justice runs as follows: *similar cases should be treated the same way, but if there are relevant differences, deviating treatments are allowed in proportion to the difference.* This general idea expresses principles of impartiality and equity.

When applying justice three purposes exist:

1. *Distribution of benefits and burdens. Distributive justice* refers to the fair distribution of costs and gains. One main topic of distributive justice is how to reward employees. We will expand on this idea by exposing the difference between egalitarianism and capitalist justice.

2. *Punishing law-breakers and those who do wrong. Retributive justice* norms aim at fair penalties for the inflicted harm. A good example of such

underlying moral principles are the three theories of product liability described in Chapter 4.

3. *Compensation for those that have suffered from a harm or injury. Compensatory justice* should impose norms that are proportional to the suffered losses and injury. Liability issues illustrate that compensatory indemnities are often the counterpart of retributive sanctions.

6.6.2 Egalitarianism and capitalist justice

Egalitarianism

Egalitarians claim that people should have an equal share of a (*micro-*) *society's burdens and benefits*. As a normative concept egalitarianism makes a strong and quite interesting claim with a long history, dating back to famous practices like ancient Sparta and still outstanding works of philosophy like Plato's *Republic*. Nowadays egalitarian theory often expresses quite noble ideas of solidarity in the public domain.

A very influential egalitarian claim was that state socialist policy should provide for equal access to educational and health services, welfare or even work. It is currently felt that social-democrat egalitarianism has been useful in providing basic welfare, but in certain rich countries this welfare state shows symptoms of decline. Especially, the redistribution of wealth is done by inefficient bureaucracies. Also, welfare policies become counterproductive, greatly contributing to the growth of the non-working part of the population. In this last decade of the twentieth century, the affluent societies of Western Europe must decide upon new distributive policies that safeguard the access of poor citizens to certain public services without suffocating the national economy.

Capitalist justice

Velasquez defines capitalist justice as follows: 'benefits should be distributed according to the contribution each individual makes to achieving the aims of his or her group (the team, firm, society, humanity, etc.)' (Velasquez, 1992, p. 93).

6.6.3 Two principles of capitalist justice

Here, the core question is: Should companies reward work effort or productivity?

Most shop assistants are often paid for the hours they work, without any direct link with their sales. Contrary to this, travelling salesmen often get high commissions for their productivity.

Individual contribution can be assessed in various ways, fitting in somewhere between the following two extremes:

1. Reward for output, i.e. rewarding productivity by applying piece rates, commissions, or other bonus systems allied to actual work results.
2. Reward for input, i.e. rewarding work efforts, which often equates to the number of hours you spend at your job.

6.7 Deontological codes for inner constituents in business

Here we discuss briefly two approaches towards corporate codes: company philosophy, and the detailed deontologic codes of conduct. They can both be classified as duty-based ethics.

6.7.1 Company philosophy

The company philosophy explains the general corporate values. It is not merely a list of deontological duties as it also includes definitions of company objectives. Such written codes formulate the basic commitments at the core of a company culture. These codes containing the corporate philosophy serve as a company constitution setting out the chief moral objectives and duties. They define a set of values the company wants to practise. The more general these principles are, the more dangerous they may become in creating the illusion that the simple incantation of these rules will guarantee moral behaviour. Practised from the top down they can be very inspiring, presenting the corporate moral vision.

In section 4.2 we mentioned the example of the Schiphol Airport Authority that started an in-company campaign in which the moral aspects were directly linked to the corporate mission statement. If carefully planned and widely spread within the corporation, allowing for feedback and congruent behaviour, such programmes can be quite effective and morally rewarding. They create value commitment.

6.7.2 Deontological codes

Deontological codes stipulate detailed duties for employees towards their company and towards suppliers or customers. They are often only relevant for one field of business operations, like the relationship between the buying department and suppliers. The Texaco guidelines define detailed rules providing against the risk of bribery. The more specific such guidelines are, the more tempting it becomes to encroach upon their authority, especially if we are not wholly committed to them. Also, experience shows that it is impossible to provide for all new temptations that suppliers may invent (in co-operation with merely rule-abiding buyers). The best course of action is not simply to control on the basis of mistrust, but to foster a positive commitment. Implementing such detailed rules involves personnel training and monitoring, because the staff should be motivated to apply the spirit behind those rules.

6.7.3 Conditions for making codes effective

In a recent Dutch study Kaptein and Klamer (1991) list six conditions for effective codes of ethics:

1. *A valid motivation for its introduction*. It should insist on important benefits for adopting and complying with the code. An 'us too' attitude is not enough.

2. *Broad acceptance within the company*. Involve representatives from all departments in the process of elaborating the code. The code should be discussed, checked and redefined before it is finally laid down.

3. *Continuous feedback*. Difficulties occur during the implementation of the code, and also norms on how to act in specific situations change. This calls for feedback. Living up to a code is not simply a matter of blindly applying rules, it is part of a process.

4. *Verification and control*. Any inconsistencies between rules and practice should be disclosed. One method of achieving this is peer discussions. New guidelines should be drawn up if the rules prove inadequate in any way.

5. *Integration into a broad company philosophy on corporate services and responsibilities*. The set of rules should be part of a wider ethical mission statement. This may involve staff training programmes, a company ethical committee or discussions with external stakeholders.

6. *Sanctions and control*. Compliance with codes needs enforcement, both positive and negative. In order to become effective, some system of sanctions must exist. Free-wheeling permissiveness would only lead to lip service. Many companies do now have severe sanctions against, for example, bribery.

6.7.4 A criticism of single-minded deontology

It is of utmost importance that codes of ethics do not remain an accessory and non-vital issue. They should be directly related to the main corporate mission statements.

If a code of ethics is only implemented as a kind of isolated Sunday sermon, while behind the scenes ruthless commercial practices go on as usual, the code will remain ineffective. However, as soon as the direct link with the corporate culture is made, and as soon as the corporate leadership commits itself to some moral principles that they actively promote and foster, then the code becomes an inspiring beacon for the corporate culture.

Narrow-minded codes with a list of employer duties will not work. Simply imposing on people a whole set of obligations without explaining their vital purpose has nothing to do with fostering the growth of a moral business community. A more high-profile idea of corporate purpose committed to public goods will be expounded in Chapter 7.

6.8 NORM by Ronald Green

Neutral, Omnipartial Rule Making (NORM) is a new method of moral reasoning. In *The Ethical Manager*, Ronald Green presents a creative mix of duty ethics and transactional ethics, leading to a coherent and sophisticated approach. This method has another interesting feature: it allows for a stakeholder model of responsibility.

However, NORM is still based on a unitarian philosophy of the relation between business and society. In most of his examples Green strikes on vital insights into moral decision-making, yet in some respects he seems to ignore the rights of corporate strategic interests, asking for a too benevolent attitude. This argument will be explained by discussing the Harlingen Hospital case already described in Chapter 2.

Finally, we will redefine the scope of application for the NORM method by incorporating it in a new concept of enlightened egoism (see section 6.7.5).

In itself NORM contains some of the best-developed principles for ethical decision-making, principles which can usefully be applied in economic legislation and for codifying voluntary codes for entire branches of corporations. In one field of moral thought, however, the method may be overstating things: it may ask too much from individual corporations.

6.8.1 An example of a value conflict in business

Green presents a simple case posing problems to adherents of outcome-based theories and to enlightened egoism. How enlightened egoism applies to in-company relations and towards competitors is not yet clear, as it may allow for radically opposed solutions.

A case entitled 'The cost of keeping a secret' presents the dilemma facing a design engineer, Philip Cortez. Half a year ago he left his job at Lifeworth, and accepted a job with their main competitor National Rubber and Tire. After six months his new employer asked him to co-operate in designing a 120,000 kilometre, puncture-proof radial tire. At his former employer, Lifeworth, 'he had been instrumental in drawing up designs for a similar tire that Lifeworth was not only very interested in producing but was also counting on to revitalize its sagging profit posture' (Green, 1994, p. 46).

When starting with Lifeworth he had signed a written agreement, promising 'to refrain from disclosing any classified information directly or indirectly to competitors for a period of two years after his termination with Lifeworth'. When he announced his departure Lifeworth's president had reminded him of this agreement, insisting on the fact that his work on the new radial was highly classified. 'Cortez had assured the president that he anticipated no conflict of interests since National had given him every reason to believe that it wanted him primarily in a managerial capacity.'

After six months at National his engineering director made it clear to Cortez that they needed his technical input on this new project. So during a talk with the director Cortez explained his dilemma:

> While sympathetic to Cortez's predicament, the director broadly hinted that refusal to provide constructive input would not only result in a substantial disservice to National but was bound to affect Cortez's standing with the firm. 'After all', the director said, 'it is very difficult to justify paying a man a handsome salary and expediting his movement up the organizational ladder when his allegiances obviously lie elsewhere.' (Ibid., pp. 46–7)

Most duty-ethical theories will give a plain answer to any question about where Phil Cortez's obligations lie. Moral duties like honouring trust and keeping promises will oblige him not to yield to the engineering director's pressure, even if that will jeopardize Phil's career at National. We believe that this is the most valid reply for other reasons too, especially from the point of view of maintaining one's reputation and self-respect. However, we have to admit that certain people adhering to a purely transactionalist and short-term view of private interest might advise a contrary solution, blurring the distinction between in-group and enlightened egoism.

It appears, therefore, that enlightened egoism still allows for considerable flaws in defining minimum obligations towards outside stakeholders.

6.8.2 Green on the impasse in business ethics theory

Green criticizes many American textbooks on business ethics for their poor ethical foundation. They waver between two irreconcilable theories, duty ethics and utilitarianism.

In practice it often happens that these two quite opposed theoretical outlooks indicate conflicting solutions for concrete dilemmas. Green thus formulates the impasse which readers of current textbooks may reach: '"Is it rights that tell us whether something is ethical" they have asked, "or is it the beneficial consequences we produce by our choices and actions?"' (Green, 1994, p. vi.).

He reviews both approaches, and comments on a utilitarian estimate of the social costs and benefits in the Phil Cortez case:

> If Phil were to break his promise to his former employer, Lifeworth, his new firm, National Rubber and Tire, would more quickly produce the radial tire. . . . Lifeworth would lose the benefit from its expenditures on research but National's gain might balance this out. Consumers would benefit by the prompt introduction of a safer tire and by the existence of two competing manufacturers, and Phil, of course, could keep his job with its handsome rewards. (Ibid., p. 79)

This is what we call a hedonistic short-term-minded reply. But not all utilitarians have to think so; according to other interpretations of utility standards the alternative solution is best.

Just as in the Pinto case other utilitarians may insist more on the danger of publicity about this abuse of confidential information:

> If Phil breaks his promise to Lifeworth, all firms that invest heavily in proprietary research will now feel threatened. . . . Utilitarians argue that these longer-term negative (or 'indirect') consequences of such practices as promise-breaking and deception are what make them so clearly unwise and immoral. (Ibid., p. 80)

Right after this passage, Green states his criticism of act utilitarianism, because of the assumption it makes that moral standards aim at preventing harmful consequences, not at respecting duties:

> this whole line of reasoning . . . hinges on people's learning of Phil's conduct, but none of this need occur if Phil and his firm actively strive to prevent it from happening. As a good utilitarian, Phil can agree to

betray Lifeworth's secrets so long as he and National succeed in making it appear that he has not done so. (Ibid.)

After portraying the conclusions of utilitarian and other outcome-based theories as leading to conclusions that defy moral common sense, Green can affirm that both theories seem to lead to a dead end:

> Although moral theorists have made great progress in clarifying the underlying presuppositions of our moral thinking, the net result of all this theorizing has been to sharpen a basic question: Does all our moral thinking rest on certain indispensable moral requirements such as fidelity, honesty, fairness, and justice [duties]; or may these requirements be set aside when they interfere with the well-being of identifiable people [outcomes]? (Ibid., p. 83)

As a good rhetorician and a valid moral philosopher, Green immediately promises that he will not leave us unsatisfied: 'Fortunately, despair is not our option. In Chapter 3, I examine a third approach to moral reasoning that seeks to resolve the conflict between deontology and utilitarianism.'

The NORM theory is based on the abstract idea of free choice, as already present in the writings of Kant. It has a universalist thrust, holding that morally acceptable rules should be impartial and acceptable to all stakeholders concerned. Its purpose is announced in the following words:

> I explore a third theoretical approach to moral choice, an approach I call *Neutral, Omnipartial Rule Making* (NORM). This approach aims at drawing the best from deontological and utilitarian theories. Like utilitarianism, NORM tries to develop the underlying logic of our moral reasoning process in terms of a basic principle or procedure for choice and then tries to carry this forward into new and difficult areas of moral decision. Like deontology, it tries to produce results more congruent with our moral common sense than does utilitarianism. (Ibid., p. 86; original emphasis)

Before explaining the proper assumptions of the NORM method, we want to comment on this pronouncement by recalling some fundamentals of our own text. First, enlightened egoism also contains a basic principle or procedure. Second, we hold that congruency with moral common sense is not the ultimate criterion in business ethics; such an argument destroys the buffer screen we drew between the economic sphere guided by relatively autonomous rational procedures, and the larger moral community of society. Although Green presents an interesting new method, he holds a unitarian view of business and society.

6.8.3 NORM

At the beginning of his third chapter, Green acknowledges his debt to Kant:

> Kant's famous guide for ethics, the Categorical Imperative, is often interpreted as a deontological principle (because it prohibits making happiness the primary objective of moral choice), but it also can be interpreted as an important early statement of a NORM-type approach. (Green, 1994, p. 87)

With this remark the author refers to the contract tradition.

The criterion for accepting an action as right is then defined as follows:

> An action is right if it *might reasonably be thought of as being accepted by all members of society as a moral rule, that is, as an abiding form of conduct known by everyone and open to everyone in similar circumstances.* (Ibid., pp. 87–8)

Green then goes on to explain that this is not relativism, as it imposes a stringent procedure aiming at initial respect for all participants. NORM expresses a principle of equity, it holds that morality aims at fair and principled settlement of disputes. This principle states as an ideal that everyone in society should approve the rules of conduct:

> Acceptable moral rules are not the result of majority will but of *free* consensus of all the people who live under them. This excludes the possibility of victimization of subgroups within a community. . . . This means that morality is ideally universal in scope, embracing all possible parties to conflicts and empowering them as moral rule-makers. Far from legitimizing the imposition of one group's values on another's, NORM requires the free consent of *all* parties affected by a form of conduct. (Ibid., p. 88)

The second point is about the possibility of reaching a free consensus on social conduct. The feasibility of this consensual approach seems quite comprised, making it unrealistic. Green himself states objections:

> People have different values and different beliefs, and they stand in such different positions of power that almost no form of conduct meets everyone's approval. Nor, as the sad history of our century reveals, is any particular act – no matter how wicked – universally condemned. (Ibid.)

In his reply Green insists that NORM contains a normative criterion, which is the procedure of impartiality. When facing opposed viewpoints we ought to apply this criterion:

take the position of each party to a dispute seriously, but [do] not identify with it uniquely, and then do the same for all other positions in the controversy. After evaluating all positions, we are better able to arrive at a decision that is objective and fair to each party. (Ibid.)

Green then discards the term 'impartiality' for implying coolness and detachment. He prefers a positive moral commitment to open-minded moral thinking. To do so he invents the word *omnipartiality*:

it suggests full, empathetic identification with the beliefs, feelings, and interests of each person our decision affects. At the same time, omnipartiality requires a stance of neutrality before competing claims. Parents exercise omnipartiality whenever they must decide between the competing claims and needs of their children. It is this approach of engaged, involved neutrality and evenhandedness that the NORM method requires. (Ibid., p. 89)

6.8.4 The contract-based social philosophy behind NORM duties

This method can be understood better if one first considers some presuppositions of this contract view of moral obligations. The idea of a social contract was first formulated by modern philosophers like Hobbes. Here the word 'modern' refers to a revolt against traditional virtue theory. As Green seems to regard man as a more co-operative and less violent being than as portrayed by Hobbes, the idea of social contract can better be explained by reference to John Locke (1632–1704). According to Locke men join together 'for the mutual preservation of their lives, liberties and estates, which I call by the general name, property' (Locke, 1948/1789, ch. 9).

The underlying idea of man seems to be one of a rational but competitive individual, who is willing to trade in order to make arrangements acceptable for all parties concerned. This is a very modern and abstract idea of human motives that dates back to Hobbes' philosophy of egoistic man. As we indicated in our previous chapter, other theories insist more on our tribal and communitarian roots; they would study morality as embedded in the culture we share with direct relatives.

Green's idea of man points to the rationalistic citizen with a normative commitment and calculative willingness to bargain according to principles of abstract equity and respect for other citizens as equal stakeholders. It stresses the principle of mutual consent based on the participant's free will. Like the Kantian ethics it risks defining rules that are too abstract, and which, although first agreed upon, have to be redefined as they are impracticable in the given circumstances. In other words, rational people can be mistaken about which rules are the best. The use of abstract free will is no guarantee of feasible and optimum solutions, as the main participants in the deal can misunderstand what is the most skilful.

6.8.5 NORM only accepts socially beneficial private concerns

We believe that the NORM method is quite applicable in the general moral community, and that it can also be applied when making laws which impose duties and constraints on the whole sphere of economic activity. But we wonder whether enlightened egoism is better suited to the specific situation in which the *individual* corporation or non-profit organization finds itself.

There is no doubt that NORM can formulate optimum rules, but it may ask for too much public benevolence from managers when they subscribe to the great responsibilities they feel towards inner constituents – shareholders, employees, or consumers.

Let us study first in detail how Neutral, Omnipartial Rule Making is applied in the Cortez case.

When Cortez faces the option of breaking his promise to his former employer, Lifeworth, he may start by formulating the moral rule implicit in his choice:

This rule might read: *An employee who has promised not to reveal proprietary information and who has been given access to it may break his promise whenever a more lucrative offer comes along or whenever he is threatened with firing by a new employer for not doing so.* Phil must then ask whether he would omnipartially accept this rule if he were to put himself in the shoes of all relevant parties: his previous employer and present employer, other employees, and members of society generally. . . . it is not hard to identify the good reasons for *not* accepting this proposed rule. In a society governed by it, employers would be far less able to trust employees, research and development would suffer or be replaced by industrial espionage, and a bidding war would ensue for employees' loyalties. Although Phil might find some support for his rule if he looked at it narrowly from his perspective or that of his new employer, there are overwhelming interests on the other side that oppose it. Ironically, in a society where this proposed rule governed everyone's behaviour, the very information that Phil's new firm seeks would probably no longer be available, since companies would either halt research or would take costly steps to prevent employees from having access to its results. Reasoning in this way, Phil must conclude that what he proposes to do cannot become a publicly known and accepted moral rule and, hence, that he cannot morally break his promise. (Green, 1994, pp. 92–3)

More generally, Green comments on duty-based rules, such as promise-keeping, by referring to omnipartial morality. The conclusion that practices like telling the truth, keeping promises and just treatment of persons are recommendable guidelines points back to their social or omnipartial utility:

> [truth telling, keeping promises and just treatment] form part of the public expectations on which we build our conduct, and because any departure from them must be considered as being approved by us all. NORM takes the mystery out of the intrinsic validity of these deontological rules and explains why deontology has been an attractive moral viewpoint. (Ibid.)

He also explains that his method allows for resolving conflict between rules:

> NORM does not always require us to uphold the standard moral rules. In each instance of choice what is important is not whether a specific rule is upheld or violated, but whether our actions *might reasonably be thought of as being accepted by anyone who looked at the matter in an informed and impartial way as an abiding form of conduct known by everyone and open to everyone in similar circumstances.* Sometimes this reasoning can lead us to make exceptions to a moral rule or to restate the rule in more specific ways. (Ibid.)

We will now apply NORM to the Harlingen Hospital case in Chapter 2. The hospital board had first decided upon the rule that whoever stole from the fee pool would be dismissed. When they saw on the hidden video camera recordings that the culprit was their only neurologist, they had to reconsider their standards because of the adverse consequences of applying equal justice in this matter.

In this particular case, the general moral rule stating 'equal justice rules for all' should run as follows, without regard for the adverse consequences: 'An employee or partner that steals from the fee pot should be dismissed, even if it implies the closing down of a department, the dismissal of innocent employees and a weaker bargaining position in the ongoing merger talks.' For society in general a moral rule like this may be acceptable; balancing all the likely consequences of applying the 'equal justice for all' rule plus the risk inherent in making an exception to this rule may well incline us to stick to this initial guideline. From the point of view of social utility, closing one department in this small hospital might be counterbalanced by improved services at the main hospital. Even the consequences for nursing staff should not be exaggerated, for they may receive priority consideration for vacancies at the main hospital.

Still our question remains: Should we ask an individual actor (private or public institution) to sacrifice its own interests in order to comply with some obligation towards uncertain social benefits? More specifically, to what extent does NORM acknowledge that separate instituton's right to pursue strategic interests?

We do not find any trace of an integration view in Green's text. This absence seldom leads to big problems, except in issues involving duties towards corporate outsiders, like the unemployed and in the Cortez example above, which presents an intricate case of competitive and moral issues. The arguments for allowing exceptions on promise-keeping rules never refer to corporate interests; rather they point towards the overwhelming concerns of larger social entities like the entire nation. In the Cortez case Green holds that under specific political conditions promise-breaking is acceptable:

> We saw that Phil is ordinarily bound to uphold the promise to his previous employer. Would this be true if the year were 1939 and Phil was a refugee to the United States whose previous employer was a German manufacturer of vital aircraft components? (Green, 1994, ch. 3)

Exceptions are made when we are confronted with a party that promotes despotism and negates the very possibility of impartial and peaceful rule-making. But how about in the ordinary business environment, where corporations are sometimes allies, but more often compete with each other? Must they always accept the best social solution, even though a far less perfect – but morally still comprehensible – rule may better serve the long-term interests of the most direct stakeholders?

A final question concerns the need for a level playing-field. In most examples NORM proves to be quite a strong ethical theory. However, what happens when some parties contest basic assumptions by pointing to implicit partialities? One example of this is the bookyear 1992–93 loss of Euro Disney ($900 million), which is four times the sum earned by Michael Eisner, CEO of the Walt Disney Corporation: $203 million revenue (in 1993). How should we handle criticisms that ask why a corporation with an overall poor performance may apply a rule which allows for massive dismissals of minor employees while the CEO gets a world record annual income? Japanese management in particular has a quite different view of just division of burdens and benefits. Although we hold NORM to be one of the best theories in business ethics, it appears to assume too easily that the moral dilemmas studied take place on a level playing-field; the method seems to lack critical awareness in relation to specific institutionalized kinds of corporate injustice.

Nevertheless Green does make a strong case in favour of employee rights, especially regarding the requirement for employees to be able to participate in big decisions affecting their own lives and futures:

> Rather than spelling out specific criteria for acceptable employer conduct, the right to participate gives employees a say in complex circumstances by moving a company closer to the basic situation of informed, omnipartial choice. (Green, 1994, p. 196)

6.9 Incorporating NORM-based rules in enlightened egoism

We may now try to redefine enlightened egoism by incorporating certain aspects of the NORM method. Adherents of a unitarian view will have no problem in applying Green's sophisticated method. We, however, will try to formulate a less high-profile and more minimalist idea of corporate responsibility.

Its main difference to NORM is that enlightened egoism still distinguishes between two types of constituencies: the directly involved parties and the outside stakeholders. Our minimalist position holds that omnipartial neutrality asks too much from our limited stretch in loyalties. Omnipartial neutrality may lead to ideal rules, but these rules do not allow much room for zealous entrepreneurs seeking to establish excellent relationships with their suppliers and consumers.

Here we not only incorporate elements of NORM, but also refer to the minimalist theory of corporate responsibility described in Chapter 4. Enlightened egoism allows for in-groups, and requires a calculated acceptance of agreed consumer requirements. It also shows willingness to dispose of the harmful consequences for other stakeholders, which can be demonstrated by environmental care and concern for employee rights, health and safety.

The following algorithm amends box 3.1, 'Neutral, Omnipartial Rule Making' in *The Ethical Manager* (Green, 1994, p. 97), and tries to give a more elaborate and complete idea of enlightened egoism. It defines enlightened egoism-2:

1. Look at the issue on the basis of a normative assumption, enlightened self-interest. Aspire to an open-minded defence of your interests, while respecting those of others.

2. Identify not only the directly involved parties, but also the outside stakeholders who may be affected by possible outcomes. Even if

consumers remain silent and are actually made up of outside non-participating stakeholders, consider them to be your chief constituency.

3. (*Condition A*) Allow for the strategic interests of the directly involved parties by defining optional win-win solutions for these inner constituencies (i.e. articulate members of the directly negotiating parties).

4. (*Condition B*) Now formulate the conduct that has to be evaluated as a moral rule. This rule prescribes a form of conduct obligatory for inner constituents, which also stipulates minimal moral rights and duties concerning the outside stakeholders, especially the silent constituency of your clients.

5. Reason omnipartially when deciding on the minimum rights you should all allow towards outside stakeholders:
   (a) put yourself in the shoes of both directly concerned and outside stakeholders;
   (b) *using as a guide their interests and all the facts you can obtain*, determine the benefit and harm which will be done to outside stakeholders, both now and in the foreseeable future, by the intended conduct.

6. Weigh up *both* the immediate effects of this conduct *and* its impact as a moral rule, taking into consideration such matters as its impact on wellbeing, and the quantity, duration, and likelihood of harms and benefits involved.

7. Ask yourself whether both the strategic outcome and the moral consequences of this proposed line of conduct merit the application of this rule. If your answer is no, regard this conduct as *ethically wrong business*. If your answer is yes, the conduct is *ethically right business*.

8. If your answer is no, try to define alternative rules that first and foremost are less harmful to outside stakeholders.

9. *In addition to Condition A* When opponents do not play this rule, and only look for their own blatant self-interest, take the following steps as necessary and return to item 3 above as soon as the outcome is strategically acceptable:
   (a) foster the development of more friendly relations, and strengthen and make the use of reasonable methods of rewarding negotiations;
   (b) menace in retaliation;
   (c) coerce, bully, flee or fight, but do this while keeping a clear idea of the interests at stake, and knowing that in the end game, reliable

co-operation should prove the best tactic (especially in the corporation–suppliers–consumer relationship).

10. At a minimal level one may check the moral consequences for outside stakeholders of applying Singer's rights for primates (see section 3.2.3) to the humans involved.

11. The resulting policy will be an example of enlightened egoism, version two. It is a quite acceptable minimum position for agents in the economic sphere.

As a final comment, enlightened egoism cannot lead to voluntary sacrifices of vital individual interests and rights. Selfless solidarity and benevolent contribution to public goods are based on other more purely *moral* principles.

6.10 References

Green, R. M. (1994) *The Ethical Manager: A new method for business ethics*, New York: Macmillan.

Kant, I. (1965/1785) *Grundlegung zur Metaphysik der Sitten*, K. Vorländer (ed.), Hamburg: F. Meiner Verlag.

Kaptein, S. P. and Klamer, H. K. (1991) *Ethische bedrijfscodes in Nederlandse bedrijven*, Nederlandse Christelijke Werkgevers (Christian Dutch Employers), internal report.

Locke, J. (1948/1789) *Second Treatise on Civil Government*, J. W. Gough (ed.), Oxford: Oxford University Press.

NRC Handelsblad (1994) 'Welvaart is de beste garantie voor mensenrechten' (Prosperity is the best safeguard for human rights), 27 May.

Sorrell, T. and Hendry, J. (1994) *Business Ethics*, Oxford: Butterworth-Heinemann.

Taylor, C. (1991) *The Ethics of Authenticity*, Cambridge, Mass.: Harvard University Press.

Velasquez, M. (1992) *Business Ethics, Concepts and Cases*, Englewood Cliffs: Prentice Hall.

7

Does this policy foster desirable skills?

7.1 Introduction

The theories in the two preceding chapters are relatively new; they were elaborated during the last three centuries. Before that time, the ethical debate in Western countries was dominated by Christian versions of virtue theory. Compared to its original form in ancient Greek virtue theory, Christianity gave the word 'virtue' a quite different meaning. In Christian theories the idea of virtue insisted on preparation for salvation, and opposed to this objective stood the vices which paved the road to hell. The Christian virtues of faith, hope and fraternal love prepared the entrapped spirit for divine grace. Christian virtue aimed at a holistic goal situated in heaven.

Our purpose in this chapter will be to examine ancient Greek virtue theory. We will show that it defines a different and very promising approach to moral quality, which has recently been reinterpreted and expanded. We will review this totally different outlook and point to its presence in management theories.

The scope of this book does not permit us to expand on concrete issues showing virtue theory's potential for post-welfare society. Nonetheless the reflective practitioner already knows the dark side of the social-democrat emphasis on distributive justice. Presently, many welfare policies are criticized for making people more dependent and less able to manage their own private affairs. Rigid duty-based bureaucracies often foster such counterproductive habits. The most illuminating examples can be found in the excesses of the social welfare state and Communist societies that foster passive dependence, diminished self-respect, personal cowardice and hypocrisy. Counterproductive social care programmes reward people that overstate their miseries and remain passive, instead of encouraging those who try to help themselves.

We hold that guiding people towards accomplished craftsmanship and personal wellbeing is one of the main tasks of leadership, both in politics and in corporations.

7.2 A first idea of classical virtue

The classical Greek outlook stresses the importance of excellent performance, which implies a different concept of moral ideals. Instead of setting deontological guidelines aimed at some airy omnipartial optimum, this approach identifies objectives that are important in community and personal life. Humans may excel in achieving public and private goods, but in order to reach these goals they need sets of public and private skills and knowledge, and these are virtues. Instead of looking for concerned parties or to establish responsibilities, this outlook focuses on the competencies needed for acquiring specific desirable goals.

The Christian outlook completely altered the original meaning of virtue. Originally, virtues were excellences in performing specific functions, that is, competencies in making and obtaining goods and realizing purposes within this world. Under the influence of Augustinian theology, the idea of classical virtue was reoriented. Public goods as well as personal objectives were subordinated to the dominant religious purpose of salvation.

For the ancient Greeks the word 'virtue' had a much wider and more neutral scope. It was applied to socially beneficial and heroic performances, but was also used to indicate a non-moral excellence in technical skills. Even tools and commodities might be called virtuous whenever they fulfilled their specific purpose. A virtuous hammer was an excellent tool for driving nails into wood. The ancient Greeks thus applied the idea of virtue to moral, natural and instrumental well-functioning.

The decline of virtue ethics was not the result of the overthrow of classical virtue theory; it was a side-effect of campaigns against traditional Christian religion and absolutist political institutions. The radical criticisms of Enlightenment philosophers paved the road for democracy and for relativism. The political movements for liberal rights attacked traditional institutions like slavery and monarchy. Following the great example set by Spinosa, Hume and Voltaire fought to demolish natural theology and succeeded in discrediting this shadow of the virtue theory. As a result of the repeated attacks against dogmatic beliefs and practices, the very idea of virtue lost credibility. In the wake of the eighteenth century, virtue theory was directly associated with reactionary conservatism and popish moralism.

The ancient Greek founders of virtue ethics did not profess the strict adherence to concrete norms based on faith, hope and love. The classical approach to virtues insisted on the particular qualities of objects and living beings in the present world. For Socrates, Plato and Aristotle the basic idea behind virtue was a more neutral one, based upon a later lost insight about excellence.

In ancient Athens virtue stood equal to excellence; it referred to a highly functional performance in respect to a specific purpose. The scope of things to which the Greeks applied virtue was also different. For them, both objects and living beings are good or virtuous when they excel with respect to their specific function. The virtue of both objects and animals consisted in performing well the function that they were meant to fulfil.

7.3 A modern interpretation of Aristotelian moral philosophy

7.3.1 DNA was unknown – his key concepts are soul, form and telos

Virtue philosophy can best be understood by looking at how Aristotle explained biological growth. Thus in order to explain why an acorn can grow into a great oak, the Greeks used the concept of soul. They knew that inside this tree seed exists a formative principle capable of using nutrients. According to Aristotle, this inner principle of change caused processes of growth and deterioration; it made the seed grow into a tree. This formative principle, which is the innate form or nature of living beings, they called the soul (*psyche*).

It is essential to realise that the word *psyche* has a wider meaning than 'mind': to have a *psyche* is simply to have life. So all living things, including plants, have soul, are 'ensouled'; they are animate, not inanimate (Latin *anima* = Greek *psyche*). Plant life is just growing, taking in nutrition, and producing seeds of new plants; plants only have 'vegetative souls'. For animals life is a matter of sense-perception, of desire and of movement; and men possess in addition the faculty of thought. Aristotle was a biologist, and he saw life as a sort of continuum from the lowest or simplest to the highest and most complex of living things. He was not at all inclined to think of the soul as a supernatural indwelling substance. This is a view that can be very tempting if one regards thought or consciousness as essential to the soul; it is not nearly so tempting to one who recognises plants too as being alive, and therefore as having souls. (Ackrill, 1981, p. 56)

The inner purpose or goal of growth was the state of flourishment, the *telos*. The *telos* for living species was identified by studying separate individuals in mature growth. From observing these well-functioning individuals, Aristotle inferred the achievable climactic stage of each species.

Here the concepts of form (*morfe*) and purpose (*telos*) may be combined. Form is the most general term for the organizing principle; it functions together with its counterpart, passive matter. In the case of living beings form is innate, it is the organizing principle or programme of the living being called the soul. All animated beings have such an innate principle or form. This form is not completely separate from the other constituent of all natural objects which is matter. For instance, the soul of the oak which contains the specific formative principle already in the acorn is not a physical substance. It is the very principle which is capable of making the acorn grow and transform itself into a magnificent tree. Here we see that matter is not separate from form, as there is only one physical substance called matter, but this matter changes due to an internal principle or form. The concept of a formative principle was introduced by Aristotle to explain the metaphysical problem of biological change: How can a thing first be this and then gradually transform into that?

Whereas for inanimate things change happened mainly under the influence of external forces, Aristotle recognized that the formative principle of living things was innate. Because of their living soul, animated beings can transform themselves. They are programmed for a natural sequence of growth and inner deterioration.

A magnificent oak is mainly made of dead wood, while the living materials in the inner bark and roots, which constitute the soul of the oak (*psyche*), still function. Confronted with this climactic stage of growth we sometimes say that such an oak is as 'oaks were meant to be', or that the 'oak is in great shape', that is, they have realized their innate souls in a full and harmonious climactic stage, their *telos*.

Especially of living things, ranging from plants to humans, Aristotle would say that they have a purpose or objective (*telos*) that originates from their soul (*psyche*). However, the way these natural dispositions are realized depends largely on nutrition and other external circumstances. For intelligent mammals the external factors that influence growth include even feedback, training and education.

Attaining the generic *telos* of one's kind is not simply granted. Only under favourable circumstances can a soul realize full growth and arrive at a stage of climax. At this point ancient philosophers say that it is as it was meant to be.

7.3.2 Virtue is defined by answering the 'What for?' question

The concepts of form and *telos* can also be explained by means of the Aristotelian distinction between four sorts of explanatory factors: material, formal, efficient and final types of explanation.

This well-known theory of four kinds of explanation can be exemplified by the artisan method for making a wooden chair:

1. The matter used is wood (the material cause).
2. The model in the mind of the carpenter is the form (the formal cause).
3. The actual manufacture of the chair results from the productive labour of the carpenter (the efficient cause).
4. The objective, goal or purpose for which the chair is made, its use is to have a commodity that people can sit on (the final cause).

The good or *telos* of the chair is external, as it is an inanimate commodity. The chair is made in order to meet a human need. The final cause of a commodity is external to the object, as it benefits persons. Thus, a tool or service is virtuous when it is apt for its use. For instance, pruning-shears are tools made for pruning roses. So, they are virtuous or excellent when they serve well their instrumental purpose, and they are 'no good' when they do not prune.

Typical of Aristotle is the claim that natural processes and productive work as well as biological growth can be explained best by reference to the final cause. This outlook studies and explains processes by looking at the goals that the process reaches.

Since Newton, modern science has accepted mechanistic explanations as a new paradigm. Yet those that are aware of recent developments in physics and in social science know that other paradigms are rising. In the case of social science and moral philosophy, the role of human intentions, perceptions and human goal-setting has challenged mechanistic approaches.

In particular, the fact that humans have more than just natural drives raises many issues. Aristotle already acknowledged the importance of human thought and speech which allow us to reformulate and develop our goals in life. A renewed version of Aristotelian philosophy can offer a way to account for them.

An example of such an account is contained in Chapter 3. The opening paragraphs of that chapter present a thoroughly updated idea of man that applies Aristotelian insights to a modern view of humans. One specific feature of our account is that it discards the notion of 'natural' human dispositions as too simplistic. In order to define the 'What for?' in human affairs such as business pursuits, we have to gain a keen understanding of the way nature and culture interact.

7.3.3 The telos of living beings is an internal good

In order to understand the original Aristotelian idea of human virtue, it is necessary to see the difference between external goods and internal purposes. Again, an internal purpose can best be explained by returning to biology. We have seen already that the *psyche* of living beings aims at a full-grown state of well-functioning. Its programme for arriving at this climactic stage is already present in its primordial nature or form. The object of growth is innate; it is an internal good.

Classical virtue theory applied the idea of well-functioning to the entire realm of living beings. Thus in order to define the virtue of a species of plants and animals, we have to look at a fine fully grown specimen. Such a specimen displays the fully developed state of being or *telos* of its kind, so it incorporates the final cause of that species. This good or objective is internal, and is not imposed upon the living being by others, but is programmed in its formative principle, that is, its soul. In its climactic stage one might see what a fully grown individual reveals about the disposition of its kind.

Even aesthetic criteria were attached to this ideal of biological development. We can admire the performances of individuals that are beautiful examples of their species. Magnificent beasts exemplify the natural virtues of their kind. Thus stuffed trophies of a great boar or a huge bear may still inspire feelings of awe and admiration; we feel that they were once examples of fine beasts.

This aesthetic outlook is by no means completely outdated. Modern environmentalists express these feelings of awe and respect for fine specimens, and even do so when they talk of plants: 'Dipterocarps are tall trees, and their trunks, if slender by some standards, are impressive growths, straight and unencumbered for dozens of meters, soaring sheer from the ground to the canopy that is so far overhead that it seems to belong to a different world' (Myers, 1992).

More explicit reference to the concept of *telos* is made by Bernard Rollin, when he defends the rights of the great apes for a life of their own. In his article 'The ascent of apes: broadening the moral community' Rollin states:

> One of the most significant steps must be the education of the general public regarding the extraordinary *telos* of the great apes – not so much in terms of their ability to, as it were, do humanly inspired 'tricks', such

as learning sign language, as marvellous and seductive as this may be. What must be of interest is not their life in relation to us, but in itself, as something to be studied – and recounted – in its own setting, with us as restrained guests who are minimally intrusive. In this, Jane Goodall is an inspiration, displaying extraordinary courage in a world where courage is a vanishing virtue. (1993, p. 216)

7.3.4 An organized view of human activities

Virtue ethics is called a *teleological* outlook, as it looks upon virtues as aiming to fulfil the *telos* for human beings – that is, the state of full development as a human being called *eudaemonia* (literally 'well spirited', durable wellbeing, happiness). This *telos* is not some external goal; it is only obtained in and through human activities, although it requires personal gifts, divine talent. Here we see that Aristotle boldly applied his concept of *telos* to human activities. Also for humans he formulated a *telos* that was already partly given as a programme for human nature.

In order to define the nature of this intrinsic good, Aristotle also referred to empirical observation. By studying existing well-functioning humans he finally draws conclusions about the supreme target that is intrinsic to human pursuits. It is important to appreciate that such research is theory laden. Aristotelian ethics studies great people in order to define what virtues make them excel. The objective of this empirical study is to gain a sound understanding of human well-functioning.

Instead of only looking at just the external physical aspects or some efficient causes, Aristotle already knew that human and organizational growth had something to do with aspirations and personal skills. Whereas modern social science sometimes seems to be happy when it has indicated significant external influences, the classical Greeks had concepts that dealt with inside development processes, the 'psychic' aspect. People and organizations tend towards objectives or goods.

One type of question Aristotle asks is about the final cause. Notable examples of such 'What for?' questions are:

☐ What is the *telos* for human fulfilment? When do we say that humans are flourishing as true human beings? What is the good life for man?

☐ What is the *telos* of this organization? When do we say that our corporation is well-functioning or successful? What is a good company? What is the objective of our public health institution? When shall we say that it is well-functioning?

Another type of question concerns the efficient causes, the skills needed. For the individual human being this 'How?' question can be formulated thus:

☐ What are the specific moral virtues which allow us to enjoy happiness?

These questions are interrelated. For individual human beings, the Aristotelian question can be resumed thus:

☐ Which virtues are characteristic of people that inspire our admiration as examples of flourishing humans?

7.3.5 Questions preceding the study of culturally transmitted virtues

Before answering this, we have to face some other questions. This is because our topic of interest is not natural biology but the philosophical understanding of human morality. This field of enquiry requires additional precaution.

Amongst others, three specific questions can be raised when one applies virtue theory to human customs.

1. Can we distinguish a final cause behind the multitude of human morality?

It is a fact that moral norms and values do not respond to one fixed set of innate rules; there is abundant evidence of how diverse moral norms are. A modern description of this diversity is provided by cross-cultural studies, although they do not provide conclusive explanations of these phenomena. Such differences between local cultures, languages and customs make it risky to infer one cause for what makes all humans excel.

The problem of cultural diversity was known to the ancient Greeks of Athens, a sea-trading city. Although some may ask if Aristotle or Plato suffered from cultural myopia, in normative ethics they both replied to this issue by developing comprehensive ideas of general human excellence. In the writings of Aristotle these ideas are checked by references to common opinions: he checks whether his general conclusions on human excellence fit with the things ordinarily said about it. Such references point to shared intuitions and commitments, which may add credibility to his general and more systematic idea of civilized man.

We now have empirical evidence that common human dispositions exist.

DNA research and ethological studies of body language reveal striking similarities.

There is also evidence that our moral norms and moral problems are not completely culture bound. One argument is that certain taboos express almost universal human values, but that in each culture transgressions of these sacred rules appear. Human failure in abiding by these taboos can be explained by normative psychology, that is, certain individuals lack self-control and inflict injuries that break the rules. Good examples are the taboos against incest and rape, which are virtually universal. Yet in all cultures transgressions appear, a phenomenon that can best be explained in terms of lack of self-control and in-group pressure. Transmission of cultural values is not completely successful anywhere. Even these powerful taboos are violated under the impulse of primitive instincts and in-group vices. Specific forms of rape and incest refer to morally powerful taboos, yet humans violate them. This universal abuse points to a malfunctioning which can best be explained as inadequate control of our cerebellum, our 'dinosaur brains'. It is a fact that humans lacking self-restraint and moral strength can cause much harm. The impulsive pursuit of false idols is a principal explanation of immoral and harmful behaviour, and this is true for both men and women. Aristotelian philosophy formulates a theory of moral wellbeing which studies the positive human objective of sane and intelligent self-control.

2. What kind of ideal is happiness? In what way does it exist?

A multitude of degrading and immoral behaviours exists. From this 'fact' many people often infer that a final cause like happiness is just an illusion. This type of argument blurs the difference between 'facts' and normative standards. Many humans believe that they do not succeed in life and are unhappy, and from this 'fact' they infer that the ideal of happiness itself is illusory. More precisely, however, the idea that a certain behaviour is debased and inhuman is not at all a fact: it is a normative judgement, as it implies reference to some, often unconscious, normative standard.

When Aristotle talks about the *telos* which is specific for the human soul, he does not make a purely descriptive statement. Rather he constructs an ideal type with the characteristic features of well-living humans. This does not mean that there is no intimate relationship with actual human behaviour, but implies that only some heroic people actually incorporate these features.

The classical philosophers – but also play writers like Aeschylus or historians such as Herodotus – provide tools for assessing morality. They all make keen studies of existing human excellences and deprivations. Yet these deprivations are only degrading because they refer to normative standards or ideals. This assumes that one has some idea of more appropriate moral action. Aristotle, then, tries to formulate a positive idea of the final cause for civilized people. He correlates his ideal with basic insights of common wisdom, explaining what makes us admire great men and women. This norm or criterion is not completely separate from descriptive reality; it is the best attainable objective in human life.

3. What is meant by calling happiness a good intrinsic to practices?

Virtue ethics distinguishes between intrinsic and extrinsic purposes. Happiness is the supreme good of human life, which is regarded as a *praxis*. The concept of human internal good is related to *praxis*, which has to be explained by opposing practices to productive work and labour. Practices are pursued because of internal goods, productive work and labour are done for external goods.

Here we refer to the Aristotelian distinction between (1) action or doing (*praxis*) and (2) production or making (*poiesis*). *Praxis* is activities which are done for their own sake; we like to perform them. Examples are playing or listening to music, being with friends just as friends, engaging in leisure activities as lovers, or participating in public debates.

Conversely, *poiesis* covers the whole domain of human productive pursuits. Productive activities are done for some external or extrinsic purpose; they produce commodities, goods or services.

7.3.6 Instrumental reason usurped control over modern self-perception

Before returning to practices, we would like to add some modern comments on the concept of *poiesis*, by referring to *The Human Condition* written by Hannah Ahrendt (1958). She introduces a distinction that may help us to obtain a better understanding of the Greek concept of *poiesis*, making or producing a commodity, a service, or a work of art.

In order to offer a realistic account of modern production Hannah Ahrendt divides *poiesis* into *productive work* and *maintenance labour*. They are different ways of achieving external goods. Modern man has problems in seeing the radical difference between *poiesis* and *praxis*, a difference which is important in order to see what happiness really means. Work and labour are different forms of making, *poiesis*. Hannah Ahrendt defines productive work as making lasting commodities according to a preconceived plan or model. Examples are making a chair, pruning a wild buxus hedge into nice forms, or team work like designing a car. Contrary to this production of relatively durable outcomes, labour is defined as a series of efforts which are necessary in order to maintain a certain quality of life, but without producing any independent product with a durable existence. Examples of labour are floor cleaning, catering and food services.

According to Hannah Ahrendt the Taylorist work methods annihilated human awareness of goods internal to practices. The independent value of practice became obscure. Agents operating in smoke-stack industries and production chains look upon themselves as animal laborans, labouring instruments which are only economic objects, no longer appreciated for their intrinsic value as participants in human practices. The only values that remain available to the labouring animal of industrial society are survival, blind competition, conspicuous consumerism and making deals based on private interest. Industrial workers feel alienated from human practices and decision-making; they perceive themselves as disposable cogs in clockwork, instrumental tools.

This manipulative outlook has direct consequences on private life. It is even applied to the more intimate human relations, regarding sexual intercourse as a matter of using each other as sex objects, instead of building durable relationships based on mutual respect, commitment, loyalty, self-sacrificing love, pleasure and tenderness.

Marcel Mauss in his *Essai sur le Don*, published in 1923, has pointed to the fact that long before modernity arrived humans participated in clan life by exchange of gifts. His view has been developed by Sahlins (1974) in his *Stone Age Economics*, which was discussed in Chapter 5. It implies that people in pre-modern communities saw themselves as members of a large family participating in practices. Individual work and labour were embedded in a wider community, fostering human actions with an intrinsic purpose. Production was related to ritual performances, and their tribal way of doing things was seen as contributing to sacred or communal purposes.

Modernity has desacrilized and isolated economic pursuits. The individual consumer with virtually unlimited desires has become the locus of interest. Any reference to more communal and social goals seems to have become obsolete. Some even think that sacred traditional values themselves are becoming objects for negotiation. For instance, even respect for physical integrity is being superseded by commercial interests, as Third World examples of organ donation can prove. Young children are kidnapped or sold in order to supply one of their kidneys; adults also sell their organs. The fact that most people feel revolted by such acts of medical piracy is an indication of our common sense of solidarity. Certain sacred communitarian virtues are still upheld.

7.3.7 A definition of the human telos: eudaemonia

Now we may return to our main questions: What are human virtues and what are they aiming at? In other words, what is their intrinsic object called *eudaemonia* or happiness?

First of all, the negative answers. Aristotle maintained that excellence as a human being is not to be found by merely studying specific productive craftsmanship. Nor can moral excellence be described by listing various material or efficient causes. This means that one cannot understand happiness only by studying conditions that actually help to be happy. A good education, training, talent, an independent financial situation and personal commitment play a role, but Aristotle maintains that one should also study the formal and final causes.

One should have an idea of where humans are heading, in their most excellent form. Most of all, one must have a positive understanding of the attainable objective aimed at in life, the final cause. Plato and Aristotle therefore designed features of our positive aim, durable human excellence.

According to Aristotle, human excellence consists of living a life appropriate to human nature. This implies the full use of those skills and powers that are distinctive of man, that is, reason and public policy-making. His insight based on final causes still remains valid, but the actual answer provided by Aristotle in his *Nicomachean Ethics* seems less satisfying to Freudian and Augustinian moralists. For all those that are still struggling with a cerebral idea of human reason, we may again refer to our exposition of the distinctive qualities of man in Chapter 3.

Here is the original answer of Aristotle:

> What a man has to do, then, is to live actively in accordance with reason (or, not without reason). But what an x and a good x have to do is the same in kind – e.g. a lyre-player and a good lyre-player, and so in general in all cases, superiority in excellence being added to what he has to do: what a lyre-player does is to play the lyre, what a good one does is to play it well. A man's good, therefore, turns out to be active living in accordance with excellence, or – if there are a number of excellences – in accordance with the best and most perfect excellence. Moreover, in a complete life. For one swallow does not make a summer, nor does one day; and similarly a man is not made blessed and *eudaemon* by one day or by a short period of time. (*Nicomachean Ethics*, book I, ch. 7; translated in Ackrill, 1981, p. 15)

The *telos* of human life is a durable state of wellbeing. In order to attain this human well-functioning a number of excellences are needed. These virtues ensure that flourishing humans can cope well with ups and downs in their personal situation; they have intellectual and practical skills that empower them to make the best out of private and community life.

The supreme purpose, *eudaemonia*, contains two important aspects. In his general idea for highest good, durable happiness, Aristotle makes a distinction between individual and public *eudaemonia*. Some people are outstanding in living happy private lives, others are great in fostering public welfare. It is to the latter that our interest will have to shift when we talk about entrepreneurial excellence. First, however, some remarks on the underlying psychology, together with a hypothesis.

7.4 Keystones of virtue ethics

In architecture an example of a keystone can be found in the middle of the ceilings of Gothic cathedrals; it is a round stone held aloft by converging arches. Virtue ethics can be represented as a mental construction with, in the nave, prudence. More exactly, this mental construction has two ceilings – one is crowned by private prudence and the other by public prudence. This image describes how we can distinguish two spheres of excellence, public and private wellbeing. So, we have to study these two keystones, which are the outstanding forms of the most eminent virtue, prudence.

7.4.1 The commanding human virtue of phronesis

Phronesis (prudence or practical wisdom) is an intellectual excellence aiming at practical objectives, either private or communal *eudaemonia*. According to Aristotle, prudence guides our thoughts and actions and helps us to succeed in life. Prudence aims at this durable well-functioning by seeking a dynamic balance between particular excellences of character and the virtues of theoretical understanding.

For the classical Greeks, prudence can sometimes mean that one has to be harsh, biased and immoderate, in order to obtain a new balance that is the most beneficial for the public or private good. From the seventeenth century onwards the word 'prudence' lost all links with magnanimous courage and strong temper; it came instead to mean cautiousness, being considerate, discreet and thrifty. This later meaning excluded the original notions of being audacious, daring and entrepreneurial.

The original wider range of meaning indicated a big difference from Christian duty ethics. Ancient Greeks emphasized that doing good is a matter of skilfully serving private and public goods, especially the fostering of a state of dynamic flourishing called *eudaemonia*, well-spiritedness.

The emotional consequence of attaining the human *telos*, like pleasure or satisfaction, does not define this good; it is just a supervening consequence. Pleasure is not something that should be desired and sought for directly, as one will then get carried away by impetuous impulses like greed, desire or anger. The best way to enjoy life is to look upon the pleasures as a non-intended accompaniment. Pleasure is produced by our cerebellum or dinosaur brains, which should not be allowed to gain control as people will then become less lean and mean. Pleasure may go along with excellence as a human being, but the real test of life is maintaining the sharp excellence of one's personal and human talents. For the individual, each period of life has its proper mix of excellences in order to be a flourishing human.

The Roman philosopher Seneca endorsed this view. He compared pleasure to the poppies that grow in a field of grain and embellish it, that is, as an addition, without having been planted or sought for. (It should be noted here that modern rational methods in agriculture have succeeded in completely removing this kind of supervening side-effect. For the first time in human history poppies are absent from the grain fields. Here the dominant idols of modern man pop up again, voracious instrumental rationality combined with a lack of sensitivity for natural beauty. Soon only a few nostalgic minds will complain about the monotony of modern grain fields. Modern people will not notice that one of the pleasures of country life has disappeared for ever.)

Striking the right balance in each moment of life not only depends on our personal enterprises and our virtues: it also depends on external circumstances and events, factors which are themselves beyond our control. Still, as most marketeers know, the great human is he or she who can turn threats into opportunities. The right functioning of prudence may then produce *eudaemonia*, durable wellbeing. Such a durable state of flourishing does not only depend on the external conditions, as it first of all results from the trained and acquired internal qualities of our will and mind, especially the latter.

7.4.2 The lawgiver as a moral entrepreneur

The prudent man or *phronimos* is not superman. He can be overwhelmed by tragic events. But in most ordinary situations and when confronted by a crisis great people are those that guide their community by making the best out of the situation. At the level of the political organization, the well-performing statesman is a person that displays lasting qualities as an intellectual and moral leader.

Both Plato and Aristotle maintained that great humans do not specifically excel in short-term success with practical affairs, because they might share that feature equally with frauds and less respectable persons. Moreover they maintained that many great people display qualities related to artistic and intellectual activities; they excel in theoretical understanding or creative expression. One specific human excellence is the contemplation of universal theories (the virtue of *thiourea*). Until recently interpreters thought that Aristotle and Plato held the purely theoretical virtues to be the best for man. They separated theoretical wisdom from durable excellence in practical affairs, and held this speculative or academic knowledge to be superior.

Contrary to this separatist view, one must point to the Aristotelian ideal of a virtuous public leader, a lawgiver that can draw upon keen theoretical knowledge while aiming at public benefit. Recent research by Richard Bodéüs (1993) has insisted on the political perspective of Aristotelian ethics:

> The description of lawgiver – the notion towards which all the elements of Aristotle's account converge and which must be understood in a quite broad sense – applies not only to those who, by acknowledged right, share in legislative work within the city, but also, it seems, by analogy, to all the educators, such as heads of households [and managers], who must set up for others and make them respect the same rules of conduct which are expressed in the laws.
>
> The essentially educational nature of legislative work is also confirmed by the conception of general justice offered us by the *Nicomachean Ethics* (v. 3). Aristotle speaks quite clearly in this respect: 'that which has been defined by legislative science [example: code of corporate conduct] possesses legal force and we say that each of its precepts is just. Now the laws, which pronounce about absolutely everything, pursue the common interest so that in a sense we call just whatever produces and preserves happiness [*eudaemonia*] and its constituent parts for the benefit of the political community'.
>
> Aristotle, who also remarks that the laws prescribe acts conforming to all the principal virtues, thereby indicates the essentially educational function of the legislative art. Hence, incidentally, the need on the part of the lawgiver, as conceived by Aristotle, to possess knowledge of ethical issues. . . . What Aristotle calls 'legislative prudence' therefore turns out to be a purely intellectual excellence. This is the reason why Plato already, in the *Statesman*, assigns 'politics' to knowledge rather than to action. Since the deliberation of the prudent lawgiver, like the deliberation of any prudent person, is backed by true general principles, we must infer that he owes his principles to experience. . . . Contrary to what occurs in the realm of action properly speaking, where the law rules from without the conduct of persons who feel their way towards right decision, since they have not yet internalized the practical principles, there are neither superior rules nor superior force able to guide a lawgiver who may be still too inexperienced to possess unerring principles of good legislation. (Bodéüs, 1993, pp. 66–7; my comments)

This recent study reminds us that distinguishing aspects does not imply a complete separation between what in the best lives is one. For responsible entrepreneurs many lessons can be learned from this outlook.

It shows that even a corporation with internal long-term planning may fail if it does not have a constructive and keen sight on its larger political and communal responsibilities.

For instance, if a corporation decides to implement stringent environmental care systems without yet being legally obliged to achieve such a level of performance, one needs legislative prudence. Certain measures will be rewarding and will also be beneficial for the environment, while others are either simply a matter of attacking symptoms or are in the long term counterproductive in international competition. Assessing desirable and undesirable consequences that are related to certain goals and methods requires careful deliberation and intellectual excellence.

7.5 A psychological structure geared towards human excellence

7.5.1 Virtues as integrative neurological patterns with specific goals

Plato and Aristotle identify three primary domains of mental well-functioning. Recently, their psychological insights have regained prominence. Here we present an amended version of their psychology, based on neurological research. But first, a word of caution. The status of this version is heuristic, that is, it seeks to formulate a hypothetical view of how the distinct operations in various brain areas become integrated. This view presents one outlook in this current debate by referring to the 'What for?' type of explanation.

According to Plato and Aristotle our soul has two principal capacities, reasonable thought and emotive compulsion. We now know that language, logic and calculation are reasonable faculties situated in various areas of the cortex, whereas the instincts and emotions are situated in the cerebellum. The classical Greeks already knew that emotions and rational behaviour were not completely disconnected. Through training and education even the strongest impulses can be partly canalized or forced to obey rational objectives. The main exceptions to this rule are motor functions like the heart beat and specific reflexes.

According to the ancient Greek philosophers, fully grown humans acquire specific virtues, durable dispositions. In modern terms one may look upon virtues as the integrating neurological patterns that are mainly located in our cortex, patterns that are constantly reshaped by feedback and reinforced by successful achievements.

Although itself located in the cortex, each cardinal virtue is the generic name for an even more integrative neurological system with a specific function. Sensory input and impulsions are processed in distinct brain areas, yet they have to be integrated in order to achieve a practical objective like learning to drink from a cup or hold a spoon. After a long period of growth and education, our mental skills have become quite vast, with well-developed local functions. The more generic skills are based on integrating links between various distinct and well-trained areas.

The virtues of successful humans can be regarded as effective integrating patterns, which have survived and have been reinforced by feedback from experience and personal development. Yet, what remains absent from the modern evolution theory of brain development is the notion of a teleological 'What for?' Neurologists only focus on the survival of the fittest, without seeing that in this context the 'fittest' can be defined as a more positive purpose. So, the following hypothetical view is only partially recognized by modern brain research.

The cardinal virtues can be seen as mental excellences. These acquired dispositions guarantee well-performance in what the Greeks postulated as the three parts of the human mind: (1) reason and its opposite (2) passion, with as an intermediate faculty (3) character or will. We will list the four cardinal virtues now. Two are called practical virtues, because they result from training and exercise. The other two are called theoretical virtues, because they are mainly acquired through teaching.

Three virtues indicate the durable perfection proper to one of the three mental faculties. Only the well-developed function of prudence is geared towards an even higher level of integration, aiming at the final good of human practice, durable happiness.

1. Temperance
The judicious use of the instincts and passions emanating from our dinosaur or cerebellum brains. Related vices are either immoderate impulsiveness or frigidity, which is the absence of any warmhearted passions. Our temperament is for a large part innate and partly acquired by a good early training, exercise and education, which has taught the child to practise self-restraint.

2. Courage
This is the generic virtue of character and will, which is partly trainable. Its more definitive form may appear only later, after childhood. These habits, such as bravery, force passions to serve practical objectives in life. They should not operate blindly, so it is a cortex faculty that allows us to make use of them.

3. Theoretical wisdom
The understanding of the truths of human life in religion and local custom. Wisdom requires teaching and prolonged cultivation. Philosophical con-

templation or *thiourea* consists of the knowledge of unchanging principles, like mathematical relationships or eternal laws. Wisdom is located in various parts of the cortex of educated people. On the other hand, the brains of idiots are totally devoid of this virtue.

4. Practical wisdom or prudence
Finally, mental excellence, the job of which was to maintain a balance between the different parts of human nature, is called practical wisdom or prudence (*phronesis*). Its proper job is to assess in concrete circumstances what the best action is. The *phronimos* is not a modest overcareful person, but a person that courageously functions according to our concept of free choice. While being aware of personal values and interests, such a person is capable of keen action due to a careful assessment of given circumstances and personal (or corporate) competencies. Emotive pulsion is not overruled, but canalized and under control.

7.5.2 *An example of high-spirited prudence in management literature*

A study of a strong character showing prudence is portrayed in Bernstein and Craft Rozen (1990):

> Now let's take a look at how the Dinosaur Brain's appetite for dominance can be channelled effectively. Even a highly competitive person in a highly competitive setting does not have to be destructive.
>
> Anne is bright and aggressive and wants to move up. Like most competitive people, she would like to win at everything, but she knows some games count more than others. She keeps her urge to win in check until she has thought through the situation and is sure that it will be to her benefit to win [she obtains insights belonging to practical wisdom]. When she fights, heads roll. She never draws her gun unless she intends to kill somebody [courage, applied with prudence].
>
> If Anne is not at war with somebody, she is a loyal and true friend [she participates in practices, she does not only relate to people in an instrumental way using them]. She has thoroughly researched the qualities that her company values: a good bottom line, a smooth-running operation, loyalty from subordinates, new ideas that aren't too radical, and a bit of deference to those above [she keenly perceives her present situation; compare our definition of free choice in Chapter 3].
>
> When another manager makes a dumb mistake, instead of blowing the whistle on him, Anne decided to spend a lot of time helping him out of the mess because she thought in the long run his loyalty would be better than his animosity [orientation towards durable results, which helps to dominate impulses].

In a meeting, another manager implied that Anne's department wasn't particularly efficient. She quietly stood up and said: 'You may have a point there. I'm willing to accept your challenge. Why don't we set criteria and just see who runs a better operation for a year? Let's figure out how we are going to measure it' [prudence and courage: turning a personal threat into an opportunity for the corporation].

That was a battle she had to win and she won it. Anne could use her Dinosaur Brain to motivate herself, but she didn't let it set goals for her. She set the goals and made her efforts count. Her Dinosaur Brain was her powerful ally, but her cortex was always in control. (Bernstein and Craft Rozen, 1990, pp. 46–7; my comments)

7.5.3 On balancing the three parts of human mind

Moral excellence or virtue as a human being does not oblige us to castrate our more natural inclinations. Contrary to what Kantians and utilitarians believe, human reason is not a cerebral tyrant nor an emotivist conscience overriding self-interested compulsion. Virtue ethics portrays human reason as learning from practice. By experience mature people can learn to cope with their passions and desires in a socially purposeful way. Inclinations and desires should be transformed not suppressed. They should be put at the service of desirable objectives in private and public life.

Virtue ethics contains a criticism of unrefined hedonistic consumerism. It also criticizes self-centred narcissism. Private desires are not the ultimate ones, they need guidance in order to make their positive contribution to private and public happiness. The commanding excellence managing our actions in a purpose-oriented and clever way is prudence.

One might even refer to a famous quote from Plato's *Phaedrus* here, which first exposed a three-part view of the human mind:

Let us compare our mental functioning (*psyche*) to the combined forces of a team of horses and their charioteer. The horses and the charioteers of the gods are entirely good and of good stock, those of other beings vary. In our case, well, in the first place the charioteer drives a pair of horses, and in the second place one of these horses is noble and good and of a stock to match, while the other is of quite opposite character and breeding. Our charioteer's job is of necessity both difficult and troublesome. (in Melling, 1987, p. 73)

David Melling comments:

The charioteer represents reason; the noble horse is *thumos* [temper], the spirited, energetic, aspiring element in the soul; the horse of degenerate stock is appetite. . . . The sense of division and conflict which is an essential aspect of human self-experience is grounded in the fundamental structure of the human soul. . . . Self-development centres rather on the establishment of order and harmony in the soul. The intellect should govern, the spirited element energize the soul's activities, the appetites be trained to seek a noble and worthy fulfilment. (Melling, 1987, pp. 73–4)

In the words of Alisdair MacIntyre (1985): 'To act virtuously is not, as Kant was later to think, to act against inclination; it is to act from cultivation of the virtues' (p. 149).

This idea of our internal psychological dynamism shows that we aspire towards a more refined existence. Our appetites can be cultivated, we are better humans when our pleasures provide something more than mere private hedonistic satisfaction. Bovines may be content with only food and shelter; we require more.

Happiness refers to human welfare and wellbeing. For corporations as well as individuals this means that whatever endangers public welfare is a vice. Vices are counterproductive extreme attitudes, often related to habits dominated by blind impulse.

7.5.4 *The doctrine of the just mean*

Aristotle states that virtues are always a mean (*mesotes*) between two extremes. The mean is the best way to reach a goal, whereas the two extreme attitudes represent vices due to overdoing or failure. Examples are bravery or courage, which is the true mean between cowardice and rashness; generosity is the mean between avarice and spendthrift, and so on. This complete doctrine of the just mean also comments that in practice people may err in their choices.

What exactly is the doctrine of the just mean? In order to make actual free choices that are both effective and efficient – that is, in order to strike the just mean – one has to meet the following criteria:

☐ The right action is a middle path between a too much and a too little.

☐ The right action aims at a goal, either internal (contemplation, action) or external (work, labour).

☐ The right action is only right for a specific agent in a specific situation.

☐ The judgement is made by an experienced person, the *phronimos* or wise human.

One of Aristotle's examples refers to appetite. The right daily food needs are not equal for all human beings. In modern terms, the triathlon athlete will need more than 5,000 calories a day to stay in shape, whereas for an old lady 1,500 calories may be her just mean.

7.5.5 Training desirable habits and reshaping skills

Aristotle knew that we should not let our dinosaur or cerebellum brains take over. Whenever we are seized by rash impulses, there are some remedies that can be applied. In general they consist of diagnosis and therapy steps. First, one should learn to recognize when the brain is dominated by dinosaur compulsion, simply because counterproductive things happen. Then the cortex may regain control by applying the general stratagem that Aristotle advised. Whenever one recognizes an inadequate response due to insufficient or excessive behaviour, one should force upon oneself to bend this response in an opposite direction. Just as one can straighten out a curved bar by bending it in the opposite direction, one may straighten out mental processes and strengthen the cortex control by prudently practising opposite behaviours.

There are some rules for creating this new balance. When imposing such therapeutic exercises, first set priorities. To this effect Aristotle declared that legislative prudence was in fact of greater priority than prudence in private life. One important condition for a happy individual life is living in a well-governed setting. This requires being aware, and organizing communal, corporate and private objectives.

Similar advice is expressed in more individualistic and competition-based terms by Bernstein and Craft Rozen:

> Whatever the emotions, you know there's Lizard Logic involved. What do you do? First, stop. Get the picture. The dinosaur brain has no perspective at all. Shift to your cortex. Ask yourself, 'What do I want to happen?' Choose your actions according to your goal. Think about how you are going to make it happen. As you are acting, ask yourself, 'Am I getting closer or farther away from the goal?'
>
> All you have to do is stop and think. If you do that, then you can be in control of an enormous primeval force within you, rather than having that force control you.
>
> Keep your cortex working when you go back to the jungle. Even if you aren't the biggest, meanest and most powerful dinosaur, you can easily be the smartest. In the end, the smartest wins. (1990, p. 245)

7.6 Revised accounts of virtue of little use for business ethics

7.6.1 Two critical statements

Now we come to a rather critical assessment of the change in emphasis that we find in modern virtue theory. Our thesis is that most of these accounts have in fact a tendency to divert the true power of virtue theory. They do so by two fundamental shifts:

(1) Instead of celebrating the virtue of outstanding flourishing humans, such as some great entrepreneur, modern theorists outline the appropriate social virtues which are considered to be desirable within a given community. Social virtues are defined by their community environment, in which critical debate on the basic assumptions of policies is not the centre of interest. The absence of strategic debate, and of glorification of legislative prudence which we called moral entrepreneurship, often leads to a kind of nostalgia. Nice communitarian and co-operative practices are promoted. Conversely, keen empire building seems less recommendable as it includes both the use of deceit and ruthlessness, and the requirement to lay people off whenever necessary.

(2) Virtue is narrowed down to moral virtue. The fact that communitarian practices are the locus of interest points back to a more basic change. The entire concept of virtue is reduced to moral virtue – the well-functioning of character, temperament and social concern as it is most beneficial within a given community. The ultimate virtue that guides man in living a successful life, *phronesis*, seems to have lost command or, at least, it remains partly hidden. As a consequence of this emphasis on virtue of character, an important insight remains concealed. Moral virtue is no longer directly dominated by personal intellectual judgement and legislative prudence.

Top people among strategic marketeers and great entrepreneurs know that certain threats sometimes call for decisive and ruthless action. Understanding and monitoring such acute changes calls for intellectual judgement and great communicative skills, and finally relies on intellectual and strategic virtues – a command function that remains out of sight in modern virtue theory.

7.6.2 The shift towards Christian compassion

An example of the shift to the promotion of more socially benevolent virtues, can be found in *Virtues and Vices* by Phillipa Foot (1978). In order to clarify this shift in the content of the celebrated human virtue, Tom Sorrell and John Hendry comment:

> There is no hint in Foot's account that true virtue attaches only to grand gestures performed by great men; on the contrary, for her, it is within the capacities of most or all adults to acquire the virtues, and, along with other twentieth century commentators, she thinks that the virtues are beneficial to those who lead relatively ordinary lives. Thus courage may be necessary for riding a bicycle in central London or for undergoing a course of medical treatment, and not only for the great ordeals of war, say. (1994, p. 45)

Modern virtue theory tends to reflect the non-political outlook of a well-educated morally concerned scholar. It often expresses social concern for less fortunate humans and stresses virtues tending towards benevolent care. In the eyes of such modern scholars certain basic concepts of human decency can be exemplified by spontaneous and unhesitating help. A critical analysis of Foot's example of split-second solicitousness may, however, reveal some less impartial assumptions, making a difference between the solicitations among in-group members and the way we manage claims from outsiders.

Maybe we are overstating this point, since most modern theorists expand on duties towards outside others. Nevertheless it still remains that our strongest feelings of love and compassion are mainly reserved for friends of durable acquaintance.

7.6.3 A more fundamental flaw in some modern accounts

In classical virtue theory there is a distinction between the so-called moral virtues that have to be trained by exercise and imitation, and the intellectual virtues that require instruction and teaching. As we explained, the Greeks considered the intellectual virtues to be the most characteristic of human excellence. They are of the utmost importance for achieving *eudaemonia*. Often modern virtue theory presents a narrow conception of moral value. Spiritual growth, duties towards yourself, and sacrifice for one's country or for one's ideals, are not put to the front. Instead, the greatest concern is for the disintegration of modern society and the predominance of instrumental reason, and in order to fight the vices of selfishness, vulgar consumerism and narcissism, modern theory stresses co-operative values and family life.

Unfortunately, what is almost lost from sight is the fact that virtue refers originally to the great human being. More moderate and day-to-day social excellence is held to be the essence of virtue.

Above all, prudence – that most vital virtue of classical ethics – remains obsolete. What is apparently forgotten is that justice can only be done by people who know what they are doing, that is, by persons possessing the intellectual excellence of prudence. Celebrating the wisdom of a great leader or of a political statesman seems to fall beyond the focus of interest.

In contrast, we try to reaffirm the classical insight that moral virtue has to be governed by keen skills of judgement and by great knowledge in order to produce just policies. Intellectual virtues, and especially prudence, are the most sublime virtues. They are in charge when people really are in good order and well-functioning.

The chief concern of many modern authors seems to be to prevent harm to relationships and foster decent practices in order to achieve private wellbeing. They insist too much on socially desired moral virtues, neglecting the keen intellectual perception of communal priorities. van Luijk evaluates this community-oriented preoccupation of modern virtue ethics thus:

> A theory of virtues is a theory of distinct and highly respected social practices. . . . Just as people find their basic identity by appropriating the mental and emotional capacities their social environment places at their disposal, so do they find their *moral identity* and their own pattern of values by adjusting themselves to the moral impulses and expectations their social group and network has to offer them. (van Luijk, 1994, p. 24)

Other texts also advance the idea that modern virtue theory stresses moral habits appreciated by local communities, while neglecting outstanding virtues of intellectual judgement. Most texts overlook the vital role of intellect, keen insight and balanced judgement present in the Aristotelian writings.

> Though revised Aristotelian accounts such as Foot's diverge from Aristotle's, they are nevertheless virtue theories and concerned with the cultivation of a few selected traits of character [sic!]. Aristotle thought of the moral virtues as character traits that corrected some typical excesses and deficiencies of human beings. (Sorrell and Hendry, 1994, p. 45)

In order to stress the fact that the so-called moral virtues are not separate items, but always require discernment and judgement when applied to practical situations, we prefer to call them *virtues of character*. Correct moral behaviour is at least, in an unconscious way, right or just, it is not contrary to what prudent and wise people would advise you to do.

7.7 Comparing virtues of character and excellence in crafts

7.7.1 Similarities

Virtues of character share features with technical excellence or craftsman-ship. Craftsmanship is the set of learned qualities we need in order to perform well in some specific trade or profession, for instance cabinet-making or accountancy. Some of these marked similarities are as follows:

- □ They are not natural gifts, but have to be trained, coached and supervised. Both are acquired.
- □ They both have to be applied with circumspection; this implies an ability for swift judgement in order to assess the given materials and circumstances, and to decide upon what is the appropriate line of action. Both excellences involve anticipation and expertise, maintained by continuous practice and mental attention. Here, a kind of intellect or expert system comes in.
- □ Character virtues and craftsmanship both organize a set of activities in a certain sequence in order to reach the objective. They are functional or purpose-oriented qualities.
- □ One more mutual characteristic is use of the feedback. The final result for both may be that certain norms and proceedings became part of an individual's personal character, they are no longer imposed by exterior authorities. Due to the fact that craftsmen internalize quality norms and procedures they like to produce quality commodities. Similarly, feed-back on moral actions can help us to improve our moral behaviour. By constantly paying attention to our functioning as human beings we can reshape our skills and adjust our insights.

Aristotle and Plato call excellence in daily life affairs 'prudence' (*phronesis*) and excellence in arts or crafts 'craftsmanship' (*technè*). The virtues of prudence and craftsmanship apply general insights, skills and methods to a concrete task, and require the understanding of relevant facts. They both represent expertise in performing practical tasks.

7.7.2 Differences

There are also some differences between character virtues guided by *phronesis* and *technè*, due to the fact that they serve different purposes.

Craftsmanship is an acquired aptitude aimed at the production of a commodity, a product that can be used. It produces a distinctive good or service. Craftsmanship aims at an *extrinsic* purpose.

As opposed to craft, the proper function of life is to create a good existence, to live excellently while maintaining a rewarding relationship with the natural and cultural environment. Good life aims at an *intrinsic* purpose.

This essential difference between human excellence and craftsmanship entails *three consequences*.

First, whereas a person may master a craft more or less correctly, Aristotle maintains that character virtues go together. A moral performance has to be seen as a whole, which is either appropriate and just or inadequate and awkward. This expresses the unity of character virtues. In moral behaviour, a deficiency in one area will necessarily frustrate the proper functioning of a real quality: 'a person with many excellent qualities can do terrible things and cause immense suffering because of a fatal flaw somewhere else in his character' (Ackrill, 1981, pp. 137–8).

This sentence can be related to a common experience in business management. Persons with the most excellent technical skills may cause disasters when they obtain management responsibilities, due to some incompetence in their character virtues. Somehow they lack balance and tuning, which finally has to do with sane judgement. Severe catastrophes, like the Pinto car burnings or the capsizing of the *Estonia* south of Finland, are related to a lack of managerial risk-awareness. In both cases involved top managers underestimated the probability of provoking harm as they narrow-mindedly pursued short-term commercial targets.

Prudence aims at balance and harmony between our various desires and feelings. Prudence is one whole excellence, which guides our activities by a constant reference to overall public goods. In order to strike at the right target in concrete circumstances it constantly applies timing, tuning, checks and counterchecks.

Secondly, whereas in technical crafts an intentional mistake is not necessarily worse than an unintentional one, in moral affairs the contrary is always true. Then, the intention to harm does matter a lot. Virtue ethics formulates this statement in a positive way: prudent behaviour implies personal commitment, the conscious will to perform well. The best strategy is to identify large risks with a moral impact, and to focus on limiting them to the utmost. Here again, there are many parallels with business. According to Taylorism, an employee does not have to understand the functioning of the whole chain in order to make a good technical contribution, and managers might be indifferent about his or her motivations as long as his or her technical output seems alright.

On the other hand, indifference about employee commitment is fatal when we introduce modern management methods like lean production and quality circles. To make these methods work, we have to explain the whole idea behind them and, even more, train and reward people for their commitment to team objectives. Modern production methods thus provide a new reason for treating employees as moral beings.

Thirdly, the training of character virtues is more complex and difficult than the learning of technical craftsmanship. A craft can be performed relatively well without involving great personal commitment, while prudence results from personal experience and commitment. Only after reflecting upon our personal mishaps and successes may we step by step acquire durable excellences of character and the virtue of practical reason. Difference in individual abilities may also explain why some will never learn and possess prudence.

Let us here indicate a parallel with management training. Business managers would like top MBA graduates to show evidence of an overall view, of leadership and of moral commitment – all this on top of many technical qualifications. This is a rigorous and complex demand. If an MBA school wants to respond to it, the relevant skills should be identified. In particular, the modern excellence of character called 'sense of social responsibility' is one of these skills. Now the question is: Can it be taught and, if so, how? Most probably it cannot be taught only in a separate course on business ethics, but should constitute an integrative part of the whole MBA programme.

Training future corporate leaders to be socially responsible implies a different understanding of 'minding one's business'. Corporate leaders should not confine themselves to the pursuit of short-term gain without caring about other consequences; ostrich policies can be quite counter-productive.

Modern management implies the capacity to mobilize human commit-ment and to make people realize the strategic considerations behind policies. It involves effective communications with the world inside and outside our own business. When the social responsibility of management is challenged, one has to respond in a convincing way. Modern business involves a moral reply to challenges in the business environment. Some MBA programmes already insist on the training of the excellences of character and mind needed for such responsible corporate leadership. One of the best examples of such an effort is the pathbreaking Leadership, Ethics, and Corporate Responsibility programme at the Harvard Business School, developed since 1987.

In the 'Epilogue' of *Can Ethics Be Taught?* Thomas R. Piper *et al.* comments on the general issues at stake in this Harvard programme:

> A strange disconnect seems to stand between, on the one hand, those ethically charged issues that we recognize as threatening to our society and, on the other hand, our professional lives. . . . Is it that we simply

don't understand the significance of these challenges to us – both as individuals and as business educators and leaders? . . . It seems, instead that the disconnect is quite purposeful. . . .

The Leadership, Ethics, and Corporate Responsibility initiative finds its meaning in the very region of this disconnect, among those questions of purpose and principle and responsibility that cynics avoid as too painful, or too risky. Its success depends on our moving beyond negativism . . . on our recognizing not only the inevitable and unhappy future consequences of our current inaction, but also the *immorality* of that inaction . . . our committing our energies to an attack on these critical challenges to our individual and collective welfare, and to a rebuilding of the trust – in leaders, in organizations, and in one another – and the sense of purpose that are so essential to the effective implementation of a strategy aimed at addressing these challenges. Here is where educators can – but do not yet – play their most important role. (Piper *et al.*, 1993, pp. 162–4)

This quotation exemplifies why the moral virtue of prudence cannot be reduced to the various virtues related to technical crafts. The reason is that moral excellence entails a higher degree of personal commitment, not as a blind faith, but as the result of reflective thought and an open-eyed estimation of public challenges.

7.7.3 Virtues of character have a final cause

Virtues of character have to be applied with judgement and guided by prudence, which functions as an acquired aptitude to choose the most appropriate actions. Prudence does not produce external commodities, but enhances our ability to live in happiness. The good achieved by living morally is not an extrinsic commodity; quality of life refers to the intrinsic good which results from living one's life happily and dynamically.

This ideal is a positive one. What it actually is can never be found by only studying primitive or inadequate forms of human growth and existence. Human excellence is a positive function. It consists of the acquired possession and exercise of typically human virtues, and its real characteristics are not fully present in preceding stages of development.

As Aristotle writes in *De partibus animalium* II. i. 646a25:

Now the order of development is the reverse of the real order. What is later in the formative process is earlier by its nature, and what comes at the end of the process is first by its nature. Thus a house, though it comes after the bricks and stone, is not there for the sake of the house [so the house is 'first by its nature']. And the same applies to materials of every kind. That this is how things are is clear if one considers examples; but it can also be shown by a general argument. Everything that comes into being is coming out of something [material] to something [the final product or grown animal], and from one principle towards another, from the primary moving cause which already has a certain nature, towards a certain form or other such end. For example, the *logos* [account or definition], the essence and form of the thing must be first. This is clear if we state the *logos* of the process. For example, the *logos* of the process of house-building includes the *logos* of a house, whereas that of a house does not include that of the process of house-building. And this holds good in all such cases. (Ackrill, 1981, p. 47)

In order to explain excellence one should focus on defining the goal, the proper purpose for these activities.

Virtue ethics does not condemn deficiencies as absolutely evil, rather it explains why attitudes and qualities fall short of the desirable goal. The shortcomings or excess is vice, yet the mean exists. The objective, end or purpose is the criterion here. Immature, incomplete or unfortunate growth is called so by reference to some idea of a more balanced and normal development.

In business many managers already apply the idea that desirable qualities should not be described by referring to bad examples, but by communicating positive goals. People will commit themselves more easily to positive targets, to policies that clearly foster both the wellbeing of the company and the wellbeing of the personnel.

7.7.4 Virtues of character qualify durable excellence

Virtue ethics holds that the good life is defined by a *set of skills or aptitudes aiming at an intrinsic purpose*. One aspires to live well; how to flourish is the question. In this project feelings of pleasure are not the core matter, what is vital is to uphold a dynamic state of well-functioning. This self-realization is not only a matter of developing particular characteristics and individual talents: it also involves a generic component called our durable realization as a human being. Finally, humans are good when they succeed in their overall life.

When Aristotle speaks about ethical qualities he never studies separate skills only at one particular moment, but sets them in a context that covers the whole span of life. As a classical Greek he maintained that definitive judgements about a person's way of life may only be made when that life is finished, that is, after the death of that person. During the individual's lifetime we can only make conditional and tentative judgements.

To give a modern example, during certain periods in his lifetime some people have admired Mr Rupert Murdoch. However, the more definitive judgements of his moral virtue are probably much less positive. On the other hand, the repetition of inspiring news about, for instance, George Soros, make it quite probable that his good reputation might last. One quotation is typical of the shrewd craftsmanship of this top speculator: 'As an investor that respects the law and the other rules of the market I cannot bother myself about the social effects of my actions' (*NRC*, 1994). Another quotation may explain why people call Soros highly respectable: 'I have money and I am concerned about the world. Already in 1979 I felt that I would make more money than I needed for my private life' (Ibid.).

7.8 Virtue theory is back in town

It is only quite recently that large audience texts, like *After Virtue* by Alisdair MacIntyre (1985), reintroduced the classical conception of virtue. Others have later indicated its relevance to business management.

Nowadays, references to the classical concept of virtue even reappear in newspapers, like the following text by H. H. Klamer (1993), secretary of the Christian Employers Organization (NCW):

> Rules on their own are not sufficient. Commitment to enforce rules is at least so important. At this point we may introduce the classical virtues: these virtues insist on our motivations for acting morally. As 'virtue' often was associated with petty decency, middle class prejudice and tutelage, we no longer dared to use this word. Yet, just as we may speak about good citizenship, we should use expressions like good employer-ship and good employeeship. Good employeeship means that we expect managers and employees to act prudently, for instance when a potential conflict of interests is at hand.

This quotation illustrates the way modern Christians may use the concept of virtue: the commitment and attitudes it entails are emphasized, while the fact that moral virtues embody well-functioning or excellence in intellectual skills is not fully underlined.

Here we have described some fundamental features of this original normative theory, our lost heritage of civilized morality. Classical virtue ethics proposes another outlook for fruitful debate on moral issues. We will now briefly indicate some modern neo-Aristotelian approaches in management theory and business ethics. Our selection may seem partial, as it ignores authors that practise ethical relativism.

7.9 Productive practices and team motivation

7.9.1 MacIntyre on goods internal to practices

A famous modern definition of virtue runs as follows: 'A virtue is an acquired human quality the possession and exercise of which enable us to achieve goods which are internal to practices and the lack of which effectively prevents us from achieving such goods' (MacIntyre, 1985, p. 191).

A core distinction here is the difference between external and internal goods. In a recent essay Alisdair MacIntyre gave an illuminating example explaining this distinction. It has serious consequences for theories of human motivation in teams and organizations. First, he states a general point concerning all human practices:

> No quality is to be accounted a virtue except in respect of its being such as to enable the achievement of three distinct kinds of goods: those internal to practices, those which are the goods of an individual life and those which are goods of the community. (MacIntyre, 1994, p. 284)

7.9.2 Crafts can foster virtues

MacIntyre then gives his example explaining the difference between internal aims and instrumental pursuits when involved in productive practices. He starts by acknowledging that until now (1994) he paid little attention to productive practices, that are 'productive crafts such as farming and fishing, architecture and construction'. He then tries to argue that other values are part of such crafts. What team members aim at should always involve another kind of aims that one may call 'aims internal to the craft or competence':

> The aim internal to such productive crafts, when they are in good order, is never only [the functional purpose] to catch fish, or to produce beef or milk, or to build houses. It is to do so in a manner consonant with the excellences of the craft, so that not only is there a good product, but the craftsperson is perfected through and in her or his activity. This is what apprentices in a craft have to learn. It is from this that the sense of a craft's dignity derives. And it from this that the virtues receive their initial, if partial, definition. (MacIntyre, 1994; my comments)

Crafts are not only work which is instrumental for some external purpose. By learning certain procedures and skills the apprentice becomes a team member, a well-performing member of a community of trained professional artisans. A craft is also a practice, it has internal goods. A key image for understanding the modern meaning of virtue, as defined by MacIntyre, is craftsmanship. He then describes an illuminating example of this by placing in opposition to each other two teams – Team I: a mechanical and instrumental team only motivated by external rewards; and Team II: a community of craftsmen motivated by goods internal to their craft and who participate in public life while seeking financial success.

7.9.3 *The instrumental perception*

Consider in this light the difference between two kinds of fishing crew. My descriptions of these will be of ideal types, defining the extremes of a spectrum on which there are many points. But that there are in fact fishing crews whose lives embody one extreme or the other is beyond doubt. (Team I) A fishing crew may be organized and understood as a purely technical and economic means to a productive end, whose aim is only or overridingly to satisfy as profitably as possible some market's demand for fish. Just as those managing its organization aim at a high level of profits [MacIntyre repeatedly criticizes the greed and narrow instrumental concepts he attributes to modern management theories], so also the individual crew members aim at a high level of reward. Not only the skills, but also the qualities of character valued by those who manage the organization, will be those well designed to achieve a high level of profitability. And each individual at work as member of such a fishing crew will value those qualities of character in her or himself or in others which are apt to produce a high level of reward for her or himself. When however the level of reward is insufficiently high, then the individual whose motivations and values are of this kind will have from her or his point of view the best of reasons for leaving his particular crew or even taking to another trade. And when the level of profitability is insufficiently high, relative to comparative return on investment elsewhere, management will from its point of view have no good reason not to fire crew members, and owners will have no good reason not to invest their money elsewhere. (MacIntyre, 1994; my comments)

7.9.4 *An intrinsicly motivated crew*

(Team II) Consider by contrast a crew whose members may well have initially joined for the sake of their wage or other share of the catch, but who have acquired from the rest of the crew an understanding of and devotion to excellence in fishing and to excellence in playing one's part as a member of such a crew [these are virtues]. Excellence of the requisite kind is a matter of skills and qualities of character required both for the fishing and for achievement of the goods of the common life of such a crew [i.e. they involve goods internal to practices and goods internal to this small community].

The dependence of each member on the qualities of character and skills of others will be accompanied by a recognition that from time to time one's own life will be in danger and that whether one drowns or not may depend upon someone else's courage. And the consequent concern of each member of the crew for the others, if it is to have the stamp of genuine concern, will characteristically have to extend to those for whom those others care: the members of their immediate families. So the interdependence of the members of a fishing crew in respect of skills, the achievement of goods and the acquisition of virtues will extend to an interdependence of the families of crew members and perhaps beyond them to the whole society of a fishing village. When someone dies at sea, fellow crew members, their families and the rest of the fishing community will share a common affliction and common responsibilities. (Ibid.; my comments)

In addition to this latter sketch of an intrinsically motivated team of craftsmen with a common mission, MacIntyre then points to the fact that they are in the practice of fishing for something more than external rewards alone by opposing economic goods to the goods internal to practices.

For the members of such a crew and the inhabitants of such a village, the goods to be achieved in attaining excellence in the activities of fishing and in one's role within the crew will, for as long as possible, outweigh the economic hardships of low wages and periods of bad catches or low prices for fish. Of course no fishing crew can ever completely ignore the economic dimensions of their enterprise. But we have enough experience of members of crews preferring to endure the hardships of economic bad times in their trade, when they could have earned far higher wages elsewhere, for us to know that the subordination of economic goods to goods of practice can be a rewarding reality. For members of such crews, continuing allegiance to one's fellow crew members and to the way of life of a fishing community will therefore not be conditional upon the economic rewards being such as to enable one to satisfy one's individual antecedent desires, those that one brought with one when first initiated into the life of a fishing crew. (Ibid.)

7.9.5 A concept of practice

Alisdair MacIntyre defines practice as any coherent and complex form of socially established co-operative human activity through which goods internal to that form of activity are realized. He adds to this that such crafts or practices realize their internal goods by trying to achieve those standards of excellence which are appropriate to, and partially definitive of, that form of activity. Finally his definition of practice concludes with its effect on the fostering of virtues of character and mind. His examples may illustrate this definition:

> Tic-tac-toe is not an example of a practice in this sense, nor is throwing a football with skill; but the game of football is, and so is chess. Bricklaying is not a practice; architecture is. Planting turnips is not a practice; farming is. (Ibid., p. 187)

7.10 Some prospects for virtue in business ethics and management theory

7.10.1 Sustainable growth as the commanding modern telos

Somehow in the back of the mind of most cultivated people an unpleasant idea keeps moving around. It is related to the growing concern for our common future. Without entering into any detail, we simply affirm here a series of statements on this public issue.

1. Corporate employees and managers are also citizens and should feel duties of stewardship.
2. Corporations can no longer see themselves as self-centred concerns, enlightened egoism has to give away to positive commitment to certain larger concerns and commitments.
3. One of the central commitments for morally responsive concerns is defining how it can contribute to sustainable growth.
4. A serious environmental care programme demonstrates the difference between the long-term objective or *telos* (sustainable growth) and the need to arrive at concrete measurable norms here and now. These concrete norms have to be constantly reformulated, while at the same time our idea of the desirable *telos* may shift too.

One small example may illustrate the third and fourth statement. In October 1994 Dutch industries protested vehemently against a decision taken by the large electric power distributors. Until recently industrialists who started to construct heat/power plants were rewarded by the monopoly of electric power distributors: they were paid between 5 and 13 cents per kilowatt for any excess power from their supplementary electricity production that they could deliver to the national network.

From the point of view of sustainable growth the construction of heat/power installations has been a notable ecological success. There are two reasons for this. They are more energy-efficient than the usual big plants. Also, a strong motivating factor was the positive ecological effect that accompanied the significant financial savings.

A third point has actually caused trouble for the electric power distributors, who own the main electric power plants. As the programme for supplementary power has overperformed, the original suppliers now suffer from overcapacity. Therefore, driven by dinosaur logic, short-term views and a self-centred conception of their concerns' interests, the national distributors now want to change the rules of the game. They want to stop private companies from building any more new heat/power installations, and to discourage them they are reducing the payment for deliveries to the national network by 12 to 13 per cent. This new norm or policy of the national distributors clearly does not foster desirable programmes, for it runs contrary to larger public interests.

7.10.2 Virtues for managers and company philosophies

All in all virtue theory may help to put isolated targets into a wider perspective. One should not just remain obsessed by instrumental well-functioning, but should make every effort to gain a wider understanding of corporate, private and social wellbeing.

We hold that the classical idea of human excellence can lead to two questions in the inner field of management ethics:

1. Does this behaviour or policy foster human growth and well-functioning?
2. Does this policy foster the development of a business community capable of fulfilling its mission in a publicly respectful way?

According to Alisdair MacIntyre, justice, courage and honesty are part of virtue ethics. His thesis is that without a whole range of key virtues we cannot obtain the goods internal to practices. Moreover these internal goods are 'not just barred to us generally, but in a very particular way' (MacIntyre, 1985, p. 191).

He demonstrates this by explaining the moral discipline involved in the performance of such a practice:

its goods can only be achieved by subordinating ourselves within the practice in our relationship to other practitioners. We have to learn to recognize what is due to whom; we have to be prepared to take whatever self-endangering risks are demanded along the way; and we have to listen carefully to what we are told about our inadequacies and to reply with the same carefulness for the facts. In other words we have to accept as necessary components of any practice with internal goods and standards of excellence the virtues of justice, courage and honesty. For not to accept these, to be willing to cheat as our imagined child was willing to cheat in his or her early days at chess, so far bars us from achieving the standards of excellence or the goods internal to that practice as it renders the practice pointless except as a device for achieving external goods. (Ibid., p. 191)

Let us now consider rule-of-thumb principles for business ethics that reflect these virtues. Each item will name one recent abuse.

(1) Honesty; a virtuous manager honours confidentiality. In the summer of 1993, the president of Volkswagen, Ferdinand Piëch, triggered a public row with GM subsidiary Opel, when he denied that Mr José Ignacio Lopez, the former Opel director of purchase, who had been working for Volkswagen since March 1993, had disclosed secret Opel projects and data to his new employer. On Opel's side there were in fact two complaints: first, the public accusation about Mr Lopez selling confidential information to their competitor Volkswagen; and second, an acute sense of having been tricked in an unfair way, because of Mr Piëch's violation of the unwritten taboo amongst car manufacturers concerning the recruitment of top managers from competitors. Most probably this second issue is now quite well understood by Volkswagen AG.

(2) The virtue of impartial justice implies that we avoid actual conflicts of interest. In 1993 and 1994 many Italian politicians were accused of accepting bribes from contractors and from even the biggest Italian firms like Fiat and Montedison. Many suicides followed, not amongst the accused politicians but amongst civil servants and company directors also involved, including very prominent captains of Italian industry like Mr Cagliari of Feruzzi.

(3) Provide a good example when building relationships by acting in good faith, including being honest in negotiations and honouring commitments. In stable business environments fair trade is simply vital if you want to stay in business. You can easily end up being sued in court for breaking the rules, since contractual rights and duties are codified by law. The most outrageous abuses flourish elsewhere, for example in politics, where power-mad tyrants still get away with breaking promises. There also we can see the outcome of compulsive hatred. From 1991 till 1994, the parties involved in the Bosnian civil war agreed truce after truce, only for one or other of the parties to break the deal as soon as it suited them. This implies an absence of mutual trust and an absence of enforcement capability. The UN and, more specifically, the West European nations played a poor role too; they just seem like impotent patriarchs unable to stop mortal revenges between clans.

7.10.3 Situationalist leadership as striking the just mean

Kenneth Blanchard, Patricia and Drea Zigarmi (1985) apply the principle of the just mean to corporate leadership in *Leadership and the One Minute Manager*. Although it is known as the theory of situational leadership, it also provides a nice example of a practical theory applying Aristotelian principles. These authors distinguish two dimensions for group performance: competence and commitment. They also distinguish four styles of leadership: delegating, supporting, coaching, and directing. Finally, they formulate a normative theory prescribing which style of leadership is best for the group with various levels of commitment and of competence.

One might regard their advice as a wise counsel on what is best in a given situation. It fits in with the doctrine of the just mean.

7.10.4 Striking the balance in ethical decision-making

Verne E. Henderson (1992) indicates that the moral decision-making process consists of four elements. This set of four interactive elements was used in an ethical algorithm. According to Henderson, moral decision-making is a matter of finding an adequate tuning between the four elements listed in Table 7.1.

Henderson indicates the lack of match between the often followed great duties and the concrete practice of business leaders.

Table 7.1 The four elements

Element	Main question	(Unethical) Example
Goals	What do you want to achieve?	Get rich
Methods	How will you pursue your goals?	Rob banks
Motives	What personal needs drive you to achieve?	Antisocial drive for financial security
Consequences	What results can you anticipate?	Make millions, buy a condominium complex in Florida, and retire early

Source: Henderson (1992).

Values in real life are like mercury, slipping away the moment you try to put your finger on them. How would you answer a newspaper reporter who asked you to name some of your values as a business leader? Words such as *honesty, fair value, contribution to society, family life, respect for the individual, corporate loyalty, or even patriotism* fall rather easily from the lips. Some of the same people who purportedly subscribe to one or more of those values are serving prison sentences. Why? Because the values that we really and truly hold as decision makers surface in the midst of crisis. If you are unaware of your values or hold them tenuously, ethical dilemmas will rip them from your grasp. (Henderson, 1992, pp. 65–6)

His algorithm offers a tool for distinguishing and co-ordinating different aspects of ethical decision-making in corporations.

7.10.5 Coping with cultural diversity in international business

A good example of a mainly descriptive study of national corporate cultures is given by Fons Trompenaars (1993) in his *Riding the Waves of Culture*. This text contains advice for managers who deal with cultural diversity. The normative standards behind his switching from descriptive to normative ethics can be interpreted as basically situationalist.

For Trompenaars, coping with different cultures is not a matter of blindly applying one's own rules, nor is it the surrender to the culture of a host country. It is a positive skill or excellence that can be acquired by trained and reflective managers. They can draw upon the decentralized capacities of their international organization if they develop a combination of skill, sensitivity and experience.

This idea applies insights formulated by virtue theory to international management. What matters is the acquisition of excellence in coping with cultural diversity; this individual skill can be trained and become part of the organization's culture.

Trompenaars describes a complex of different outcomes that may result from international managers understanding local cultures. Getting acquainted with other cultures provides a first outcome, as it results in personal growth. Abroad we may learn different ways of doing things and a greater capacity to respect local customs.

Rather than there being 'one best way of organising' there are several ways, some very much more culturally appropriate and effective than others, but all of them giving international managers additional strings on their bow if they are willing and able to clarify the reactions of foreign cultures. (Trompenaars, 1993, p. 20)

So, a broadened personal experience acquired through confrontation with different cultures enriches our personal skills.

This personal skill may serve a company egoism, so from the point of view of virtue theory this may be one-sided. The individual manager may forget about public goods, and be motivated by private or corporate self-centred greed.

Trompenaars asks for:

> the genuinely international organisation, sometimes called the transnational, in which each national culture contributes its own particular insights and strengths to the solution of world-wide issues and the company is able to draw on whatever it is that nations do best. (Ibid., pp. 11–12)

In the end Trompenaars shows his sociological background by frequently using the concept of system optimalization. Still, his perspective may also be interpreted as a truly philosophical plea for a kind of purposeful transnationalism, which assumes an ideal of educating universal human potentials in a more balanced way.

Three more quotes to illustrate this interpretation:

> International and transnational structures allow us to *synthesise the advantages of all cultures while avoiding their excesses*. Families are quite capable of nurturing independence and encouraging achievement. Managing across cultures gives you more possible pathways to your goal. (Ibid., p. 174)

> I have argued the essential *complementarity* of values. To post an individualist to collectivised Singapore can help to make that collectivism more responsive to individuals and the reverse would be true of posting a Singaporean to America. (Ibid., p. 175)

This second quote reminds us of Aristotle's remarks on how to redress wrong habits. To Aristotle a vice is an excess or deprivation which should be redressed in the same way as crooked branches: by forcefully bending them to grow in the opposite direction.

> World culture is a myriad of different ways of creating the integrity without which life and business cannot be conducted. There are no universal answers but there are universal questions or dilemmas, and that is where we all need to start. (Ibid., p. 177)

This last quote underestimates the purport of his own descriptive theory, and cannot explain on the basis of which standards Trompenaars gives advice.

His standards basically aim at the success of a company. It can be obtained by becoming truly transnational:

Collectivist cultures with a synchronous view of time, like Germany and Japan, are typically long-term strategically. . . . Within the international or transnational structure a microcosm of international economic competition is going on. We would be foolish not to notice who is winning or why, and to fail to apply the lessons. (Ibid., p. 174)

This ultimate aim is questionable for many business ethicists who stress the need for intrinsic moral motives. The external pressure exacted by international competition may provide a spur, but in the end operating from a transnational frame of mind has to become second nature, a moral commitment. It may then become a virtuous practice, also serving higher public goods like mutual tolerance and the empowering of peaceful approaches to the real issues of modern society.

7.11 References

Ackrill, J. L. (1981) *Aristotle the Philosopher*, Oxford: Oxford University Press. By permission of Oxford University Press.

Ahrendt, H. (1958) *The Human Condition*, Chicago: The University of Chicago Press.

Bernstein, A. J. and Craft Rozen, S. (1990) *Dinosaur Brains: Dealing with all those impossible people at work*, New York: Ballantine. Copyright © 1990 by Albert J. Bernstein and Sydney Craft Rozen. Reprinted by permission of John Wiley & Sons, Inc.

Blanchard, K., Zigarmi, P. and Zigarmi, D. (1985) *Leadership and the One Minute Manager*, New York: Morrow.

Bodéüs, R. (1993) *The Political Dimensions of Aristotle's Ethics*, Albany, NY: SUNY.

Foot, P. (1978) *Virtues and Vices*, Oxford: Blackwell.

Henderson, V. (1992) *What's Ethical in Business?*, New York: McGraw-Hill. Reprinted with permission of McGraw-Hill, Inc.

Klamer, H. H. (1993) 'Moraal in bedrijf' (Morals in business), *De Volkskrant*, 10 December.

MacIntyre, A. (1985) *After Virtue: A study in moral theory*, 2nd edn, London: Duckworth.

MacIntyre, A. (1994) 'A partial response to my critics', in J. Horton and S. Mendus (eds), *After MacIntyre*, Cambridge: Polity Press.

Melling, D. (1987) *Understanding Plato*, Oxford: Oxford University Press. By permission of Oxford University Press.

Myers, N. (1992) *The Primary Source: Tropical forests & our future*, New York: W. W. Norton.

NRC Handelsblad (1994) interview with George Soros taken from *Die Zeit*, 4 January.

Piper, Th. R., Gentile, M. C. and Parks, S. D. (1993) *Can Ethics Be Taught?*:

Perspectives, challenges, and approaches at Harvard Business School, Boston: Harvard Business School Press.

Rollin, B. (1993) 'The ascent of apes: broadening the moral community', in P. Cavallieri and P. Singer (eds), *The Great Ape Project: Equality beyond humanity*, London: Fourth Estate.

Sahlins, M. (1974) *Stone Age Economics*, London: Tavistock.

Sorrell, T. and Hendry, J. (1994) *Business Ethics*, Oxford: Butterworth-Heinemann.

Trompenaars, F. (1993) *Riding the Waves of Culture*, London: Nicholas Brealey Publishing Ltd.

van Luijk, H. (1994) 'Business ethics: the field and its importance', in B. Harvey (ed.), *Business Ethics: A European approach*, Hemel Hempstead: Prentice Hall.

Index